Grím Reader

<u>**FROM THE CELLS & SECRET MINDS OF SERIAL KILLERS**</u>

TED BUNDY + JOHN WAYNE GACY + GARY HEIDNIK

OTTIS TOOLE + ARTHUR SHAWCROSS

Grim Reader

Printed in the United States of America. First printing, August 2021.

ISBN: 978-0-578-96250-4

Reaper art from *Welcome to Fear City: A Survival Guide* (NYPD, 1975)

Inquiries via:

www.TheeGrimReader.com

Grim Reader

In Memory Of

Pioneering homicide Investigator

Robert D. 'Bob' Keppel

June 15, 1944 – June 14, 2021

❖

Because I could not stop for Death –
He kindly stopped for me –
The Carriage held but just Ourselves –
And Immortality.

Emily Dickinson

Grim Reader

Chapters:

P10 P39
P12 P40
P13 P41
P13 P44
P14 P45
P15 P47
P19 P102
P19 P105
P22 P106
P23 P107
P26 P108
P27 P109
P29 P112
P30 P115
P32 P117
P33 P121
P34 P123
P35
P36
P37
P38

Grim Reader

Editor's Note: This title's content was painstakingly edited for clarity, however grammatical, punctuation and spelling quirks remain as intact as possible, in the effort to capture the 'voice' of each character. Certain identities found in The Grim Reader's penultimate chapter have been disguised to preserve both the reputations and secrets of private persons.

TAKES ONE TO CATCH ONE:

TED BUNDY PROFILES THE RIVERMAN

𝕴n 1978, while representing himself at a Floridian capital murder trial, Ted Bundy submitted a cheese sandwich on white bread as Exhibit A to a Motion demanding luncheon befitting an officer of the Court.

"I cannot be expected to function properly or continue to participate in these proceedings on a one-sandwich lunch," grumbled Bundy – soon to be condemned by bite-mark evidence – in disgust. "*Wherefore,* I move the Court to direct the County Sheriff to bring me an adequate noon meal, which is sufficient and wholesome, to support a person presenting a defense…".

Jailhouse mayonnaise oozed out onto the lined yellow margin beside Bundy's hand-scribbled grievance, but his dramatics were from hunger, so to speak. Bundy's trial Judge reminded him he was there under indictment, not as a prosecutor or the Police, or even as a real lawyer. Which made sense to everyone in the courtroom but Ted Bundy who'd already pretended to be so many different people that he struggled mightily to remember his rightful place.

Enter the Green River Killer. Or, more precisely, investigators from the State of Washington who'd once looked hard at Bundy as a suspect in multiple unsolved 1970s murders but who had themselves a new nut case to crack: one who, while still very much at-large, was already being credited with stealing more female lives than Bundy himself was even suspected of.

About their cold cases in Washington State, Bundy stubbornly refused all comment; still convinced he could outwit the system, Bundy didn't wish to overcomplicate his efforts avoiding execution in Florida by attracting new charges out west. But with the focus now shifted to 1980s victims who Bundy couldn't have killed from his cot on death row, 'Ted' offered to assist the newly formed Task Force. *And here now, for the first time in publication, are Theodore Robert Bundy's unfiltered letters to Police actively hunting for the Green River Killer in King County, Washington.*

Just a few short years after twelve jurors saw through Ted Bundy's lawyerly charade and sentenced him to death by electrocution for the murders of two Tallahassee sorority sisters, Bundy detected yet another prime opportunity to be someone other than himself; other than a warehoused killer in a suffocatingly hot prison cell, waiting to have his posterior stuffed with cotton then be strapped into an unforgiving oak chair.

Within communiqués exchanged between natural-born nemeses, Theodore Robert Bundy posed as a sage, a clairvoyant, a defense attorney, a devil's advocate and as Hannibal Lecter, all in a drawn-out attempt to manipulate serial profiler Robert D. 'Bob' Keppel and the future U.S. Congressman David 'Dave' Reichert, each official point men in the Green River Killer investigation. And who each, by some miracle, kept their composure while exposed to Bundy's posturing, volatility and – potentially most frustrating of all – his compulsive misspelling of the word 'homicide'. But serial gaffes notwithstanding, who knew – except Bundy and the prolific, elusive Riverman – that he was right? Or, at bare minimum, close.

On November 30, 2001, twelve years after Ted Bundy's grisly execution robbed him of both bragging rights and bargaining chips, Gary Leon Ridgway – *a Green River Killer suspect first identified in 1983* – was apprehended by Washington State with assistance from DNA specimens collected from Ridgway two years before a desperate Bundy, mortified at the very idea of meeting his own maker, was escorted to the death chamber.

In June of 2021, Bob Keppel, too, passed. The letters which follow were entrusted by him to the AOC Archives more than twenty years earlier, with the understanding they would not be disseminated until after his death.

Ted Bundy
Box 747
Starke, Florida
32091

January 28, 1985

Hi Bob,

I just received your letter of January 23, 1985, a few minutes ago. I am not going to allow myself to procrastinate writing to you any longer.

I apologize for taking so long to write to you. On January 15 I was determined to turn over a new leaf and answer your letters and begin to express the enormous number of thoughts and ideas concerning the Green River case that have occurred to me since our meeting in October, 1984. After writing over 20 pages to you, I read what I had written and began having serious doubts that I was telling you anything worthwhile. For instance, I rambled on for 17 pages on the shortcomings and inherent incompleteness of victim lists in the Green River case in particular and serial murder cases in general. I was consumed by the misgiving that I was wasting your time in addition to feelings of my own lack of articulation on the subject. So I put the letter down and haven't been able to get back into it, even though not a day passed that I did not think about it.

The topic I had chosen to discuss in the letter was this: The Riverman's Victims: some thoughts on how many he has actually killed and how he selects and abducts his victims.

The letter I received from you today, which had enclosed with it an article on similar cases in Portland, tended to confirm many of my thoughts on the subject. When I read the article about the Portland area murders I knew I was on the right track, and I felt a renewed sense of urgency to get down to the business of giving you my point of view on the problems you face trying to solve such cases.

I will get back to my letter of January 15 and with some luck and effort I hope to mail it to you this week. For now, I want to briefly list my major reactions to the article on the Portland cases:

4

1. I considered that the statements by the Portland detectives may not represent their true feelings. Even if you and they were certain that there <u>was</u> a link between the Portland and Green River cases my advice to you would be not to admit it in public, even to downplay the speculation. I'd do this because I wouldn't want the Riverman to think I was on to his activity in the Portland area. I wouldn't want to drive him away.

If, in fact, the Riverman is active around Portland, let him think you're not on to him, and let him believe that he is relatively free to do his thing there, as opposed to, say, Pacific Highway South where he has received such intense publicity. Let him think he has gone far enough to escape the heat, and then place those areas where Portland prostitutes hang out under intense surveillance, similar to the kind we discussed during our meeting. Maybe even decoys could be used. Take the offensive.

2. If anyone in law enforcement in Portland or Seattle really believes that the Riverman isn't responsible for one or more of the Portland area murders, he ought to go live in a tent on Mt. St. Helens. It makes sense for the Riverman to go hunting in the Portland area because:

   a. It has a large population of prostitutes
   b. It is a short drive from the Seattle/Tacoma area. Let's assume the Riverman works. If he does, he could easily drive to Portland after getting off work, do his thing and be back home in time to get a few hours sleep before going to work again. It would be nothing for him to drive to Portland.
   c. In fact, one would expect the Riverman to drive and drive around a great deal. Mobility is one of the hallmarks of such a series of murders. The Riverman may in fact be familiar with the problems police have in linking murders committed hundreds of miles apart,

not to mention that there have undoubtedly been murders in King and Prince the Riverman has committed and are known to the police that have not yet been linked to him. With a three or four hour drive, the Riverman could easily range between Vancouver, B.C. and Portland. I would expect him to range that far…frequently, not just to avoid detection but to discover new hunting grounds. The Riverman is a hunter and his kind of hunting means driving.

3. I can understand the desire to list as official Green River victims only those victims where there is the highest degree of certainty that they were victims of a common assailant. Unfortunately, in practical terms, that has resulted in a victim list limited to victims found in King County. But the Green River murders have never been and are not now solely a King County problem.

The Riverman isn't a compulsive robot. His car and the freeway system have allowed him to roam throughout the Pacific Northwest, as I noted above. State and county lines don't deter him. I know that sounds ridiculously obvious, but why then can't Portland authorities recognize that the Riverman has almost certainly killed in their town? Maybe they do recognize this, though. I don't know.

4. I also understand that there is no hard, indisputable evidence to link the Portland murders to the Green River murders. But does there need to be at this point? These cases are in the ballpark geographically, timewise, and demographically. They fit. They don't have to fit exactly. Like I said, the Riverman isn't a robot. There are going to be certain variations in his behavior. They may appear random and disassociated to you, but to him, for whatever reason, whatever exigency, they made sense. Not all his victims need be

prostitutes. Not all are going to be strangled the same way or left in the same way.

5. So what do you do about the Portland cases and other cases outside of King County?

The article you sent said, "*Investigators have a system of rating certain factors before they add names to the Green River list.*" That's the first I heard about such a rating system. I guess there's no great harm in such a rating system, as long as you realize that it's got to be flawed in that there's no way it can account for all the variations in the Riverman's modus operandi, the constant evolution of his personality, and hence, all the victims he has actually killed. There is no harm unless it prevents you from looking outside King County to obvious links to Tacoma and Portland, for example.

Here's what I suggest:

a) Have an "A List" of dead and missing and a "B List". Your "A List" would contain the names of dead and missing persons that are <u>probably</u> victims of the Riverman. Basically, your "A List" includes the 28 victims whose remains have been found and are official Green River Victims and the list of 10-15 names of young women officially listed as missing in the Green River case. The "B List" would contain names of dead or missing persons who are <u>possibly</u> connected with the Green River case.

b) So what criteria would I used to determine who might <u>possibly</u> be a Green River victim? My rating system would definitely be broader, less restrictive than the one mentioned in the Portland article. I believe it is far more dangerous, from an investigator's point of view, to have a victim list that is <u>too small</u>, than one that is <u>too large</u>.

If a murder victim:

1) Was found between Vancouver, B.C. and Portland, Oregon;
2) In 1981, 1982, 1983, or 1984;

3) In an outdoor and out-of-the-way, but not necessarily remote, location;
4) who was between 15 and 25 years old
5) asphyxiated to death, and
6) whose body was nude or partially clad,

then I would put her on the "B list. You notice that I have avoided a requirement of being a prostitute. I have a number of reasons for this, which I will explain in a later letter, but for now I'll say that just because a murder victim wasn't known or believed to be a prostitute doesn't mean she wasn't one or that the Riverman didn't think she was one for some reason.

Among those I would include on my "B List" of possible Green River victims are:

1. Leann Wilcox, Tacoma, found 1-22-82

2. Unidentified body, La Connor, [found] March 1982

3. Virginia Taylor, North Seattle, found January 29, 1982

4. Joan Connor, North Seattle, found February 1982

5. Oneida Peterson, Snohomish County, found February 8, 1982

6. Theresa Kline, North Seattle, found April 22, 1982

7. Trina Hunter, Portland, found December 6, 1982

8. Linda Rule, North Seattle, found September 26, 1982

9. Joanne Hovland, Everett, found June 5, 1983

10. Kimberley Reames, Tacoma, found June 13, 1983

11. Essie Jackson, Portland, found March 23, 1983

12. Kimberly Ramsey, Portland, found October 26, 1984

13. _____ Anderson, Tacoma found August 12, 1984

14. Vickie Williams, Portland, found _____.

I am sure you can think of any number of reasons why many of these 14 girls shouldn't be linked to the Riverman. I am dealing only with the most superficial facts when I listed them. The point is, however, to keep in mind that there are many of the Riverman's victims that aren't on the official Green River victim lists, who weren't found in King County. Fact is, there are undoubtedly victims of the Riverman who won't appear on anyone's list. Such being the inherent incompleteness of lists. The important thing is to make the lists as complete and <u>inclusive</u> as possible.

Why?

A list never went out and arrested anyone. Lists and computers won't solve [these] cases. What I am attempting to illustrate by discussing lists and such is to show that the Riverman has not confined himself to King County. He has ranged all over the Pacific Northwest and that certainly includes Portland.

If the Riverman is still alive, healthy and free and living in the Pacific Northwest, he continues to go about his killing ways. In 1984, if 1982 and 1983 are any indicators, he has killed between 10 and 20 more. There will be more in 1985.

What I am saying is to look at the "big picture" to help you decide where and how to look for the Riverman <u>today</u>. Portland is one logical place to focus on.

Ask yourself, where would the Green River case be today if it weren't for the sensation of those five bodies found in the Green River in a couple months time? I'll bet there wouldn't be a Task Force, let alone an investigation. Portland hasn't had a shocking series of discoveries such as those that occurred in the Green River, but that doesn't mean the Riverman couldn't have killed just as many young women in the Portland area as he has in the Seattle area. Runaways and prostitutes are just as hard to trace and just as <u>mobile</u> in Portland as Seattle.

Thanks for writing.

I received your letters of November 30 and December 4, 1984.

Thanks.

If there are any questions you have about the things I have said and written about the Green River case, please don't hesitate to ask.

I should have the long letter I mentioned to you earlier in the mail later this week.

Take care.   Sincerely,

                                                    ted

(noun) drudgery: hard menial or dull work
(adj) menial: (of work) not requiring much skill and lacking prestige.

❖

                                        February 3, 1985

Hi,

When I wrote to you on January 28 I mentioned a letter I had started writing to you on January 15 on the subject of the Riverman's victims: some thoughts on expanding the number of victims believed to be involved and how he selects and abducts his victims. The January 15 letter got stalled, but I began working on it again on January 29 and it grew to over 60 pages with 40 footnotes. The thing has become unmanageable. There may be some stuff in it you might find useful but it seemed lost among the verbiage. My verbosity is not just an embarrassment, but a waste of your time. So I've decided to rewrite, restructure and edit the thing to see if I can make it more useful to you.

I sure could use a word processor right now. I could whip this mess in to shape in a day. As it stands now, I must write it by hand which is not only a drudgery, but an exercise in illegibility.

I have had some more thoughts on the Portland murders, their probable link to the Green River murders, and some things that come to mind whereby the Portland situation could be turned to your advantage. While it would be helpful to view my suggestions in the context of the more comprehensive treatment I've been working on, I don't want to delay sending along these thoughts about Portland. I'll send them along now and hope they make sense on their own.

treasure trove

(supporting) (adj)
(noun) Footnote (exactly this): an ancillary (additional) piece of information printed at the bottom of a page.
(noun) verbiage: speech or writing that uses too many words or excessively technical expressions.
(noun) verbosity: the quality of using more words than needed/wordiness

10

The article you sent me in your January 23 letter ("Has Green River Killer's grip spread to Portland?", Seattle Times, January 1, 1988) helped crystalize some thinking I've been doing about Portland for several months. I realize there's a great deal I don't know about the Portland cases. I realize that not only isn't there any conclusive proof that says that the same person who killed the Green River victims also killed one or more of the Portland victims…but there are also certain differences between the Green River and Portland cases.

But I realize this too: there are differences between the murders officially listed in the Green River case. Two of the major factors that link the 45 or so official victims together are the areas where they disappeared from (downtown Seattle area and Pacific Highway South/south King County) and/or the places where their bodies/remains were found (south, southeast, and eastern King County).

As I said in my January 28 letter, the Riverman didn't stop at the King County line any more than I-5 does. He could easily range from Vancouver, B.C. to Portland, Oregon, looking for victims and most certainly has. The Riverman was just as mindful of the links between prostitution activity between Seattle, Tacoma and Portland as the newspaper that reported the fact.

There's no question in my mind that the Riverman has searched for and killed victims in the Portland area. Is there any doubt in your mind? It's one of the few things I can state with any certainty in this matter.

Sure, there is some question whether he killed any one or more of the seven girls listed in the article in the Portland case. But please don't let the differences between the Portland cases and the Green River cases throw you. Why?

Because the Riverman is human; he is prone to inconsistency and change. Even among the Green River cases you find some in the river, some buried, some in the mountains, some by the airport, some nude, some partially clad (one, Christensen, was fully clothed), and a couple who may not even have been prostitutes.

If you believe the Riverman worked the Portland area, then the differences between the Portland and Green River cases become less important than the similarities evident in at least four of the Portland cases: Trina Hunter's, Tonja Harry's, Essie Jackson's and Kimberly Ramsey's.

And there are probably a number of others who have yet to be found. These four are in the Riverman's ballpark, young prostitutes asphyxiated and found in out-of-the-way places.

Okay, I realize that talking about a connection between the Portland and Green River cases is hardly a brilliant deduction. It's a connection that certainly isn't lost on the girls who work Portland's streets. The reason I am pushing the likelihood of such a connection so hard is because I believe the Portland situation offers the Green River Task Force a unique opportunity to look for the Riverman in the "here-and-now" instead of sifting through mountains of cold, two and three year-old clues.

If, I say "*if*" Kimberly Ramsey, the latest Portland victim who disappeared on October 26, 1984, is one of the Riverman's victims, she represents by far the freshest and most recent of all his victims known to the public. While the trail of the Riverman grew cold in the Seattle/Tacoma area during 1984, with no officially confirmed kills occurring during that period, the Ramsey case would indicate that the Riverman is still active in the Portland area at least.

Just as important, he may be seeking victims there with a certain confidence and sense of impunity that comes from knowing certain murders and disappearances in the Portland area he is responsible for have not been linked to the Green River murders. He couldn't be blamed if he felt he had escaped much of the heat caused by the publicity and investigation in the Seattle area.

One of your very best chances to catch this guy is by focusing your investigation on the area where he is still seeking out victims. This is why I am so enthusiastic about the otherwise sad news from Portland.

And here are my suggestions, for what they are worth. I don't for a moment believe that you haven't thought of them already.

(in spite of)

1. Notwithstanding a quote in the Portland article by Lt. Rob Aichele (a Portland detective who said, "*No one believes we have a serial killer involved. My personal belief is that the deaths are a byproduct of prostitution.*") police in Portland must be convinced that the Riverman almost certainly has and probably still is cruising Portland's streets looking for victims. In my opinion, the arguments supporting this proposition are

(adj) injurious: causing or likely to cause damage or harm.

(noun) (immunity)

impunity: exemption from punishment or freedom from the injurious consequences of an action

(noun) proposition: plan of action (proposal).

undeniable. Portland and Task Force investigators should join forces to <u>actively</u> hunt for the Riverman in that city.

2. Police spokesmen with the Task Force and Portland authorities should continue to deny and downplay any involvement by the Green River killer in the Portland murders. The Riverman must believe his activities in the Portland area have escaped attention. He must not be driven away from Portland or otherwise be made more cautious by news that the police know he's working in Portland.

3. Begin street and area surveillance of those parts of Portland (e.g. Northeast Union Avenue) where prostitutes are known to hang out. There are certain behaviors I'd look for in the men seen cruising those areas that could set the Riverman apart, and I'll discuss these in detail in the letter I'm writing on how he selects his victims. Of course, one obvious thing to look for are vehicles with Washington plates, although its entirely likely he has taken precautions to hide the Washington origins of his vehicle.

4. Go back and do thorough searches of the areas where the bodies of Hunter, Harry, Jackson and Ramsey were found. The experience in the Green River murders, of course, indicates the possibility that other victims may have been disposed of in these areas.

5. Do a detailed study of men arrested for crimes against women (e.g. assault, rape, kidnapping, etc.) since 1981, especially those involving prostitutes, in Multnomah County. Compare with a similar study in King and Prince Counties and look for men arrested in Washington and Oregon.

6. Develop a list of names of men picked up in Multnomah County for soliciting since 1981 and compare with a similar list of names developed in King and Prince Counties and cross reference with arrest listings above.

7. Question Portland prostitutes about men who have approached them with any unusual proposals or offers, including any who claimed to be police officers. I know this covers a lot of ground, especially considering the nature of the streetwalkers' profession, but I feel like there is potential here. I know if I read such interviews I would spot lines and ruses of the kind the Riverman might use. Have them pay special attention to men

who approach them on foot while the prostitute in question is by herself, alone.

8. Policemen passing as hookers. I recognize that this is a dangerous and controversial suggestion. In addition to the obvious danger, it would be a little like looking for a needle in a haystack, but in my opinion, I think there are things these decoys could do to draw the Riverman to them.

Policemen passing as hookers pose as special problem for the Riverman and one of which I am sure he is very mindful, and one for which he uses all his unique intuitive and observational skills to guard against. This threat doesn't appear to have deterred him in the past, though.

Anyway, done properly a undercover cop could overcome the Riverman's apprehensions. First, I would undertake a thorough study of all that is known about the appearance of the known Riverman victims just prior to their disappearances. Hairstyle, jewelry, make-up and type, style and color of clothing would be studied to see if the Riverman showed any kind of preference in the appearance of his victims. (I have not read or heard anything regarding the way the victims looked and dressed when they were last seen, and I believe it is critical to understanding the Riverman.)

The decoys would then dress and look in a way most likely to attract the Riverman.

I would have the decoys live in seedy, nearby motels.

I would have them move around alone and on foot as much as possible, make lots of calls from phone booths, shop in nearby convenience stores, and eat alone in fast food places. Occasional encounters/pickups would be staged to make it appear as though they are working.

They would have to be made up to appear as though they were in their late teens or early 20s.

I would have at least one decoy working night and day since we know that in the past at least, the data indicate he worked day and night.

Of course, there are many more details involved here, not the least of which is how far a decoy goes with someone who approaches her before her backup moves in.

9. Reevaluate stolen car incident. Back in September or October, 1984, before our meeting, I read a story in the Tacoma News Tribune, about an incident in Portland about a man in a car stolen in Seattle who tried to pick up some Portland prostitutes. I can't remember now all that the article said but I counted it as something related to the Green River case. It sounded too crude, too messy to be the Riverman. I remember that we discussed the incident when you met with me and you seemed to dismiss it too. Did you have specific reasons for dismissing its possible relevance?

Unless the man driving the car was arrested, I would take another look at that incident. Someday, even the Riverman is going to make a horrendous, amateurish mistake, act stupidly and impulsively, do something out of character and foolish. He probably already has at least once. Could the stolen car incident have been one of those times?

10. Missing persons study. A list of all women between 15 and 30 who have been reported as missing in Multnomah County since 1982 should be compiled. A special attempt should be made to see which of the missing women had records for prostitution. There are many flaws inherent in such a study but it may be possible, flaws notwithstanding, to detect a pattern in the disappearances.

Well, there you are, my ten easy steps to hunting for the Riverman in Portland. I welcome your questions and comments.

As I asked in my last letter, where would the Green River investigation be today if it hadn't been for the five bodies discovered in the Green River in July and August, 1982, a sensation that galvanized both public concern and the police investigation? I submit that it'd be lacking far more than just a name. Portland hasn't had it's "Green River", which doesn't mean there isn't a series problem down there.

P.S. Outline of my *non-profile* of the Riverman: it's really a "non-profile", since my experience has always been that profiles are generally misleading, pretentious and somewhat irrelevant to the issue of apprehension.

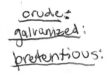

I'll send it to you after I've finished this piece on my thoughts on how the Riverman selects and apprehends his victims.

Sincerely,

ted

P.S.S. I need some input from you. The more I have, the more I give. You help me, I help you. Below are a few things I'd like you to do.

1. Would you mind letting me know what, if any, reservations you have to believing that a link exists between the Portland and the Green River cases.

2. How about giving me a call? I'd call you but I am not allowed to make outgoing calls. Sometimes more is accomplished by talking than writing. Maybe it could be a conference call so that you and other Task Force members could question me about what I have said and written about the Green River case. I am sure it could be arranged if you contacted Superintendent Duggar and stressed the importance of the call. Or you could work through the F.B.I. again.

3. Do you have any detailed info on what some of the victims were last seen wearing that you could share with me.

4. Are you sure there have been no reliable reports by prostitutes along Pacific Highway South in 1982 and 1983, who say they were approached by a man passing as a vice cop?

5. Were the records of the Red Lion Inn checked to determine whether or not either Constance Noan or someone she could have been with were registered there or seen there?

6. Has there been any attempt to compare hairs and fibers between the Portland and the Green River cases?

❖

Hi Dave,

I thought it was about time to write to you directly. I have written to you and Bob three times since our meeting in November, 1984, and sent them to Bob at his address. I hope you have had a chance to see those letters, dated November 18, 1984; January 28, 1985; and February 3, 1985.

The last two letters I sent to Bob concerned my thoughts on the likelihood of a link between the Green River murders and several murders in the Portland area that have occurred since 1982. I had been <u>unaware</u> of the Portland murders until I read an article Bob sent me on January 23, 1985, entitled "Has the Green River killer's deadly grip spread to Portland?" (Seattle Times, January 1, 1985). I suggest that a more pertinent question would have been, *"Has the Green River Killer been commuting to Portland all along?"*

Anyway, in my last letter I outlined eleven ideas to expand the search for the Riverman to Portland.

I am working simultaneously on two other letters. One deals with my thoughts on how the Riverman selects and abducts his victims. My thoughts on this subject have changed somewhat since our meeting, but my attempt to put them on paper has proven a little frustrating. My initial draft ran over 60 pages with 40 footnotes. It was poorly written and wordy and I am now in the process of redrafting it.

I am also working on an outline of my impressions of the Riverman, the unique, understandable, surprisingly normal everyday person that he is. Only the faintest of outlines emerge from my reading of the facts and circumstances of the cases, but some bread outlines do emerge.

In the meantime, I decided to write to you today and express some ideas on a matter you and Bob asked me to give some thought to: lists of names and other data that when analyzed by computer might yield the names of possible suspects.

Late last year, Bob sent me a coded list of some 31 lists (A thru AE) compiled at some point during the investigation of the disappearances and deaths of Linda Healey et al, back in the mid-1970s. That list-analysis

17

approach is something of a long-shot, but I guess a lot of things are in such an investigation.

What puzzles me about the Healey list of lists is that it appears, in part at least, to have been compiled after my arrest in Salt Lake City in October, 1975. It seems to me that the value of such an analysis is not what it says when it's been drawn up with a particular suspect in mind, but what it says when you have no suspects worthy of the name.

Let me put it this way: if you had a first name, description, and make and model of a vehicle of a man who was seen with one of the Green River victims immediately before her disappearance...and a number of known possible suspects in your files fitting that description and driving such a vehicle, what would you do? Would you say, *"We have too many suspects fitting this description, let's try to narrow them down by seeing how many also appear on one or two or three other lists?"* Maybe a thinning of such a list would be warranted, but it also might be like peeling an already peeled potato.

What I am saying is that this kind of thing can be pushed too far. I don't think it should be expected to be able to narrow a list of several hundred down to five or ten. If you had the names of 50 or 100 or 200 or 300 men fitting such a description, wouldn't it be better to try to question them all than reduce the size of the list and risk eliminating the man you're looking for?

We'll discuss the Healey list analysis in more detail later.

Among the lists of names/data I'd be interested in seeing analyzed in the Green River investigation are:

> 1. A list of names of persons in King, Prince, Snohomish, and Thurston Counties who have been arrested in 1980 for violent crimes against women; e.g. assault, rape, kidnapping, attempted murder, etc.

Hardly a brilliant thought, I know. You have probably been doing this for some time. What surprises me about the 31 lists in the Healey list of lists is there no mention of a list of persons arrested for violent crimes against women. There may be a perfectly good explanation for this, but I can't think of one.

Obviously, the vast majority of men who are arrested for rape, assault or some other violent crime against a woman are not serial murderers or on the way to becoming serial murderers. In the Green River case, for example, there is a very good chance that the Riverman has no criminal record of violence against women at all, but there is an equally good chance he does. *statistics??*

A criminal record of violence short of murder in the case of a serial killer like the Riverman would be indicative of a number of things:

a. Prior to committing his first murder an act of violence may represent a link in the chain of increasingly violent behavior ultimately resulting in murder. As I think I've mentioned to you before, there is no doubt in my mind that the Riverman didn't just wake up some morning in early July, 1982, and decide <u>for the first time</u> to go out and harm a young prostitute, which turned out to be Wendy Coffield. In my opinion, and that's all it is, the Riverman could have been killing people for six months to a year at least prior to July, 1982, and could have been displaying gradually more violent non-lethal behavior long before that.

b. It may be that before he killed his first victims the Riverman may have intended to kill someone but his lack of skill and exposure resulted in his committing acts of violence, for which he may have been arrested, which fell short of his goal. In this context acts of violence can be seen as part of a trial-and-error learning experience that helped him become a proficient and elusive killer.

c. Once the Riverman had begun killing, an act of violence short of murder could represent any one of three things:

   1) Something happened that prevented him from killing his intended victims as he had planned,
   2) He made a conscious decision to spare his victim, or
   3) He may be the type of individual who exhibits non-lethal violent behavior toward some

victims but when it comes to prostitutes he kills.

This is all guess work, I admit. A criminal record of violence for a serial killer like the Riverman could represent any combination of the above factors.

Anyway, when compiling this list of men arrested for some sort of act or acts of violence against women, you would certainly want to focus on and flag these cases where the victim was a hooker.

2. A list of names of persons arrested in the King, Prince, Snohomish and Thurston Counties for impersonating police officers since 1980.
3. A list of men who have purchased handguns in the above listed four counties since 1980.
4. A list of the names of persons stopped for driving stolen vehicles or vehicles with missing, stolen or altered license plates in areas of prostitution such as a Pacific Highway South since 1980.

This list brings to mind the steps the Riverman might take to prevent being identified should the vehicle he is driving be reported while he is looking for or abducting a victim. It has got to be a major consideration for someone as wary as the Riverman. It is highly unlikely that he pulls up to the curb nearby where an intended victim is standing driving his own car which displays license plates registered to him. So how could he avoid identification through the vehicle he was driving?

I'll discuss this much more thoroughly in my letter on how I think he selects, approaches and abducts his victims. But for now I'll summarize somewhat by saying that one technique he may use is to park his vehicle in a location that is out of the line of sight of passing cars, pedestrians and occupants of nearby buildings. I doubt that this is the only precaution taken, however. Additional steps he may take, if the car he is driving is in fact his, is to remove or alter the plates or to replace the legal plates with stolen ones. He may even have purchased a vehicle under an assumed name so that while it is not stolen nor using stolen plates, neither can it be traced to him.

Of course, there is also the possibility the Riverman has stolen a vehicle prior to abducting each one of his victims. I wouldn't put it past him to use a stolen vehicle now and then, but for him to have done so <u>every</u> time he has gone looking for a victim for the past three years is highly unlikely. The risk of being caught stealing or driving a stolen vehicle would be very high when you consider the dozens of vehicles he would have to have stolen and the thousands of miles of cruising he would have to have done in them in high crime areas looking for victims. Keep in mind that the 45 or so official Green River Killer Victims represent only a fraction of the total number of times he has had to steal vehicles in the past three years. Not only has he certainly killed more than those 45, but these were times when he went out hunting that he came up empty-handed for one reason or another. Stealing 60, 70, 80, 100 vehicles over a three year period would seem to create an unacceptably high risk of arrest when you consider the steps he could take to conceal the true ownership of his own vehicle.

Since there is a chance he may have used a stolen vehicle once in a while, I propose the following study: compile a list of all vehicles stolen in King and Prince Counties on the day of and the day before each of the disappearances in the Green River case. For Wendy Coffield, for example, vehicles stolen on July 7 and 8, 1982, would be listed. I would want to know make, model, year and where the vehicle was stolen from and where it was found.

It sounds like a fairly major undertaking for an issue of questionable relevancy. It may not be worth it. The data may not even be available.

Finally, I wouldn't say that he has never driven right up to one of his victims as he was making his approach to abduct her (one of his victims was hitchhiking, for instance), but for many reasons I think that such a practice would be an exception to the rule.

5. Mental patients' printout: I am not very enthusiastic about such a listing but don't want to overlook it. The Healey list of lists included mental patients. While including them won't hurt, doing so should be done with the following qualifications: 1) mental patients show no greater propensity for violent criminal behavior than the general population, and 2) I believe it is highly unlikely that the Riverman has suffered or is suffering from the kind of mental disturbance that would bring him to the attention of mental health

professionals. There's always a possibility, though, hence the mental patient list.

Why do I believe he doesn't have a recorded history of mental problems? For starters, he has committed between 40 and 60 murders over a three-year period, and he has not been caught and has left very little in the way of clues. This by itself isn't conclusive and must be considered in light of other things. The manner in which he has gone about systematically abducting, asphyxiating and disposing of his victims is evidence of a highly controlled, quiet, relatively rational individual. He has had to be very well disciplined and conscious of what is going on around him.

Furthermore, a certain presence of calm and normality has been essential to him being able to lure and abduct his victims, most of whom were aware of a killer stalking them. And from what I know about the murders, there is a lack of the kind of extremely bizarre acting out (taunting the police, mutilating the victims) that would suggest a severe impairment of mental capacities.

The Riverman has his problems, which sounds like an understatement I suppose, but those distorted mental processes which underlie his violent behavior would appear, from the facts and circumstances of the case, to be as well integrated as they are hidden from view of those around him.

There you have my lists. Now, what I would do in addition to this is to develop a duplicate set of lists for Multnomah County (Portland, Oregon). As I discussed at some length in my letters of January 28 and February 3, the likelihood that the Riverman has been active in the Portland area is so high as to approach certainty. Cross-referencing the Oregon and Washington lists could develop an important list: possible suspects with significant contacts in both states.

I hope this has been of some value to you. Please share it with Bob when you have a chance. If you have any questions, don't hesitate to ask. Maybe you and Bob could arrange a call to me so we can go beyond the limitations of the written word.

Best Regards,

ted

 laughable! were you really a serial killer?

P.S. – When studying a list of unsolved homocides of young women between 197(?) and 1983, which Bob sent me, I noticed that there are only two cases listed in 1981: one involved a white female named Carter found at Fort Lewis on January 18, 1981, and the other involved a 27 year old woman named Quaschik found in the Spokane River on April 14, 1981. Did either Carter or Quaschik have a record for prostitution? How comprehensive is this listing for 1981?

Were people who may have been traveling along the road that runs near where Opal Mills was found on the evening of July 12 questioned about any vehicles they may have seen parked along the roadside?

I am sure he immediately recognized what a close call he had, and, in my opinion, didn't come any where close to that area of the Green River for months if ever.

One closing footnote. By placing a large rock over Cynthia Hinds body to keep it submerged, the Riverman displayed the extraordinary lengths, revealingly inept the use of the rock was, he would go to hide his victims.

P.P.S. I would appreciate it if you would send me a few stamps. I'm running low on postage, and these letters to you and Bob put a drain on my already meager supply. Thanks.

Ted Bundy
069063 R2N3
Florida State Prison
Box 747
Starke, Florida 32091

March 21, 1985

Dear Bob,

I wrote you letters on January 28, 1985 (12 pages) and again on February 3, 1985. I wrote to Dave on February 5, 1985 (16 pages). I haven't heard from you or Dave since I wrote to you. I would like to know if you received those letters, and, if you did, did you send me a reply.

 revealingly:
inept:

23

I would like to know your reaction to my most recent letters. There is a good deal more I have to send you but I am awaiting word from you before I write again. I would like our correspondence to be as much like a dialogue as possible.

Take care,   Best Regards,

ted

P.S. – Please address any future letters to me in the form I have written in the upper right-hand corner of this letter. Recent changes in prison regulations require the lengthier address I have written above. Thanks.

Ted Bundy
069063   R2N3
Florida State Prison
Box 747
Starke, Florida 32091

April 17, 1985

Dear Bob,

I have received and read your letter of March 19, 1985, as well as the enclosed newspaper articles describing the two latest finds in the Green River case. What with the arrival of Spring in the Northwest more of the Riverman's victims should turn up. And based upon past behavior, this is the time of year when he should be expected to be more active. So I imagine that you and Dave and company will be busier than ever.

I realize that you are very busy, as I said, and that the time you have to correspond with me and respond to my letters is quite limited. On the other hand, I hope you can understand that its hard for me to figure out what to write to you about when I know so little about the current concerns of the

Green River investigators. I also realize that I cannot be trusted with confidential information. That's the way it is. No problem.

So I've reached the point where I don't know what else to write to you concerning the Green River murders. I have already expressed most of my ideas on the case. Sure, I could go on hypothesizing but I'm not sure what value it would be. I'd rather not waste your time and mine.

Let me put it this way: if there is anything specific you'd like me to comment on concerning the Green River investigation or any specific questions you have stemming from what I've said or write about the case, please feel free to ask. If I can come up with any additional thoughts I think might be of value to you, I will write them down and send them along as I have in the past.

Regarding the comments you made in your

April 25, 1985

I put this letter aside a little over a week ago, hoping for some new insight and appreciation. I can't say I came up with anything, so I'd better finish off this one as best I can and send it on its way.

Picking up where I left off, regarding your comments made in your March 19 letter about the list of lists used in the Healy et al investigation in 1974, I wouldn't go so far as to say I'm puzzled by the list and the analysis of it. Sure I have some questions about it, and I would challenge some of the things you have said about the use of the list. For example, I can see my name appearing on two, maybe three lists, but not the five you allege. But whether my name was on one or ten lists may not be relevant at this point. I don't want to get in the position of debating this aspect of the 1974 investigation.

The important point as I see it is that people in law enforcement have learned something from the use of the lists ten years ago and that today they may use such an investigative tool more effectively because of that experience. As you know, names on lists is not evidence of the kind that could prove useful in a trial. At best it's a tool that can bring focus an investigation on possible suspects. With this in mind, investigators in those

1974 cases cannot be faulted for limiting their investigation of me prior to my arrest in Utah in August, 1975.

There's more to this business of the use of lists in 1974 cases, and some day we'll have a chance to discuss it in more detail perhaps.

You also mentioned the incompleteness of your list of murder victims in the Pacific Northwest in 1981. To the extent that this incompleteness is due to the failure of agencies to report crimes, it is abominable and an unfortunate fact of life in your business. I doubt that even ViCAP will change that.

But there's more to this problem of incompleteness than the failure of agencies to report. Take the Green River case, for example. There are some 45 known victims and missing persons officially believed to be victims of the Riverman. I think you would agree that it's safe to assume he has killed considerably more than 45 people. He almost certainly killed prior to July, 1982, and has continued to kill since December, 1983. The obvious problem you encounter in such an investigation is linking [homocides that] differ or vary in location and modus operandi.

Still, this only addresses part of the problem of incompleteness. Even if you were 100% sure you'd included all cases with known victims whose remains had been found [and could be linked to] a certain perpetrator, there's always a problem in a Green River kind of serial murder case that all the victims are not found and may never be found, and that in all probability there are victims in the Green River case whose remains have not been found and are not even believed to be possible victims.

I'm sure this is frequently on your mind. What you are doing with the Green River case is only the tip of the proverbial iceberg. And while it is not usually productive to generalize in serial murder cases, I think that there's a significant tendency in serial murder cases that a number of the victims of a serial murderer are not found. Let's say that the percentage is somewhere between 25% and 50% that are found. In the Green River case the percentage is around 30% and probably far higher. Sure, there are cases that are exceptions to such a tendency, cases where all the victims in a given murder series are found. But I think such cases are exceptions.

Well, I've rambled on again. I guess you could say, "*So what?*" What can you do, except keep it in mind? There are any number of possible explanations for the phenomenon of unknown and missing victims in series

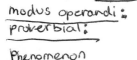
modus operandi:
proverbial:

Phenomenon

26

murders, of bodies disposed of and never found, and if you're interested I could elaborate.

Before I forget to mention it, thanks for the stamps.

Please take note of my new, revised address at the beginning of the letter.

Take care.   Best Regards,

                                         ted

Dear Bob,

Its almost time I got off my ass and at least acknowledged receiving your last two letters. Those would be your letters of May 29 and August 12. I apologize for the delay. I just find it hard to get motivated these days to write to anyone about anything. If I had a word processor, things might be different.

I don't anticipate this being an extensive reply to your letters. I'll write what I can write now and get into the rest some other time.

Your August 12 letter and enclosures focused mainly on developments related to the discovery of the remains of two women in the Portland area who were on the Green River missing list. That the Riverman is now conclusively linked to activity in the Portland area shouldn't really surprise anyone, but that the bodies of two women last believed to be in the Seattle area were found near Portland is….well…a novel twist. You called the discovery of the remains of Bush and Sherill "*a dynamic and interesting dimension.*" That is it. And it is probably by no means the most novel, dynamic and interesting development to be unearthed in the cases, considering the fact you're just scratching the surface at this point.

You asked if these new facts would change my mind about the likelihood of the Riverman living in the Tacoma area. No, not really.

Something else about the locations of the remains interested me. The Riverman seemed to be intent on leaving them in King County. Like I

unearthed (uncovered):

said, it "seemed" that way. This said to me that not only did he live south of the Pacific Highway South area, he lived outside of King County. He disposed of the bodies where he did because he didn't want to leave them close to home. So I looked at this and my gut reaction was that between July, 1982, and December, 1983, the Riverman probably lived in Pierce or maybe Thurston Counties.

The discovery of the remains of Bush and Sherill doesn't change my initial impressions for a number of reasons. To begin with, if the Riverman had lived in Portland during 1982 and 1983 I'd expect to see many more victims remains scattered between Portland and Seattle. Instead virtually all the <u>official</u> Green River victims (I emphasize "official" because there are undoubtedly many more victims of this man) were left in King County.

My second reason for thinking the Riverman didn't live in Portland (at least not continuously) during 1982 and 1983 has to do with his level of activity in the Seattle area during that time. He must have spent an enormous amount of time cruising and looking around the Pacific Highway South area for example. It would appear that at times he was looking for victims on a daily basis. And you must keep in mind that it's unlikely that every time he went looking he found a suitable victim under suitable circumstances.

Considering all of this and the fact he abducted his victims day and night seven days a week, says to me that he wasn't doing all this and commuting the four hours or so it takes to drive from Portland to Seattle, too.

I think its clear now that Bush and Sherill's remains have been discovered that he was active in the Portland area in 1982 and 1983 at least. But from the facts and circumstances I am aware of, extremely limited though they are, the Riverman was making the occasional commute from Washington to Oregon and back rather than vice versa.

(Refer to my earlier letters on the subject of his travels to Portland for more of my reasoning on why he'd do this.)

Okay, so why did he dump Bush's and Sherill's bodies near Portland, assuming he picked them up and abducted them near Seattle?

I sure as hell don't know. I don't even have a good idea. But I'll tell you this much: the Riverman had a very good reason for taking them there, even though it is not apparent now. I'm not saying the Riverman understands the reason necessarily. Let me put it this way: as I think I have noted before, the Riverman is not the stereotypical, maniacal, compulsive, mad slasher type. He was (and hopefully still is) a thinking, learning, changing, dynamic person. There were variations in his behavior just like there are in yours and mine. He's going to change. He's going to be inconsistent at times. He's not a robot. His mind works much the same as yours does. At the same time he is unique, as you are. Think about it.

So while taking Bush and Sherill to Portland made sense to him at the time, you'll never know exactly why until he tells you. The important thing is that an undeniable link has been made revealing the Riverman's presence in the Portland area. He is certainly responsible for the deaths of many more people in N.W. Oregon than Bush and Sherill. And as I mentioned in an earlier letter extending your investigation to Portland opens things up. You might say it warms things up.

Well, that's the essence of my response to your August 12 letter. One additional observation for the hell of it, though. The newspaper clippings you sent about the discovery of Bush and Sherill mentioned that the F.B.I. was contemplating becoming involved. Like the F.B.I. could make a difference. I can't imagine anyone around the Task Force is holding their breath waiting for the F.B.I. to come to the rescue. Or if a small handful of F.B.I. agents didn't already have more than enough to do to keep them busy.

It always amazes me how the press and the public think F.B.I. involvement is some kind of panacea, providing some special insight, some resource, some magic to do what local agencies can't accomplish. Such is the F.B.I. myth. Considering the massive resources devoted to the Green River case anything the F.B.I. could contribute would seem to me to be marginal. Besides too many cooks can spoil the broth.

It's all academic anyway since I can't imagine there being any evidence sufficient to establish an interstate crime that would pave the way for the F.B.I. coming in. The irony is they've probably been unofficially involved in one way or another for some time.

Okay. Now as to your May 29 letter.

29

In the second paragraph you asked me to get into the business of *"where is the Riverman now?"*, *"what's going through his mind now?"*, *"what's his behavior like now?"*

I guess that's what it comes down to: the Riverman here and now. He's certainly not the same person today as he was in '82, '83, or '84. But I know of not one shred of fact or circumstance upon which to base any inference or speculation, theory, whatever...as to what he's like today that would be useful to someone, like yourself, who's looking for him.

I realize that you want to go beyond what you called the "traditional theories". We discussed some of these last year when you were here. I am sure that the people in the Task Force have formulated more of these theories than they care to remember. I've thought a lot about some meaningful way to approach this. I have some ideas, but nothing that particularly impresses me. Let me work on it some more.

What I have to say is not of much relevance to the Green River case, anyway, and is best left to another time. Ultimately, however, law enforcement people and social scientists are going to have to develop better ways of studying and tracking missing persons. For all the talk about missing persons these days, the data is shockingly poor, contradictory and unreliable.

I have an idea how I'd study missing person records in order to grasp the real number who are likely victims of "foul play". A proper review of missing persons files of agencies in the Pacific Northwest would, I believe, be revealing and could in some instances alert authorities to patterns of what might be called "silent serial murders".

In your letter of May 29 you asked about my current status following the decision by the Florida Supreme Court in the Leach case. The legal battles now go into the Federal Courts. There is no timetable as such. I have many options, however, and I plan to fully exercise them all. It's fair to say you'll have ample advance notice in the event the folks here in Florida set a specific date to murder me.

I suggested this once before but you never let me know what you thought of it, so I'll propose it again. I think it could prove useful if we talked on the phone now and then. Writing is fine as far as it goes but it can't provide the subtle and spontaneous give and take a conversation can.

Speculation:
inference:
foul play:
ample:

30

Of course, there are problems with confidentiality. Don't hesitate to call if you think it might be of some value.

The best way for me to share my thoughts is if you're in the area again someday and you could come see me? I'd welcome the opportunity.

Have you given any more thought to my idea of a serial murder movie festival? I know it sounds outrageous but I'm telling you you'd have them coming out of the woodwork. I have written to you in detail about it, although we discussed it briefly. Maybe I didn't make myself clear. It's an idea whose time has come, Bob. Talk about a pro-active technique. I don't see how you can't afford not to use such a novel approach especially considering how old and cold most of the tips and leads in the investigation have become. You can't be worried about starting a controversy in the community. Not at this point. Besides it can be defused.

People interested in fishing and skiing, for example, go to see movies about fishing and skiing. People who kill serially go to see movies about serial killing. It's that simple.

Would [it] be a waste of time for me to go into the details?

I've got to go. Take care.

Best Regards

ted

❖

March 4, 1986

Dear Bob,

Thank you for your letter of February 13, 1986, and the clippings you enclosed with it. The Green River murder investigation has taken on mythical proportions. We're talking about 56 investigators, including 10 F.B.I. persons, two million dollars in computer stuff, the recent find of a two-year-old pile of bones, and a wise old head named Pierce Brooks. It's certainly more than I'm capable of comprehending.

All the Task Force needs is an acupuncturist and nutritionist and it could go on tour. Seriously, I wonder if it is too big for its own good.

I've read the positive predictions about 1986 being the year the Riverman is caught, etc. etc. Putting on a confident face is one thing but if your man is out there watching all this he has a pretty good idea if the investigation is on track or just spinning its wheels.

I heard that a few weeks ago there was a rather sensational search of a potential suspect's house, complete with live televised accounts. If it did happen that way, it would be most unfortunate in my opinion. I'd sure like to know what it was that convinced the Task Force to go after someone like that.

It wasn't old Melvyn Foster, was it? Has he been cleared or is he still a suspect of some kind. I intended to write to you last year about my thoughts on Mr. Foster, but there were other things I wanted to write you about which took precedence. In any event, I believe I expressed to you when you were here that dear Melvyn didn't seem to fit the bill. Just my gut reaction, mind you. I understand that you cannot afford to take anything for granted.

The impression that I was forming of the Riverman back in November, 1984, and which has continued to take shape, was that the Riverman wasn't out to play games with you. He wasn't going to tease you or play games with you or leave Lincoln Continentals laying around for you. He wasn't going to get in your face like Melvyn because, believe it or not, he didn't and doesn't want to get caught.

I'm not saying Melvyn never thought of taking some young girl off and doing away with her, but he doesn't seem to me like the type who's crossed over the line to actually do it, certainly not with the intensity and proficiency with which the Riverman has done it. Just because Melvyn contacted the police back in 1973 about the Devine girl doesn't mean any more than he's had a longstanding fascination with such things. He didn't kill the Devine girl; he just got off on talking about her.

You asked about my suggestion of talking by phone. Since I made the suggestion I've thought more about it. We wouldn't have much time; maybe only ½ hour or so. But, if something comes up you'd like to discuss by phone, call Superintendent Richard Duggar and he'll make the necessary arrangements, if they can be made.

I won't press you anymore to hold a serial murder movie festival. It's obviously up to you. I think you're missing something, though. You

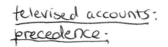

televised accounts:
precedence:

don't have many pro active tactics available to you at this stage. It's time to take a few risks, calculated risks, and really what are you risking? This doesn't violate any one's rights any more than any suspect's rights are violated in the course of an investigation. Where there's a will, there's a way, multiple screen movie theaters notwithstanding. Let me quote you something from the August, 1985, F.B.I. Bulletin (p. 5), which reported findings of a study on serial murders: "Their (the 36 subjects studied) visual interests (pornography, fetishism, and voyeurism) reinforced the sex and aggression." For the serial murderer one form of voyeurism is watching a movie of someone committing serial murder.

So much for my words of wisdom about the Green River case. With all the folks now on the Task Force I'm sure there's no lack of ideas.

Perhaps I can be of more value in commenting on your project to centralize data about homocides in Washington State.

What comes to mind first is the question of whether or not you and the office of Attorney General have the legal authority to appeal to local agencies to supply such information. Secondly, if you have the legal authority, do you have the funds and the administrative apparatus to effectively do the job.

Sure, I can see the value of having data on all unsolved and solved homocides on one computer so that summaries of the data can be distributed around the state. It'll be a massive undertaking. Every law enforcement agency around the state without exception will have to search their records back 10, 20 years. (How far back do you want to go is one basic question).

So let's say this can be done. What are you going to produce?

Last year you sent me a couple lists of unsolved homocides, which, though interesting are more noteworthy for their shortcomings. They're examples of what not to do. For example, you sent me one list which appears to contain homocides occurring between 1973 and 1983. What defined what homocides were placed on the list? Who compiled it? What area does it cover? The list is clearly incomplete. Why? What's its purpose?

The 1973-1983 list may be someone's personal working list. It appears to contain only the unsolved cases of young women in Western Washington, although 3 Spokane homocides have been included. What your data base would do would be to assure the reader that the list was

thorough and credible. You would also be able to provide them
uniform format and a better selection of information about each crim

The problem with uniformity is one I noticed when receiving
various lists of alleged Green River victims. It's also evident in another
you sent me which appears to cover unsolved homocides an
disappearances of young women in California, Oregon, Washington and
British Columbia between 1969 and 1975. Again, it is hard to say what the
purpose of the list is. It is seriously very incomplete. Who's responsible for
the list? What were its sources? There are, for instance, several missing
persons on the list. Are these all the young women missing under
mysterious circumstances in those jurisdictions between 1969 and 1975?
And so on.

The point is that a uniform state-wide system of reporting could
take the guesswork out of such lists.

One idea before I forget: somehow your data bank should make
provision for people missing under suspicious circumstances. It will
probably have to be a fairly well defined criteria for what "suspicious"
disappearance is. As you know many murder victims, especially serial
murder victims, are often listed as missing before it's known that they're
murder victims, the Green River case being a good example. If your
computer system is going to attempt to identify a pattern of serial murders,
among other things, it should be capable of making connections between
actual murder victims and missing person.

I've gone over the State of Oregon Homocide Report you sent me
a couple times. It's about as thorough a report as I can imagine. I have only
one suggestion. The category of "Activity When Last Seen" could be
reworked. Currently, the activity category mixes activities and places.
Places last seen and activity when last seen should probably be separate and
analyzed closely in conjunction with the modus operandi section.

The place and activity categories are important for reasons other
than those of linking similar cases and searching for witnesses. They are
important because they can also yield insight into modus operandi. How, in
fact, could the victim have been abducted under these conditions?

Summarizing these reports in some meaningful way so that
investigators can more efficiently scan a listing of unsolved homocides is
going to be a challenge. I'd supply the following information:

1. Sex & age of victim
2. Investigating Agency
3. Date missing
4. Date found
5. Activity when last seen

No, no. Let me start again.

1. Sex, age, race, height, weight & name of victim
2. Cause of death
3. Condition of body (clothed, nude, mutilated, decomposed, etc.)
4. Date found
5. Location when found
6. Type of location (River, beside road, abandoned house, in bushes, buried, in water, etc.)
7. Date missing
8. Last known location and activity before disappearance/death
9. Investigating agency

You get the picture. I can see where it'd take a lot of work to put the information into a form that is readable, neat.

Having access to all this kind of information and being able to link cases are two different things, of course. All this data is only as good as the person interpreting it, and there are a number of factors which inhibit an investigator from officially linking a case in his jurisdiction to a series murder investigation somewhere else, as you have seen in the Green River case. And there are going to be times when (no matter how skilled the analyst) cases won't be linked which were committed by the same individual, because of what appear to be distinguishing characteristics. If a perpetrator consciously or unconsciously varies some critical variable, then the entire premise of consistency and similarity is confounded. A lot of data doesn't make one clairvoyant under such circumstances. The serial murderer who is thoughtful enough to leave police a truly unique "signature" is definitely the exception to the rule.

One last thing. It occurred to me when I was thinking about the Devine girl earlier. I worked in Olympia for a few months in 1973 and again during the Summer of '74. I became quite familiar [with the] area around Olympia: the rural areas, backroads, dirt roads, places where people illegally dumped

35

refuse. Anyway, in 1974 while I was checking out these off-the-road locations I found what appeared to be human skeletal remains in two separate places. I wasn't sure though. I forgot all about it until a while ago. I never had occasion to mention it really.

I'm almost certain there'd be nothing left there but if you want to send me a detailed map of the Lacy area I'll try to pinpoint the scene. I'd also appreciate it if you could send me some of the crime scene photos in the Devine case, including a couple that show her face. The ones I saw don't show her face.

Thanks.   Take care.

Best Regards,

ted

P.S. – Even as crude as that list you sent me covering the period of 1973 to 1983 is, it reveals a couple of interesting patterns: the three women strangled in their homes in the Kent-Bellevue area in 1980; the four women found strangled in Snohomish County between 1980-83; the five found strangled to death in the Spokane River. I'm sure there are more patterns but I have a feeling the list isn't complete. There isn't enough information either.

Do you have a more complete list of unsolved murders in Washington and Oregon between 1980 and 1985?

And finally, how about this proposal: how about you and I sitting together and going over all the unsolved homocides in Washington in the past 10 years or so and seeing what cases we could link? I guarantee you it would be worth your while. I would be disappointed if you don't take me up on the offer at your earliest opportunity. Let me know.

August 3, 1986

Dear Bob,

I received your letter of June 5, 1986, at a time when there was a death warrant pending against me, as you know. I felt then that it would be best to delay answering until calmer conditions prevailed.

crude:
prevail:

36

Considering your last letter and what has transpired between us since we [met] in November. 1984, I don't see any benefit from us continuing to write to each other.

When I first contacted the Green River Task Force in 1984 I was disappointed when I was informed that you had been assigned as my liaison with the Task Force. I had no animosity toward you, but I know that you had been an investigator in certain cases where I was a suspect. I felt that these unsolved cases would naturally tend to preoccupy you and perhaps detract somewhat from what I had to say about Green River. I won't say that you didn't give full consideration to my comments and observations, but I never felt that we established a dialogue in the Green River case. There could have been a number of reasons for this, but I think this was in part due to your continuing concern about these other cases.

In your letters you constantly referred to or inferred about the cases in the mid 70's. I don't blame you. However, I made it very clear in my initial letter to the Task Force that I was in no way interested in discussing those cases. I meant it. I wasn't playing games with you. This initiative on my part was not and is not some subtle or subconscious way of easing into a discussion about the mid-70's cases or any other cases, except Green River.

What your last letter indicated to me is that we really have no where else to go. I was very surprised that you would bring such a proposal to me. My offers to help first the Task Force and then your state-wide, unsolved homocides project were genuine and explicit. I did not appreciate your attempt to crudely manipulate me by questioning the sincerity and value of my efforts. I know I should have expected this but I didn't expect that you would so badly misread me.

I am not going to play games and I don't want you to feel that you have to play games with me. The only way I can see for us to avoid such unproductive involvement is for us to stop communicating. We both have better uses for our time.

I wish you the best in your work on the Task Force, with the A.G.'s Office, and in your life generally.

peace,

ted

transpired:

liason:

detract:

infer:

crudely:

❖

37

February 16, 1987

Dear Bob,

I must ask that we postpone our meeting scheduled for February 27. Circumstances are such that it should be postponed indefinitely. I hope that this change of plans does not inconvenience you. It will, at least, save the state some money, and give you a couple of days that I am sure you will have no trouble filling with other activities.

One of the reasons that I feel the need to cancel our meeting involves the possibility that a visit by my Washington, D.C. attorneys will conflict with our meeting. My attorneys will be in Atlanta on February 25 for oral arguments in one of my case before the 11th Circuit Court of Appeals. They indicated that they have tentatively planned to come see me following oral arguments. It would be a mess if you and my attorneys showed up on the same day. I wouldn't want you to come all the way across the country and risk encountering my attorneys, who if they knew I planned to meet with you, would insist that I not do so.

I am sorry about this. I realize that you are very busy. You can hardly be expected to organize and re-organize your schedule around the last minute plans of my attorneys. As things stand now, I feel it is best if we just put our plans for a meeting on ice indefinitely.

I hope things are going very well for you.

peace,

ted

P.S. – Thank you for your January 28 letter and for explaining in it what you meant by "solvability factors".

July 6, 1987

Dear Bob,

I apologize for not writing promptly to answer your February 23 and May 22 letters. Today I received your July 2 letter. Thank you for your

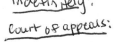

38

letters and your patience. I have all three letters in front of me. I will go over them now.

Your February 23 letter:

Because of some misinformation in the press a couple months ago, which falsely stated I had been studied by the F.B.I., my attorneys became aware that I had in fact been in contact with Bill Hagmaier. They were not previously aware of this and were not pleased. They gave me a direct order not to communicate with people in law enforcement. That is they're job and, for the time being, I will have to honor their instructions on this.

Given the situation, I do not know when we will be able to meet again. I am confident that someday we will be able to.

You asked if I had any ideas on lists of names that could be used to develop suspects. I have nothing further to add to what I wrote to you on the subject in several earlier letters. I know so very little about what's really happening in the case/investigation that anything I would say would be elementary. I will say this much: looking for names of persons, whose names show up on lists developed in the key metropolitan areas (Portland, Tacoma, Seattle and Vancouver, B.C.)) has a lot of potential. Wait…I don't think I worded that clearly, but you get the idea. The more areas where a given person's name turns up, the higher his suspect status.

Your May 22 letter:

You briefly discussed Ronald Holmes and enclosed a news clipping about statements he is making.

What Holmes is saying around the country is so patently and outrageously preposterous that anyone who knows about serial murder and/or my background will quickly identify Holmes as a charlatan. Of course, most people do not understand the nature of serial murder and do not know me, and this is true of people in local law enforcement who attend seminars and conferences only to be misled by Holmes who is himself tragically uninformed about the problem.

And he hasn't confined himself to lying about and otherwise misrepresenting and distorting Ted Bundy. I happen to know that people at the F.B.I. are very unhappy about how Holmes has misused and falsified

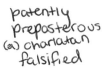

patently
preposterous
(a) charlatan
   falsified

information related to subjects they have studied. Holmes seems to have gone off the deep end.

I must admit that I didn't in any way expect this kind of bizarre conduct on the part of Holmes when I first agreed to meet him. He supplied me with a curriculum vita, which showed him to be a well-established professor and researcher, a man of credibility and honor. In his letters he came across as an open minded, mild-mannered and humble academician. So I agree to meet with him so long as he promised, which he did in writing and in person, that all of our communications would be held in confidence. I wanted to see what kind of person he was, and if he was legitimate. I hoped to provide such general background information (not about myself but about the reality of serial murder) to help guide his research.

I genuinely wanted to make a contribution, notwithstanding the *(in spite of)* limitations I had to remain cognizant of.

You know how your last meetings with me went. Well, my meeting with Holmes was far more general because he didn't have 1% of the knowledge and experience with serial murder you had. I didn't discuss my background or the allegations about me, not so much as a single case, not in the first, second or third person, not directly or indirectly. During that meeting, and in subsequent correspondence, it became clear that Holmes did not have the kind of capabilities needed to make use of my knowledge. But what has totally surprised me is that he has so brazenly fabricated such a ludicrous account of the meeting. (Fortunately, I saved letters he wrote to me after the meeting, which support my version of the facts.)

That about does it for the mad professor, except to say that I, too, hope to find a proper forum for the truth, although I know this will not be easy since it is my experience that the system and the people who operate it are not primarily interested in the truth and may even be adverse to it.

Your July 2 letter:

You mentioned the discovery of the remains of Cindy Anne Smith. You said Smith disappeared about the time police located the remains of an unidentified victim not far away and that Smith was found ½ mile from Yvonne Antosh.

You wondered if I thought those coincidences were/are significant. I rather doubt that the Riverman drove by the discovery site and then boldly

curriculum vita   *·*   correspondence

bizarre   brazenly   40

cognizant   ludicrous

allegations   subsequent

adverse

went off to abduct Smith. (Besides, the information I have shows that the unidentified victim was found March 21, 1984, not March 24). But, who knows. Only the man himself.

The fact that the Antosh and Smith dump sites where close together could mean the same person did both murders, or that Smith's murderer was a copy cat. Yvonne Antosh was discovered October 16, 1983, and no doubt the discovery was well-publicized. The fact that Smith wasn't closer to the Antosh site may only mean the copycat didn't know exactly where Yvonne Antosh had been dumped. Again, there's no way to say for sure if it was the Riverman or someone else.

With the discovery of remains of victims, like Smith's, the Green River murders continue to haunt the Pacific Northwest, and yet the investigation is about as cold as a murder investigation can get. I can only see one way that that case can be satisfactorily resolved, and that seems highly unlikely: the man will have to be convinced to give himself up.

I don't have much time. I have one more matter I've been wanting to write about. I saw a news item in the April 25, 1987 edition of the St. Pete Times about a Morris Solomon, who was arrested in Sacramento for the murder of six prostitutes, some or all of whom were buried on his property. You must certainly have checked him out long ago, especially since he had a history of violence against women including his 1977 acquittal for the murder of a prostitute. The man was loose on the West Coast for the better part of the next 10 years after his 1977 murder trial. He may have been cleared in the Green River case, but he represents one kind of individual who is in the Green River ballpark. There are undoubtedly more Morris Solomon types out there. With their criminal records, I am sure those you can identify are at the top of your list. Then there are all the new ones without the criminal records…

I wish you the best.

peace,

ted

acquittal ❧

41

February 11, 1988

Dear Bob,

Thank you for your letter of February 2. You said you plan to be in Jacksonville the week of February 22. I am interested in meeting with you while you are in the area. You said you could come by the 22nd, 23rd, or both. How about the 22nd? I may have an attorney interview on the 23rd. The best time would be after 11:00 a.m. I only get two periods of outdoor exercise a week and one of them is 8-10 Monday mornings. I would suggest asking the prison to schedule you from 11:00 to 5:00. That way we'll have the time if we need it, and if we don't, we don't. It's up to you.

As to what we can discuss, the Homocide Assistance Program questionnaire would be one good topic. It is so very thorough, however, that I am not sure what I can add.

You said we could also talk about the information in my July 6, 1987, letter. I don't recall the letter, although I do remember writing in one of my last letters to you, as you noted, something about the Riverman turning himself in. I must say that it is highly unlikely he would do so, but at this point in the investigation there's no point in not turning over all the stones. Nothing ventured nothing gained. I have no doubt that you and many in the Task Force have contemplated a scenario or two designed to prompt the man to give himself up. And I'll bet that conventional law enforcement (not to mention political) considerations find such tactics objectionable to one degree or another for one reason or another. The hope that good old (and new) investigative practices will identify this guy springs eternal. Maybe this year…

I would be interested in going over with you any of the cases you mentioned in your November 21, 1986, letter, plus any of the unsolved cases in the Pacific Northwest since 1982, which may be related to King County Green River cases. Actually, I don't know what you'll feel comfortable bringing. Bring as much as you want, but nothing prior to 1976 please. I won't discuss anything prior to 1976. Do we understand each other on this? Please let me know what you can do and when you can come.

peace,

ted

42

Grim Reader

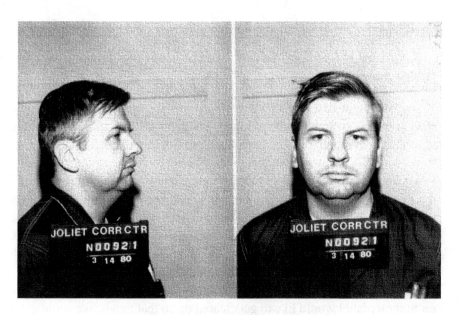

TICKET TO CLOWN TOWN:

THE LOST JOHN WAYNE GACY TAPES

Jim Jurzak's desk sat littered with neatly-creased business cards, each dusted with the powdery residues of the preceding day's party, and the Chicagoland personal injury attorney's West Randolph Street offices' primary furnishings were teetering accumulations of unanswered legal briefs, buttressed by rubber-banded bricks of ignored correspondence.

Amid this widely scattered debris of a thus-far undistinguished law career sat an unusual letter: a relic of infamous Chicagoan John Wayne Gacy's early incarceration. Its densely packed sentences addressed a different Second City lawyer and were potentially most notable to Jurzak for being so different from those which Gacy obsessively mailed to him on the daily: jammed with demands, foot-stomping tantrums and the caustic accusations of a sociopath clawing to keep breathing against increasingly poor odds. What this letter contained, instead, was John Gacy's *confession*.

John Gacy N00921
Lock Box 711
Menard, Illinois 62259

Dear Ralph,

Thought that I would get a letter off to you, since visiting, and talking with you on the phone. I realise where your coming from when you say, when it comes to civil matters, that your not interested. That your more interested in the criminal matters. When I told you that I was depressed, it [was] only because when I see all the things that I had worked hard for all disappear like it was nothing, I get upset. As you know I have a 73 years old mother, and I don't like to see her worry or want for anything. Maybe you don't know it, but I used to send money every month, up to $2,900, since I have been in here all she receives is Social Security. So when I ask about the civil things its only because I would like to get things out of the way for her, so she don't worry or have to want for anything. The property on Summerdale I would like to get cleared up so that maybe we could get it sold. My mother worry about having to pay the taxes, because her name is on the property. Then there is the money owed under the old mortgage. I know that recovering my personal property is going to be hard, but if they were able to get some of it back, at least they could sell it, and get some cash for it. I don't understand all the laws, but since my mother and sister have there names on the property, and they were not charged with a crime, certainly they should have rights to what was there's. The same goes for PDM's personal property, they were not charged with a crime. I would think that legally they could be paid for the damage or missing property. The wrongful destruction of the house can not be justified by those search warrants. Even you said that they weren't any good, but because of who I am they won't do anything about it. But what about those people who were not charged with a crime, they are entitled to what was there's. While much can't be done for what was mine, certainly they should get what's coming to them. I have never been selfish, and I am not looking out for myself now, I just feel that others shouldn't be hurt by me. So I hope you understand where I am coming from, and why I am pushing the civil stuff, it's not for me. All you have to do is keep me busy with what you think I could help you with.

Sometimes my memory is clear, and sometimes I can't remember things, and I try hard to write them down when I do. You asked one question when you were here, that I don't feel I gave you a fair answer to.

Civil matters
Criminal matters

45

Remember when you asked if the other side has come out, while being here, well I told you no. Well at times I am not sure, when I have been alone or getting tired, I sometimes feel like the other side wants to come out, that's one of the reasons I asked to be taken off the night medication. I got to tell you that I am scared, when I think that it is happening because I don't know if he will kill me.

The same with depression. I try to stay away from that, because of suicide and the thoughts of it. It's like I said, I am afraid of myself, because I don't know what could happen. That's another reason for keeping busy, keep my mind off of it. I sometimes think I would like to bring out the other side just to find out if I could control that side, or learn anything from it. Dr. Lawrence Freedman said that if I tried hard enough I could put more of the whole picture together. I just wonder if I should push it alone. I wish I was working with Freedman and [Helen] Morrison, because they seem to be putting the puzzle together better than anyone else. I want to know what triggers it, and if I can control it. It might answer some of the questions that I have, in wondering what cause what happen and what the reason were. I know that it wasn't sexually motivation. I think that the theory that Rappaport was coming with fit it best, about wanting to punish them by transferring the guilt from me to the victim, because they were dumb and stupid. The other reason is maybe I could find out just how many I am responsible for and like I believe that there are more than what was found. Also I know from my feelings that others were involved, but I only know and remember the one that Rossi was present for. Its like a great big puzzle and the pieces are missing.

I don't know what you think of all this, and would like to hear your comments on it. It seems that we just get started [when] you come down, and the visit is over. I wish sometime when you come down that we could visit for a longer period of time. There are so many things that we didn't get into on this last visit, and there is so much I don't understand. Like with the law and my case, if things were done illegally why can't they be overturned. Wrong is wrong no matter what kind of case it is. I think that I am entitled to fair rights just like anyone else. They should not be allowed to profit from their own mistakes. Hindsights is great, but it has no place in the law. That's why I asked about Paul Kelly, wondering if he could get into researching more on the illegal search warrants and fill in all the loopholes to force them to uphold the law. Or make them change it.

I think that I am willing to do the right thing even if they cut me loose. I still want to know what happens, the Why, the what, the how, and what triggers it, can it be controlled, or will it take me over.

Well I have bent your ear long enough, enclosed is the legal papers that are for Ira Moltz, I hope that you can light a fire under him and at least get some of the things out of the way. Bye for now. Thanks again for coming down and the lunch. Don't forget about the picture I asked for, just make sure that they are close ups and that they are at least 3x5.

Sincerely,

J.W. Gacy

Fast forward twelve years. John Wayne Gacy is Jurzak's client, and his burden; not in efforts to halt Gacy's looming execution date or the civil lawsuit over who ought to pay Gacy's room and board – a well-timed ploy by the Attorney General to distract Gacy from more critical appeals. Instead Jurzak's role was to root out cash Gacy could use to hire lawyers actually qualified to enter those courtroom battles. A '1-900' line was one scheme Jurzak was particularly bullish on: a concept he helped birth, evidently. Callers would fork over $2 per-minute to hear Gacy reply to scores of pre-recorded questions while improbably declaring his innocence. Jurzak's job was to make crime pay, in spades if possible. Though sometimes his job was to locate Gacy's favorite porn novels. To smuggle Gacy's oil paintings. To plot against Gacy's legitimate attorneys. To defraud Gacy's enemies, both real and imagined. Or to supervise an impressionable young student's retrieval from an airport, then his hand-delivery to Gacy at Menard Prison. But Jurzak's job-in-chief was that very first thing: to monetize a serial killer.

It would all prove hypothetical. On May 10, 1994, Jurzak's cash cow lost his fight at the pointy end of a lethal injection without ever milking his fortune, and without even knowing his own lawyer's name: the sly substitution of a single letter transformed 'James Jorzak, Ambulance Chaser' into 'Jim *Jurzak*, Attorney-at-Law' and this sleight-of-hand prevented anyone (least of all Gacy) from suspecting his dad was Judge Richard Jorzak, who with one pen stroke demolished Gacy's death house: the ranch-style grave marker atop his burial ground. The senior Jorzak's

consolation
raze
hallowed

albeit nepotistic
clandestine
transcribed

order deprived Gacy's family of *"what's there's"* *and* had Gacy caught wind of this lightly veiled truth it would have meant an abrupt end to their association. Also the end of 1-900 revenues, the end of profits from art exhibitions marketing Gacy's clown portraits at obscene prices, the end of Gacy's book sales and the end of interview requests from Geraldo Rivera; all signaling the beginning of his life as a never-was enslaved to some very unflattering addictions. Cocaine. Streetwalkers. Heroin. And, in that order.

Jorzak sat balding and bloodshot amid his rapidly expanding chaos. When his desk phone rang at the appointed hour and an automated voice announced a collect call from death row he'd promptly hit 'record', a habit now grown to Nixonian proportions. As Gacy's execution date neared, Jorzak tried selling recordings he'd made to the tabloid Inside Edition for twenty-five grand. Gacy's confession letter, too. He'd split the money (or so he'd propose) with the killer's spitting-image nephew, Edward, a blackout drunk who Jorzak prophesied was a lengthy prison sentence waiting to happen. Not that day or that year, maybe, but eventually. Again, all academic because at the end there were no TV producers cutting Jim Jorzak checks. It was almost as if the world had heard enough from John Wayne Gacy for a while. And from his mouthpiece, too.

But there was an Only-In-Chicago-style consolation prize awaiting Jorzak: a black robe and rosewood gavel, like those Dad wielded when he summoned the backhoes to raze Gacy's hellish homestead. Soon, criminal defendants were paraded before the junior Jorzak, only 31 years old, never suspecting that in their presiding's hallowed (albeit nepotistic) chambers, atop – or, at best, hiding just within – the desk that would decide their fates lay business cards dusted with the residues of last night's party. Amid persistent rebuke from colleagues Jorzak died in office, age 40. Unlike Gacy's death, obituaries failed to say if drugs played any role in his demise.

These conversations, transcribed from clandestine recordings, are the legacy Jim Jorzak leaves behind. These, and a single prediction that took decades to come true. In 2012, John Wayne Gacy's nephew, Edward Kasper – Jorzak's on-tape collaborator – was sentenced to serve 24 years in the Illinois state prison system for committing deviant sexual assault upon a 12-year-old child.

For the record, he, too, proclaims his innocence.

TAPE 1:

James Jorzak and Unidentified Male Caller

Jorzak: The fact that what?

Unknown: Robert Piest, the one they were looking for. They didn't know that they had a serial killer situation.

Jorzak: They were just looking for the one. Right…right. I thought it was that Gacy invited them over for dinner or something and while they were there one of them went into the john to take a piss and there was a heating duct near the toilet. When the heat went on it…

Unk: That's in one of the books.

Jorzak: Yeah, it's in John's book. You don't think that happened?

Unk: I don't think so. It might have happened somewhat.

Jorzak: I've heard three or four different versions of this already.

Unk: Well, the one where the heat comes on and the odor comes up and the guy says, "*I've smelled that odor in morgues*", I always wonder in the back of my mind if his suspicions were already strong enough that he cooked up that as an excuse for a warrant…

Jorzak: Right! Right! You know what, that's probably what it was.

Unk: On the other hand, meanwhile, they had already discovered all of those rings and wallets and stuff.

Jorzak: Were they in his house? One of the times they went in there when he wasn't home?

Unk: They got in there twice, they were in there several times – one time by [Gacy's] invitation but I think the first time they went in was in search of Piest. They didn't know what they were looking for. They were looking for anything that would give them a clue. They found the wallets and rings and other stuff that was just suspicious because it didn't belong to anyone that they knew of. But they were still just looking for one kid…

[RECORDING STOPS]

49

[CALL RESUMES]

Jorzak: Hello? Sorry about that.

Unk: So Kozenczak sees a receipt laying on the top of the trash or someplace and just on a hunch he picks the thing up and sticks it in his pocket.

Jorzak: Wow.

Unk: Then when they got back they found out that it had been in Piest's pocket.

Jorzak: It was like a dry-cleaning receipt?

Unk: Uh, photo processing. Photo processing.

Jorzak: Oh, Piest had been picking up pictures.

Unk: I think that on the basis of that, that might have been...I don't know if that was the one that got them the warrant or not.

Jorzak: When they found the coat...They found the coat and then they found the receipt, right?

Unk: No, no, I think the other way around. They found the receipt and I think that they might have been the basis of their.... [TAPE ENDS]

TAPE 2:

James Jorzak and John Wayne Gacy

Jorzak: ...those are your copyrighted materials.

Gacy: Ninety-five percent of that fifty percent I was supposed to get from that other character belongs to me. He was being paid a fee as an overseer. Five thousand dollars. I don't know if he told you that 'cause that was cut and dry and way up front.

Jorzak: Well, yeah. I believe that that goes into the expenses portion, right? So should I leave that out of expenses, or...?

Gacy: No, just give him a flat five thousand dollars.

Jorzak: This covers his expenses?

Gacy: Well, for him taking the time to oversee it 'cause I figure he's got his own life, his own job, and he's got to be taken away from that so I paid him for that. But the rest of those funds are supposed to be paid over to my sister who is handling my estate. She handles everything that belongs to me.

Jorzak: To be honest, John, he's never... I don't want to go into that. Whatever agreement as to where the funds are going, I really don't...I don't...I'm not going to concern myself with that. I'm just, I'm helping to facilitate these actions and things Edward brings to me and, uh...

Gacy: Yeah, but you've got to be paid from somewhere...

Jorzak: Pardon me?

Gacy: Lawyers have to be paid from somewhere.

Jorzak: Well absolutely, for something... When I help him to do something that winds up...materializes into something that is profitable, I expect to get paid. And he understands that too, like with the, uh...

Gacy: The "1" number?

Jorzak: Exactly.

Gacy: Yeah, the "1" number.

Jorzak: Yeah, I know. Exactly.

Gacy: Yeah, well, you understand, my understanding is Missouri only has thirty percent of that.

Jorzak: Missouri only has thirty? Are you talking about Deacon? In Illinois?

Gacy: No, no. He's supposed to have thirty. Oh, okay, so he's out.

Jorzak: I got a release from him.

Gacy: So you got a release from him, but that doesn't automatically take that thirty percent that was there and send it over to Missouri, you know that?

Jorzak: Oh, no, absolutely not. That goes back into the one hundred percent, or the full amount. That's all.

Gacy: Exactly, but that thirty percent was supposed to be handed over to Hannibal to handle the, *heh*! To handle the, *heh*! To handle their phone bills...

Jorzak: Exactly.

Gacy: To cover their expenses. That is so that Edward could be more dependent...*independent* over there.

Jorzak: Thirty percent, I think, would buy most of the real estate in Hannibal, Missouri if this turns out the way we foresee it.

Gacy: I'm surprised that it's not going better in the coastal states, not here.

Jorzak: Well, exactly, on both coasts, and I think it's going to – and in the northeast, I think. You know, Seattle.

Gacy: Well, I haven't got it yet but I'm supposed to be getting copies of the flyer that has been put out in Florida. It's coming out of Bensonville.

Jorzak: Uh, coming out of...it's, uh...

Gacy: Shane Bugbee out of, uh...

Jorzak: Shane Bugbee. He sent out the flyer. Right. And that's the one...

Gacy: He happened to send it to a couple of my friends down in... I've got people.

Jorzak: It has the wrong number on it.

Gacy: Well, it might have the wrong number on it, but I know...

Jorzak: Do you have one of those, John?

Gacy: No, I haven't got the flyer yet. You get a flyer yet?

Jorzak: I had him fax me as soon as I heard about it. I called over to that comic book place, uh... Mike Johnson's, and I said, "*Get one over to me as soon as possible.*"

Gacy: And what did they do?

Jorzak: Let me go grab it, hold on. Hold on. God, I found it, with all of my materials, fortunately this one wasn't...

Gacy: That's the one put out by Tri-Star...

Jorzak: *Tri-Star*? What is Tri-Star? No, this is the one that I had Shane Bugbee fax to me. It says – do you want me to read it to you? Um, probably not a good idea, but…

Gacy: No, I don't think it's necessary. Anyhow, they are the ones who are behind that, right?

Jorzak: Well, yeah. Because as I told you…

Gacy: And how can they have a…a tape?

Jorzak: How can they have a tape?

Gacy: Yeah, in other words…

Jorzak: Well, we gave them certain limited information because, number one, and this was a while back – you know how long we've been trying to do this, facilitate this whole thing.

Gacy: Yeah.

Jorzak: Uh, Bill Hellmer apparently had connections with UPI, the Associated Press, and other major media sources who he was going to issue the press releases to, which we would design, uh, before they went out. Now, Mike Johnson has, apparently, connections in these underground magazines and certain periodicals that he convinced us there was a market for this type of line. So he was authorized, uh…when we told him. That's where this whole problem lies, is that we didn't authorize this thing to go out, and it has the wrong number on it, too. But, as I said, we did give them limited information and their part was to issue this information when we authorized it. So that is where my whole problem with this arises. They jumped the gun. Something with that article that came out last…

Gacy: Well, yeah, right away, the Attorney General's office is checking into me to find out if I'm profiteering off of this…

Jorzak: Yeah.

Gacy: …and of course, I had a meeting with the [Department of Corrections] officials, and since I'm a ward of the state they want my permission so they can go ahead and sue. You see, I did not give permission for them to record my voice. Whoever they are investigating…

Jorzak: [It] says "*A granted phone interview*" at the beginning of it, and, uh...

Gacy: Where is it granted?

Jorzak: Well, that is what I am suggesting. At the very beginning of the tape it says, "*this is a granted phone interview*", and that is what my understanding was from the beginning, uh...

Gacy: I never gave permission. You see, like when you got on this phone with me, they inform me right up front that this phone call is being recorded.

Jorzak: Right, exactly.

Gacy: Nobody has ever done that to me from my end so, therefore, I am not committed to knowing that anything I am saying, even to you right now, is being recorded. I have never given no permission and there is nothing in writing that I have permission or granted a phone interview to anybody.

Jorzak: Um, let's see, as we discussed the other day, this whole project is geared towards...it's just a thought...you are expressing, or getting out your opinion of what took place.

Gacy: That was the object of 'A Question of Doubt', also. To get 'Q of D' made public. Edward, since last April, has been in charge of 'They Call Him Mr. Gacy II'. It also is a factual book that was particularly set up to cut down the movie and it was also to put more factual info on the street for more people.

Jorzak: Was that a paperback, John? Was that the third?

Gacy: No, it's the second one. It's the second one that's out.

Jorzak: I've got 'They Call Him Mr. Gacy' then 'More Letters To Mr. Gacy'.

Gacy: 'More Letters to Mr. Gacy'. If you look in the first part of the book, it's loaded with nothing but letters about the movie. There is actually a legal filing that was filed in the Federal Courts.

Jorzak: I saw that.

Gacy: That's actually a copy of the pro se petition that was filed. It was deliberately put into the book so that the public would be enlightened. However...

Jorzak: Same with the F.B.I., uh, correspondence. That was here somewhere, too. Even in '84 they were still looking into… they still had an ongoing investigation.

Gacy: As late as ninety-one they had an ongoing investigation. But the thing of it is, is that the book hasn't moved. And Edward took it over in April, and for the amount that Edward has sold I could have sold them right from here for five bucks apiece. He jacked them up to $19.95 and then didn't do distribution or advertising, so they haven't gone nowhere.

Jorzak: Who originally coordinated the publishing of this thing?

Gacy: I did.

Jorzak: You did? Because early on I heard some comments regarding how it was poorly done, and that it's – please don't misunderstand me, I don't mean to offend…

Gacy: Well, I don't get offended by anything. I would rather you speak frankly to me. Originally, well, let me give you the brief story. Originally, the first 'Mr. Gacy' book was put out by a guy in Colorado. He just took a bunch of my letters and said, *"Do you realize? All of the letters are addressed to 'Mr. Gacy'?"* And he says, *"They're interesting!"* He says, *"these are fascinating people"* and *"they're well-known people."* But I said, *"O.K."* I gave him six thousand letters and said, *"Pick out some"*. And he put them together as a book. These were about this, this, and that, and I said, *"No. I don't want them all one-sided. I don't want to slant opinions."*

Jorzak: Right. Right. Exactly.

Gacy: Give them a cross-section.

Jorzak: Yeah.

Gacy: Then he wanted to re-write my letters. He said, *"You've got typing errors in yours."* I says, *"So what?"*

Jorzak: That's the real…

Gacy: That's the real me.

Jorzak: That's what people want to see.

Gacy: So I says, *"No, leave my letters just the way they're written."*

Jorzak: The only… the point that I was making…

Gacy: But they weren't organized. They weren't *correlated*.

Jorzak: They weren't organized and also…

Gacy: Notice in the second book they are more correlated.

Jorzak: And instead of taking a black marker, they should have whited that out. That's the only feedback that I heard. I mean, to be honest, the artwork itself on the cover should sell them, in my opinion. It's, uh… I didn't know when this thing was published, I wasn't involved in it.

Gacy: 1988.

Jorzak: O.K. I didn't have any input so I can't really sit here and say, *this should have been done or that should have been done.* All I can tell you is what feedback I've heard…

Gacy: The people find the book interesting with the letters but the thing is is that the first book was disorganized as all hell. It's the exact opposite of the way I am as a person.

Jorzak: Yeah, I know that.

Gacy: Now, if you do take a look at number two – now number two is all organized. One letter right after another, so in other words…

Jorzak: They're in chronological order, too.

Gacy: Yeah. That's the way the first one should have been laid out.

Jorzak: Exactly. That was, uh…

Gacy: On the first one, uh, they printed up a thousand books, right?

Jorzak: Yeah.

Gacy: And they can't account for eight hundred of them and I've got two hundred of them.

Jorzak: Who's "they"? Edward?

Gacy: No that was Clell Cunningham and Craig Bowlby out of New York.

Jorzak: Bowlby?

Gacy: See that's how the first book came out. O.K. so I finally says, "*When am I gonna get payment back for what I advanced from my art money?*" 'Cause all this was done through my art money. They still owe me $765.00 there.

Jorzak: To this day?

Gacy: Yeah. From eighty-eight.

Jorzak: Jesus.

Gacy: But they were able to buy themselves a new computer and all that, word processor and all that. And they took that out of the funds that were taken in from the book money. So, then I finally got two hundred and I sent them down to Rick Staton in Baton Rouge. Well, then, that's when I was coming out with 'More Letters to Mr. Gacy'. Only I laid it out and put it all together. And I says, "*Rick, all you have to do is take this to the printer. I will send you the money from Arkansas and you get it printed up.*" He printed it up, but then he started playing games. So finally, Ed and Shawn Jackson ended up with it. If you know you're talking about 1000 books, believe it or not these people can't account for a thousand books. Edward's had them since April.

Jorzak: That's silly, but it seems to me, John... And again, you know I've only been involved in this for a short time but with all of these characters you've dealt with in the past who have, uh...

Gacy: Everybody's out to make a buck off me.

Jorzak: Exactly. Exactly. And that's why I say, uh...I might be a little biased because I am close with Edward and have gotten to know him real well, but I'll tell you one thing. Out of all these other people, Ed's by far, by far more honest and more capable of handling these things.

Gacy: But you don't understand...

Jorzak: Can I just finish, just real briefly, John? I think it comes with experience, and Edward is, uh, simply... you can't blame him for, uh... action or inaction if he doesn't have the background to know. That's why, I think, he brought me in. That's why he has talked to other people who he feels can help him. He is making the effort. The points, you know, that you're making regarding the number of books and not distributing them, I agree with you one hundred percent. The solution, I think, is...uh, pointing him in the right direction and giving him, or telling him, exactly who in your best judgement he should, uh, address this matter with or what particular parties or businesses or whatever he should contact. And that's, um, I think that's the best way to do it. All of us have to advise him on our best judgements from what we know, what he should do in the given situation as applies to these books and the other matters that we're working on, too. When you have an honest, uh…core, when you are an ethical person, in nature, then that to me at least…uh, and I'm not… Again, John, I know that you think I'm just tooting his horn, but I'm not. I'm giving you my impression… as opposed to these other people who you've mentioned.

Gacy: Let me go a step further with Edward…the reason I picked Edward out of the family is that I know he's got business sense. In fact I know that if he didn't have the bottle to lean on, he would be making big money. He's got the ability to do it. The idea that he is at odds with the family… I went *against* the family and went with Edward. I was told to stay away from Edward. *"Edward's gonna rip me off"* and *"Edward's gonna do this… Edward's got a problem with the bottle and he'll just screw you around."* The only thing that I laid out with Edward is don't lie to me. If you've got a problem, bring it to me.

Jorzak: That's right, be honest. Yep, that's…

Gacy: That I can handle, because I can't handle the rest. But the thing of it is, that has not been the problem with Edward. It's just that there has been a lot of procrastination. Back in April of last year he took these books and I says, *"Put some ads in some underground papers. Just little ads. You watch, they will sell."* I gave him a whole listing of the underground zines. You don't need Mike Johnson. Fuck Mike Johnson. Go to these zines yourself. You can get an ad space in their little paper for a dollar or two.

Jorzak: That's a good idea, and it's not too late to do it, either.

Gacy: I sent him a package in the mail. When he gets to Hannibal he'll have…

Jorzak: He has a list of those magazines?

Gacy: Oh yeah! I'm in contact with the underground magazines 'cause I give them interviews all the time. Yeah, out of New York – the satanic crowd, the heavy metal crowd. I mean, these are fuckin' weirdos out of left field!

58

Jorzak: Exactly. Now that's the perfect market for the…

Gacy: Oh yeah!

Jorzak: …the 1-900 line. They're gonna call it. They don't even think. They'll call it immediately.

Gacy: Yes. Yes. Just so they can run around in their cut-off jeans and pot-smoke and say, "*I talked to John Gacy.*"

Jorzak: Exactly. Or, "Look at *this* article, or *this.*"

Gacy: I told Edward. I've got the biggest following.

Jorzak: Absolutely. No, you've got these young heavy-metal kids sittin' around smoking pot, then one of them brings out this book and it's a real big deal for them. You know, like I said, just for the artwork alone on the cover, it's a very…. There's a market there. In any case, I just made a note to bring up the rest of that with Ed as soon as I talk to him.

Gacy: But do you see, I keep sending him all of these lists and names. I don't know what he's been doing with them, see. I keep telling him, 'cause I says, "*I've got a hell of a following. Not only in this country but in the foreign countries.*"

Jorzak: No doubt about it.

Gacy: Have you ever heard of G.G. Allin?

Jorzak: Sounds familiar.

Gacy: He's a punk rocker who just O.D.'d on stage. He's the one who used to ejaculate on the stage. He'd call this entertainment. He'd drink his own urine, get blowjobs on the stage…

Jorzak: Kind of like Iggy Pop, right?

Gacy: Yeah, only this guy was most flamboyant. He thought he was God and that everyone else was his following. He used to go out in the crowd and beat up his audience. Used to cut himself with razor blades on the stage.

Jorzak: Oh yeah, I heard of him.

Gacy: This guy's way out in left field, but the thing of it is, he has visited me a couple of times here at the prison. He actually visited me. Brought a girl down who wanted to give me a blowjob.

Jorzak: No kidding.

Gacy: Fuck, yeah. Well, nothing wrong with that. But the thing of it is, is that he... Then he goes and tells his audience that John Gacy is a father figure to him.

Jorzak: Then you've got his whole audience...

Gacy: Right.

Jorzak: ...knocking at your door.

Gacy: Exactly. That's where I sold a lot of my artwork, you see.

Jorzak: It's a known fact that, all it is is a matter of giving them an opportunity. That's what is bothering me so much about hearing Snake – that's what we are calling Mike Johnson – *Snake and Worm* – if you don't mind that I'm calling him that...

Gacy: By the way, did you get ahold of Worm and get those copied?

Jorzak: They are in the mail. They *are* in the mail. I wrote a letter and sent that down. That's why I wish I would have held off until today. I could have sent off this 1-900 thing, too, to you. I have the first set of originals. I have them in our evidence vault so I'll hold them until further instructed. You have a copy of the originals that he gave me and also a copy of the...

Gacy: You were supposed to get the original back.

Jorzak: Right. That's what I told him. I said, *"Where is the original?"* He wrote something in there. Hold on a minute. Now the second set of questions, he gave me a xerox copy of them. No, I had a xerox copy in my own file of the second set of questions. And on top of it, it had his initials on it, 'W.J.H.' or whatever. Then it had a date and it said, 'Second Copy'. This is the one I had. Then he is telling me that he didn't know about any second set of questions.

Gacy: There are one hundred and forty-seven questions.

Jorzak: John, I know. And that's why I'm saying...first he's trying to B.S. me that I have everything because he gave me the originals. The first set.

He gave me the originals and a xerox copy thinking I was going to say, "*O.K. here's both sets.*" You know? So in any case, right away I called him back and said "*There's only one set here.*" He's like, "That's everything, page one through eight." I said, "Wait a second. I got a copy of the second set from you. It has your initials on the top page." Then I said, "*Bill, I'm gonna hang up the phone. I don't want to hear anything. I want you to find them. I want them on my desk by Monday morning, at the latest.*" This was yesterday. So, he calls me back and tells me that this guy in, what the hell is his name... Maycroft. Maycroft has the originals, the second set of originals. So at least he acknowledges their existence. I assume you talked to Maycroft.

Gacy: Well, I talk to Maycroft almost every week. Maycroft says he doesn't have much contact with Bill. He keeps asking me what's up with those...

Jorzak: Well, Edward was sitting right here yesterday when I talked to...Ed's going to talk to Maycroft about it and make sure that what...

Gacy: Just tell him that you know that this guy's pulling him into it.

Jorzak: That's right.

Gacy: You don't need that. But aside from that, did you ever talk to Greenlees?

Jorzak: No, I have not talked to him, John.

Gacy: Adam – er, Greenlees is supposed to have the files on the housing lawsuit.

Jorzak: Okay.

Gacy: He has the files on it.

Jorzak: That's the materials that you gave them?

Gacy: Sure. When Keefe was down here on the 22nd of December, er...the 21st of December he picked it all up.

Jorzak: Okay. Do you think that Greenlees is there now?

Gacy: No. I tried calling just a little while ago. He wasn't in.

Jorzak: What's the best time to reach him?

Gacy: I don't know. I can only call until…

Jorzak: Does he have a private number?

Gacy: …till one-thirty. I just got that one number for him. You got his number, don't you?

Jorzak: Oh yeah, I got his number.

Gacy: That's the only number I have for him. And you put a recording there, because he's supposed to be handling – 'cause he knew Greg Adamski was handling some of that stuff so he was supposed to get those files to him. But Adamski has not been keeping in touch with Greenlees and Keefe, and that's why I sent a letter to Adamski, letting Adamski go.

Jorzak: You gotta do what you gotta do.

Gacy: Yeah. It's just a matter of a lack of communication. They tell you one thing and they're not doing it. I'm a real simple guy to get along with…

Jorzak: I know…

Gacy: …and what bugs me more than anything are the little fucking things. Like right now, with Edward… Edward, two months ago told me that I had ten copies of 'Question of Doubt' coming from Mike Johnson. Ten books were going to be put in the hands of the people that I asked. As of this day they are still not in those peoples' hands. Why?

Jorzak: Well, that's the whole dilemma. That's why…

Gacy: Edward is running around like a chicken with his head cut off.

Jorzak: Not necessarily.

Gacy: He's got his books, but he doesn't…he hasn't sent them back. He asked each one of these people that had the wrong book to send the book back. We're talking about four or five people. You mean to tell me in a fucking months' time that he can't get four or five books back to these people? Now all these people are hounding my ass again and I figure, it's such frivolous bullshit.

Jorzak: Well it all goes, in my opinion, it all goes back to Mike Johnson – "Snake" – if he were doing what he agreed to do…

Gacy: None of this would have happened.

Jorzak: None of this would have happened. That's what pisses me off the most and that's why I'm behind any effort to, you know, er…cut him down and put a stop to that. I don't care what recourse he takes.

Gacy: I don't see where he's got any recourse. Let him keep holding on to it. *Let him keep holding on to it.* You just can't tell me those books aren't printed. I'm not stupid.

Jorzak: My understanding is that they are printed, but they're not bound.

Gacy: Yeah, well the thing of it is, is that those signed letters that they bind in there is what makes the book worth…

Jorzak: That's another thing. Johnson, uh…he was supposed to, uh, come in here yesterday with the, uh, letters that you supplied him. Now I know this is gonna, uh…this is not going to sit well with you, and it didn't sit well with me, either. I told him straight to his face. He said that he only received four hundred and eighty of the, uh…

Gacy: Five hundred and fifty.

Jorzak: That's what I told him. I said, *"Come on, now. You mean…"* …

Gacy: Why would he wait so long to tell me that?

Jorzak: That was the second thing I said. I said, first of all, *"You know how meticulous John is with details. Now, I can see 548 or 552, but there is no way that he omitted seventy letters, from that, that…That just does not sit well and it didn't happen, so don't even go into it."* I told him. I said the same thing you said: any retailer is going to count the…take note of the merchandise, in inventory, when it comes in.

Gacy: Keep in mind that it was sent to him in May, by Certified Mail. And it was told to him, *"Here's three hundred. Here's two fifty. You have the total amount there."*

Jorzak: That was my next question. Um, how you sent them to Johnson because he mentioned something about stacks of fifty or packets of fifty. In some of them there were forty-eight, in some of them there were thirty-seven…

Gacy: He's full of shit.

Jorzak: That's what I thought. I said…

Gacy: So how many did he actually end up giving you?

Jorzak: No, that's, that's the whole point. He didn't come in here with anything. He came in here with another bullshit story.

Gacy: Well, why didn't he bring the 448? That's about the time I would have taken him out to the elevator shaft and says, *"Either I get the letters or you go down the shaft!"*

Jorzak: Hah! Or down the stairway. Yeah!

Gacy: Yeah!

Jorzak: John, believe me. I am at that point.

Gacy: The thing of it is, either shit or get off the pot. That's, that's…

Jorzak: That's the bottom line.

Gacy: You wanna know what's interesting? You see, I brought this to his attention in…brought this to Edward's attention in May, but Edward kept saying, *"Trust him. Trust him. He's doing what he can but he's running into problems."* That ain't our problem. But that's all it's been.

Jorzak: There's no question, uh, over the last months, what his intention is.

Gacy: Oh yeah, I told him that I'm not going to die in May and they're gonna be sorry. What are they gonna do? Wait until next September?

Jorzak: Yeah, well, Ha! Ha! Ha! That's what I said to Edward. I said, because Ed and I went over – John I don't know if you feel comfortable – I don't think you feel uncomfortable – but my gut feeling is…

Gacy: Everybody wants me to die.

Jorzak: No, no, but there's no way in hell that this May 10th date, uh, is going to happen. And that's just my gut feeling.

Gacy: All you have to do is talk to the legal community.

Jorzak: I mean, it's ridiculous. And, uh, so, but we don't want to let Johnson know that. We don't want to let him know anything.

Gacy: Why do you think he's holding onto the books right now?

Jorzak: Well, John, I told him straight to his face. I says, "*Mike.*" I said, "*Now, let's proceed with the understanding that the game's over. Ed and John understand. And, again, we're proceeding with the understanding that you are going to hold of with distributing any books, or any significant number of books, until John is gone. And then, when the price has peaked, that's when you're going to sell…*

Gacy: I'm gonna put more… I'm gonna put more pressure on him.

Jorzak: I told him straight to his face.

Gacy: I'm gonna put more pressure on him right now, from the outside. I'm gonna say that most of the paintings he has is stolen. I'm gonna put it out through the underground network. Watch what happens.

Jorzak: Either stolen or forged or bogus or something.

Gacy: Yeah.

Jorzak: Yeah, that's a good idea. That's a real good idea. If I can do anything to facilitate that, let me know.

Gacy: Oh no, no. Somebody just wrote me a letter telling me that he's got a 'Death Wish'. I'm gonna tell him that I never did a 'Death Wish'.

Jorzak: I missed you, what…what is that?

Gacy: Death Wish painting.

Jorzak: Oh…oh!

Gacy: All of my paintings are registered and numbered. You know, but thing of it is, is that whole series that he's got, you know, he's selling it as an "exclusive series", and I'm going to tell that individual – 'cause he asked me to verify the number – I'm gonna tell him that he can get the same painting from me for thirty three bucks.

Jorzak: Well, if you want, John, I can have somebody call someone from the Attorney General's office – because that's consumer fraud, essentially. What he's perpetrating. And, uh, if he has any merchandise that he has for sale that is not, in fact, what he is purporting it to be, then he's going to have problems. And, uh…

Gacy: Yeah, all I have to do is disown the knowledge of it. Because I'm gonna – this letter that I got from Illinois – I'm gonna put it out that this guy is selling phony stuff. I'm also gonna put it out in Michigan and also in Indiana and I know that it will filter right back to Mr. Hellmer and Mr. Johnson.

Jorzak: And will it be relatively... Will they know it's coming from you, or no?

Gacy: No, no, no, no, no. They're gonna hear...

Jorzak: Their own community is gonna...

Gacy: ...that they're gonna be told, until we put a fast one over on Johnson.

Jorzak: Good. Good.

Gacy: Give me something else to worry about.

Jorzak: Well, John, that's my whole, uh...perception of all of this. That's why they're "Snake" and "Worm". They're trying to detract, er, they're trying to divert our attention from the book by doing these other things.

Gacy: But you can see, in the meantime...

Jorzak: That's why we have to do the same things to them, and uh....

Gacy: Jim, the other thing... [RECORDING STOPS]

[CALL RESUMES]

Jorzak: ...Mike Johnson.

Gacy: So, in other words, it hasn't – again, I'm pissed, so I'm gonna tell you right now. In other words, no complaint has been filed yet, so therefore I have to hire another attorney to get a complaint filed, because I will do that.

Jorzak: Well, John, you can do that...

Gacy: But you see, it's been three fucking months of this jacking around shit. They can jack someone else around.

Jorzak: Okay. Well, I'm not gonna sign the complaint. Ed's gonna sign the complaint.

Gacy: Yeah, well, we've been playing this fucking game for three fuckin', four fuckin' weeks, at least. *"You sign it. No, I can't sign it. Let Greenlees sign it."* Fuck all that shit. I'm out of room on this shit.

Jorzak: Right, well…

Gacy: You know what I mean?

Jorzak: Right. And that's why, uh…

Gacy: It's just, just jacking me around and I don't like being jacked around. I shoot square with people and they're not doing the same with me.

Jorzak: Well, um, the problem with…uh, 'cause I talked to somebody about what would be the best way of proceeding with this and, um…since we didn't have any report number or general offense report, we're going to have a hard time filing a theft…um, reporting them as stolen now. Um, even though we said that they were in his possession and that, um, that's basically what we're telling them – that the paintings were at his store on North Avenue and then they disappeared. But we didn't make a complaint at that time. So that's why it's difficult now to make a theft report. Or a report for possession of stolen property. Now, that's not saying we can't do it, but that's…these are the problems that we're looking at also, and uh…

Gacy: I'll talk to Greenlees and Keefe and I want Edward out of my life. I'm tired of this shit. I told you about it and told you about it. You guys apparently think I'm some kind of an asshole that can be treated this way.

Jorzak: No, no. That's not true.

Gacy: Yes, it is, Jimmy. I'm tired of it. I've made it fuckin' clear a month ago that this shit has got to move.

Jorzak: Okay, well…

Gacy: Nobody is going against him because I think everybody's in fuckin' cahoots with him. Everybody's gonna split that fifty grand each. Fuck all that.

Jorzak: That's ridiculous. I'm not getting anything out of it, John.

Gacy: Do you understand what it is to sit in a nine by twelve cell, er…an eight by nine cell, with all this fuckin' frustration? When all you get is fuckin' stories? One right after another? Enough of the fuckin' stories! Shit, I get enough of that from the State side.

Jorzak: John, I know that. Do you want, the only thing I can tell you at this point is that it's not gonna be easy filing a complaint. If you want…

Gacy: Why the fuck? You're the lawyers, you're the ones that drew up papers that was supposed to have tied him up in knots where those books couldn't go nowhere. All of a sudden those fuckin' books are all over the goddamn country!

Jorzak: John, we're looking at civil versus criminal here. We're talking about a criminal complaint right now.

Gacy: And I say he can't…the books in Wisconsin are stolen.

Jorzak: Well, uh, they didn't find it. Did you see that, uh, report in the Tribune yesterday? Here it is, it said: "*John Gacy's lawyers are not the only ones racing the clock as aides of Attorney General Burris have stepped up the ongoing search for Gacy's prison painting [profits], interviewing art collectors in hopes of recovering the costs of Gacy's incarceration. Neal Trickell, a Monroe, Wisconsin collector who acquired seventeen Gacy paintings last December found Police officers on his doorstep Friday. The cop, acting at the behest of Burris' office, wanted to know if Gacy got money for the paintings. Not from Trickell, who said he swapped for them, giving up two antique police tear gas guns. Burris' suit to recoup the cost of warehousing Gacy for nearly 15 years, is scheduled for trial April 25th. If Gacy has profited through sales of paintings and charges to callers who phone to hear a jailhouse recording of Gacy on a "900" number, Burris says taxpayers should be reimbursed.*" That was in yesterday's Tribune. So, uh, apparently, uh, this…the Police were at his house. I don't know what type of, uh, warrant or what type of investigation, you know, what they did there…but they didn't mention any books. All they did was mention the paintings. Uh, now, I don't know whether he's acting as a kind of a broker for the books, because as you said, uh, when your friend in Lacrosse, Wisconsin called and asked if Edward was involved in it and he said "*No*", Ed's not, that Mr. Snake is handling it. I would suspect that he probably doesn't have any books on the property. He probably…

Gacy: They requested books and he said he had ten of them.

Jorzak: Oh, okay. He said he had ten on the property.

Gacy: Out of the 159 that were on his list. [*SOUND OF TOUCH TONE DIALING*] I gotta go. I gotta get off the phone 'cause I'm gonna handle some other calls. I'm hot that this shit ain't being done right and, again, I'm at the point with this frustration of just walking away from it all.

Jorzak: Alright. John, let me do this. I'm gonna leave a message for Ed. We're gonna go to Belmont-Western Police Station…

Gacy: I was told that three weeks ago. Fuck all that.

Jorzak: I just talked to a Commander there yesterday on another matter so, uh, now he owes me a favor. And so I'm, uh, I'm gonna use it here. So I'll go in there tomorrow with that and I'll…

Gacy: Edward lied to me again when he told me that it was…he was filing it last week when I talked to him. See, it's this I can't handle no more.

Jorzak: I know he's been working on a lot of other things, John, you know, with Greenlees and Adamski…

Gacy: They're getting all that material from Randy White and the other stuff I'm working on right here. That's with the dates and the addresses and stuff.

Jorzak: Right. Right. And I know that he's been, you know, concentrating on that a lot. Um, as far as…

Gacy: No, but this was a week before that. This was a week before he had that meeting with them. He had already told me this and it wasn't done. So that, that ends it, and I will inform my sister of the same. I'm just tired of it! As far as the deal that Adamski just cut, I'm gonna kill that, too. I don't give a fuck if nobody gets any of that six-hundred thou. I gave them something that between you lawyers were supposed to split three-hundred grand. And fuck it. I'm walking away from it, and I'm gonna just tell you why. It's all this little fucking nit-picking bullshit, everybody trying to get their fuckin' hands on something.

Jorzak Well, I'm not trying to get my hands on anything.

Gacy: I don't… Don't you understand? I'm frustrated. And I have to take it out on anybody I can get ahold of. And when I learn this shit and this hasn't happened.

Jorzak: John, you said yourself a long time ago, you said to me, if I had a financial interest in this, you better believe that I'd be working on it faster, er, quicker. And I'm not saying…

Gacy: Since last November nothing has been done. You got to wonder why nobody is going after Mike Johnson, not since last November. That should have been shut down last November. All I've asked is that all this shit be cut down.

Jorzak: Well, he's certainly laying low, I mean, since then. He's not, uh, you know…he's been in hiding half the time.

Gacy: The books are all over the fucking country!

Jorzak: Where else have you found them?

Gacy: I just told Edward last week. There was the guy in New York, this Shane Bugbee, he's puttin' them out as if he's got free reign on them. I gotta go.

Jorzak: Alright. I'll talk to you.

Gacy: Bye.

[TAPE ENDS]

TAPE 3:

Edward Kasper and John Wayne Gacy

[OPERATOR] *…COLLECT CALL AND IS SUBJECT TO BEING MONITORED AND RECORDED…*

Kasper: Okay, um, this is being quoted from, uh, a newspaper. Because, I, I, I, I know of something that was quoted in a newspaper, but that's all I know… [CALL DISCONNECTS]

BUSY SIGNAL

TO ACCEPT THE CALL, DIAL THREE, OR SAY 'YES, I ACCEPT' AT THE TONE...

Kasper: Yeah. Hello? Hello?

Gacy: Are you done cutting off the phone?

Kasper: That's not me! That's them!

[OPERATOR] *THANK YOU FOR ACCEPTING THIS COLLECT CALL...*

Kasper: That's them, that's not me. What's...okay...now, Adamski...

Gacy: Where the hell are you? I can't even hear you.

Kasper: I'm in the office.

Gacy: You're not by the phone.

Kasper: Yes, I am. Right by the phone. I don't know, you know. We get good and bad connections. Today was good. Now, this one's bad.

[OPERATOR] *THIS IS A COLLECT CALL AND IS SUBJECT TO BEING MONITORED AND RECORDED...*

Kasper: I can hear you. I can hear you pretty good.

Gacy: Yeah, 'cause I put my mouth right next to the phone.

Kasper: Well, that's where mine is.

Gacy: Oh, okay. You apparently don't know what the hell is going on. There is...I still have not gotten all the goddamn files on this room and board lawsuit, and as of Monday I'm going into court and dismiss Adamski as the attorney of record.

Kasper: Okay.

Gacy: He was supposed to cross-file. He never sent me a copy of the cross-filing. He was supposed to get this goddamn stuff from the State on Discovery and has not done that yet. But he's got time to go give fucking news conferences out in California, doesn't he?

Kasper: Discovery? Uh, okay. That's the master file. Alright.

Gacy: Also, the stuff at the warehouse is being copied again at Adamski's office, so says Karen Conti. You said it wasn't, and you told me that I'd have an affidavit signed by these people that it wasn't.

Kasper: Yeah...

Gacy: Edward! I don't give a fuck, you...you...where is my copy of the xerox? And where is my sister Karen's copy of the xerox of those things?

Kasper: I told you. I told you I haven't received the original from them, but I do have it. Now, um, as for another copy, copies are being done at the office. I don't know how the hell they could even think of doing something like that. You have no idea the mountain...The other day it was four boxes just packed full of stuff. There's no way their copier would even handle it.

Gacy: If they're not copying it, that's fine. But the thing of it is, is why is all this other shit not getting done? Why am I told that the room and board lawsuit, that nothing's going forward on it? He hasn't started any of the depositions. I don't even think he's going to be a good litigator for me. He shouldn't be the one to be in front of the camera, givin' interviews, talkin' about thirty thousand dollars I made last year. Where the hell did I make thirty thousand dollars? And don't tell me that he's misquoted again. Because that same bullshit of tellin' em that I'm the one that signed the "900" contract has still got me irked. I still intend to, to become a State witness on that "900" shit. And if for no other reason than to burden the attorneys. You know, I don't understand why these guys keep playing these stupid fucking games. I got six weeks left to live and instead of fucking putting it together...there's more money than can be handled if you fucking do the right thing. And instead, all I got is jagoffs around me. I hope you know, Edward, that the stuff you're working on with Greenlees and Keefe...

Kasper: Yeah?

Gacy: ...and, and Randy White is all confidential. But the thing of it is, is that here's a guy that... he's like a treasure chest of information. I don't want you even sharing it with these other guys.

Kasper: No, I won't. I won't.

Gacy: Greelees is impressed with that stuff coming from...

Kasper: White. I know he is.

Gacy: ....White. Because Adamski... now, now Greenlees had told Adamski *"no news conferences about what we're gonna file."*

Kasper: Right!

Gacy: Yeah well then how come fucking Greg Adamski tells somebody in a New York newspaper that I was in New York at the time of one of the murders? What the fuck is he releasing this shit ahead of time for?

Kasper: I don't know.

Gacy: Now don't tell me that the reporter misquoted him. I know you're not gonna say it, but I mean, I'm frustrated.

Kasper: No, I understand.

Gacy: Understand where I'm coming from. I'm not mad at you but I'm trying to...

Kasper: I know.

Gacy: ...get it across to you that we're not playing with fucking people that are playing up to par.

Kasper: Well, that's...I told you Greenlees was hot at him.

Gacy: He's pissed! Yeah, he's pissed at him!

Kasper: Yeah.

Gacy: Also, he was supposed to get a copy of that 'eighty-twenty-nine' thing. And he's never gotten a copy of that, either. All he told him was that it's not making money, and I've got somebody down there in Florida checking on it.

Kasper: Uh, you'll find that out for sure. Ha! Ha! Ha!

Gacy: I cannot believe that nobody ran the number. Nowhere. In advertisements.

Kasper: No one...it just went out. There was no money to do it. In fact, uh, the advertising that's been done is owed for. [*UNINTELLIGIBLE BACKGROUND CONVERSATION*] Huh?

Gacy: I'm talking to the mailman.

Kasper: Oh! Ha! Ha! Ha!

Gacy: Alright, listen. Seriously, on this other stuff. Adamski is out. I definitely think we got to dump him.

Kasper: Well, this, this is ridiculous. You know, I agree with you one hundred percent.

Gacy: No! I can't have...you can't have leaks like that. He refuses to play ball. He wants to be the most talked about attorney in Hollywood. Well, Hollywood's off. Here's Cornerstone Television contacting me.

Kasper: Who would you, uh, could we get to take over the room and board lawsuit, then? You can't do it on your own.

Gacy: Yeah, well, if that's what I have to do, that's what I gotta do. Why do you think I asked you what was happening with Patrick Tuite?

Kasper: Well, Patrick Tuite is criminal law. He wouldn't touch the room and board lawsuit.

Gacy: All these guys know people who would jump on these things.

Kasper: Uh, Okay. You want...

Gacy: I've got news for you. You guys have never even contacted Patrick Tuite.

Kasper: What did I tell you? I told you that today!

Gacy: What?

Kasper: I said no one talked to him yet.

Gacy: Yeah, but I've been told that weeks ago, that you...yeah, well, Adamski said "*You want him?*" He says, "*I'll get him for ya.*" And I had James Jurzak tell me the same thing, but it never happened. 'Cause Jim Jurzak's the one that came up with the idea of, uh, if we can get some money together, we could approach Pat Tuite.

Kasper: Right. Right. Right. Now, just slow down for one second about it, okay? I told you if the funds could be raised to pay his retainer... He is a friend of Jim's dad...and Jim's, and I'm sure that if he was asked to handle it there wouldn't be a problem with it, but there would still be a problem with the retainer. That's...I think that's where you keep getting mixed up.

74

Jim is more than happy to go to Tuite and ask him, but it was still a matter of getting a retainer…

Gacy: Do you agree that Adamski's go to go then?

Kasper: Yes, I do. I agree that… I think I do. I agree that Adamski has to go.

Gacy: He's just grandstanding.

Kasper: Right, but before we do it, um, before…

Gacy: I told him he has until Monday to get me copies of his cross-filing with the State of Illinois and I'm still looking for that master file he was supposed to file for all that stuff. I am yet to see that.

Kasper: Do you want me to ask Jim to see if he can find someone?

Gacy: No. No. No. No. No. Because you just talk to Greenlees and let Greenlees find somebody.

Kasper: Let Greenlees find someone. No, alright…that's fine. I'm just… It's an option we can use.

Gacy: And I'm still finding out who this attorney in Beverly Hills was, that was told he wasn't needed. You can bet the shit will roll when I hear that one, too. I'll know as soon as my guy in California gets back to me.

Kasper: Uh, alright. What, uh…

Gacy: Fuckin' fifteen letters tonight again.

Kasper: That's not very many.

Gacy: Fifteen letters? Let's see how many you answer a night.

Kasper: Ha! Ha! Ha! Ha! Ha! No fair…

Gacy: I just noticed another thing.

Kasper: …I don't answer them!

Gacy: They sent out three of your packages, but they didn't send out the big packages and I want to know what the fuck is going on.

Kasper: They did what?

Gacy: Well, normally I get the…uh…

Kasper: The slips out? Yeah.

Gacy: …the slips back the next day.

Kasper: But the big one didn't go out.

Gacy: The big one's going to you. No, they sent out a small one to Jurzak, a small one to Greenlees.

Kasper: They're probably rifling through it to see, uh…

Gacy: Well, I should have the slips by tomorrow, 'cause if I don't have them by tomorrow the shit's gonna hit the fan.

Kasper: Yeah.

Gacy: Did anybody, uh, make any contact with [*Deputy Prison Director*] Leo Meyer?

Kasper: I talked to…immediately after I got off the telephone with you, I talked for about thirty minutes with David Keefe. And David Keefe said, "*O.K.*" He says, "*Let me kick this around for a couple of minutes in my mind.*" He said, "*I really think the best way to handle it the first time around is that I make some friendly phonecalls to, um, Hopkins and Meyer…*

Gacy: Hopkins is not even here today.

Kasper: Okay. Hopkins, Meyer…

Gacy: He's off on Friday and Saturday, by the way.

Kasper: Okay. He's off Fridays and Saturdays? Uh, so he said, "*Otherwise,*" he says, "*what they're gonna do is*", um, "*feel hair standing up on their neck.*"

Gacy: No, I mean, do you see…I am so…this is what pisses me off. Hopkins can only tell you one thing: "*I follow orders.*"

Kasper: Right.

Gacy: Paige can only tell you: "*I'm, we're following orders that came from Springfield.*"

Kasper: Right.

Gacy: Why did you not understand that I said to go to Leo Meyer? 'Cause this is the fucking asshole that did it?

Kasper: I told him. I told him to go to Leo Meyer. Keefe said he never takes his phonecalls.

Gacy: Then I've got news for you. If Meyer don't wanna take your phonecalls, then you call the Director, Howard Peters. And Howard Peters' office will take the call. And if he's... Complain to them, *"Why they don't take the call?"*

Kasper: Okay.

Gacy: That's the way you go. You don't go down the ladder, you go up the ladder. Okay, now you're sending that to Randy White and Randy White is already doing stuff.

Kasper: Right.

Gacy: But again, everything you're getting from them is strictly to be tunneled that way.

Kasper: Right. I understand that. With no problems. Have you talked to your sister in Arkansas this week at all?

Gacy: No.

Kasper: I just wanted to know if she got the packages I sent her.

Gacy: No. I would get a postcard from her if I do.

Kasper: I would hope so. Okay. Alright. Anything else?

Gacy: No. Just like I'm telling you. I'm just trying to...

Kasper: I'm gonna...I'm definitely gonna call Adamski. He will take my fuckin' phonecall this time. 'Cause I called him once already tonight.

Gacy: Well, the bullshit...I'm telling you, he's only responsible for one thing to do.

Kasper: Right.

Gacy: Fuck all these goddamn interviews and contacts. If he hadn't got any of them cut yet and if he hasn't got any of the up-front money, what the hell good are they? Don't you understand? If we had the money already in, that this money can be used for this room and board lawsuit?

Kasper: I understand that.

Gacy: You talked to him about bringing Patrick Tuite in. Don't you think Patrick Tuite would jump in if the money was put up front?

Kasper: Oh, I'm sure. Of course. That's what I've been saying all along.

Gacy: Yeah, and right away... I mean, when he's telling me he's got King World for six figures. And I told him only half of it goes to Karen. The rest of it is to be split between you and the attorneys. And I think the amount that he was talking about was nearly three hundred thousand dollars. And do you know how much money each one person would get for that?

Kasper: Sure. Sure. Right.

Gacy: And we're still jerking around?

Kasper: See, I never heard my name in that jumble. Ha! Ha! Ha!

Gacy: Oh yes! I told them to put you in with it. See, only because you're working with Keefe and them. I'm telling you to be open and honest with those guys, because they're the ones that are gonna do the legal fighting.

Kasper: Right.

Gacy: Not Adamski.

Kasper: Right. Fuck that, I... It just pisses me off, the fact that it pisses me off. I'm gonna have to take a step back and, uh, calm down for a few minutes and then I'm gonna call them.

Gacy: He's not there yet. He's still in California. Karen Conti says she's gonna be back at the office at five or six o'clock. I just talked to...

Kasper: He'll be back in his office tonight.

Gacy: Good. Because I gave her an ultimatum that if I don't have copies of his cross-filing with the attorneys with the room and board lawsuit and all that stuff by Monday – in my hands – to take a walk. And I'm meaning it. And don't think he can work it around by talking to you to talk to me...

Kasper: No. I want him gone. No...

Gacy: Because I, I think he's causing too much chaos and too much dissention. They, we, he had talked to Greenlees and Keefe and said he wouldn't give no more interviews without first clearing it, and what the fuck does he do? He's got one in New York and one in California. Where the hell are they coming from?

Kasper: They must be coming from him if they're quoting him.

Gacy: Yeah. As far as I'm concerned, he can be history.

Kasper: Well, I agree with you. One hundred percent. If, if that, if those are the only two guidelines you gave him, um, for a deadline on Monday, um, I think you were being too lenient. Ha! Ha! But if that's the case, I support you...

Gacy: Well, he'll get back to his office tonight and he can put his overnight express letter in the mail and I will get it on Monday.

Kasper: Right. That's right, you will. If he, well if he sends it out Saturday or Sunday you'll get it.

Gacy: If it even exists, Edward. If it even exists. And the same thing with all those other releases that those other people were supposed to sign. And Greenlees is supposed to get the ones that I told you that he talked to you about.

Kasper: Right, he gets the originals.

Gacy: Fuck Green... Greenlees says, you know... I told you to give copies of this "900" split thing and all that other shit to Greenlees, and he has yet to receive it.

Kasper: Well, I talked to him. I talked to him yesterday 'cause they had to cancel out today and, uh, reschedule for Sunday or Monday.

Gacy: What's that?

Kasper: Um, to start going over everything. 'Cause they had some other stuff...

Gacy: Yeah, I know. They met with you the other day. You wouldn't take a ride from them because you gotta go someplace secretive you don't want them to know about. Where the hell do you go that you don't want anybody to know you?

Kasper: What the fuck? No! *Ha! Ha! Ha!* This is exactly…

Gacy: They offered you a ride and you said *"No"* …

Kasper: They offered me a ride, exactly, they offered me a ride and I said…

Gacy: But you don't know where you're going.

Kasper: …and I…would you listen to me? I said *"No"* … [RECORDING STOPS]

[CALL RESUMES]

Kasper: I have an affidavit in front of me that Adamski signed.

Gacy: What affidavit?

Kasper: When I left the prison, I was hotter than hell, okay?

Gacy: About what?

Kasper: About what we talked about regarding the attorneys. So, I figure the best way…

Gacy: No, no, no…

Kasper: What?

Gacy: Wait a minute! I still don't understand what you're upset about. It ain't your case. My life is not your life.

Kasper: I understand that.

Gacy: But you have no right to control it, either.

Kasper: I'm not. I'm not controlling it. All I wanted to do was get something in writing that said that they were not, um, they were not making any deals without your knowledge. That they were not…

Gacy: They're not making any deals and they're not keeping my sister informed of anything.

Kasper: *"Number Three. I acknowledge my obligation as attorney and agent of John Wayne Gacy to fully disclose all materials and facts and observe my duty of loyalty to him at all times."* That's number three.

"Number Four...I have not entered into any agreement, oral or written, with the National Enquirer Magazine, Dianne Sawyer, ABC News, Geraldo Rivera or Tribune Entertainment Company, pertaining to my client, John Wayne Gacy, his case, conversations, name, likeness, or any aspect of any relationship with him, including the sale or conveyance of any last statement...".

Gacy: Yeah, but my sister doesn't have a copy of that.

Kasper: I just, I just had it made yesterday. It was faxed over to Adamski's office and he signed it. I just got it now, okay?

Gacy: But it has not been sent to my sister.

Kasper: Im gonna... I'm gonna send it today!

Gacy: My sister is the only legal party.

Kasper: I just got here! I had this done. I just got here. I got it in my hand. I'm gonna send it to you.

Gacy: Because the thing of it is, is that the next thing I'm gonna tell you, you're not gonna like it, either...

Kasper: What?

Gacy: And that is that I want you to back away from my life.

Kasper: What?

Gacy: You can be my nephew, but you cannot be involved in anything involved in my case, because I think they're using you. I think they're gonna hurt you in the long run and I don't want to see it happen. Don't you agree? *Don't you agree?*

Kasper: [emotional] No, I don't.

Gacy: The more you're involved, the more they're there. You see, if I have control over who's involved then I know what is going on. Jurzak is not doing anything for me or the family, and I want him out of it, too. You can do the same affidavit on him.

Kasper: I will. Him, Pierce, Adamski...

Gacy: But Edward, I'm telling you… No, Pierce ain't doing nothing. Pierce don't want no part of this bullshit. At least, I don't think so.

Kasper: But he's still gonna sign one, and I'm gonna do one also, to you.

Gacy: I don't really give a fuck about you. You understand what I am saying?

Kasper: Yeah, but I want it all the way across the board, because I'm…

Gacy: It ain't the point. It ain't the point. You see, I'm gonna die, Ed. I told you that. And I'm not gonna fight the case no more. And the only reason I'm doing that is because of all the shit I've been put through. I can't handle it no more, Edward. Don't you understand that?

Kasper: I do, but…

Gacy: No, you don't. I don't think you understand where I'm coming from.

Kasper: No, I do in a way, but…

Gacy: No, I thought I had faith in people and every fuckin' time I turn around Adamski's lying to me, through his teeth. If he wasn't lying, don't you think I have a right to see everything that is being done on my behalf? But what I'm trying to tell you is the only reason I'm asking you to step out of it is because I think you're going to be used as an excuse. See, because, I mean Jurzak tells me one thing about you. Then I've got Adamski telling me another thing about you. And you're just getting caught in the middle of it.

Kasper: Yeah…that's probably true. Why do you think I had the affidavit drawn up?

Gacy: They're fuckin' both lying to you! Edward! They're lying to me! If they're lying to me they're lying to you. Well, I had Adamski come down here last Thursday and I asked him, "*Where are the Motions? I want to see copies of the stamped Motions.*" He went right back to his office, we talked the next day, he says, "*I'll put them in the mail.*" I says, "*Okay.*" And here's another fucking night and I still haven't got them. Why? He's so fucking important he hasn't got no time to do it. If he's that important and he's got that many things going on, then get the hell out of my life. Do you understand this? I don't want to hear this shit that he's out to save my life because I'm telling you something: he's doing everything to fuck up my life. You're right there, right in his office. Write these things down...

Kasper: I am.

Gacy: Go over to his office when he's going to be in his office. Ask to see the cross-complaint he filed on the room and board lawsuit. There is none. Ask to see the Motions requesting to see the Department of Corrections' papers. For the master file, for John Wayne Gacy's master file from June of...it should say 'From June of 1988 till 1994.' You ask to see a copy of the Motion, not his word that he's having it taken care of.

Kasper: No, no. A copy of the Motion.

Gacy: Ask Adamski to show you the Motions, or you ask that an extension of two weeks should be given on the trial, to push back, because everything has not come in yet. You haven't got the state's Discovery. If he hasn't got the state's Discovery, how the hell...what's he gonna do? Get the state's Discovery on April 7th? And then you have no time to look over all of this... You realize that Motion from the D.O.C. is something like seven or eight hundred pages?

Kasper: It's that big, huh?

Gacy: Yeah. And I told him in December to get it for me. 'Cause I need to go through and pick out the stuff that he can use...that is favorable to me. And what do I get? I get my dick in my hand. Don't let the sonofabitch tell you how great he is or what he has done for me. And another thing. The reason the photocopying is taking so long over at the warehouse...

Kasper: Yeah?

Gacy: ...is 'cause Adamski is making an extra set of copies so that Jurzak can sell them. Edward, do you have David Keefe's phone number?

Kasper: I...I'm trying to find my book.

Gacy: He's the one who's supposed to be talking to Leo Meyer to find out about...to straighten this thing out about the visits... [TAPE ENDS]

TAPE 4:

Ed Kasper, John Wayne Gacy and James Jorzak

Kasper: …I wanted to make sure you were getting what you wanted, that's all.

Gacy: Well, the thing of it is, is, if you look inside any of them books, just like that stuff I had sent to you, 'cause I found another one had six or eight stories in it. And, of course, these are different books. I think they are a hundred fifty-eight pages, or something like that. And, of course also, you've got the novel stuff which has brother to brother, father to uncle. You know what I am talking about?

Kasper: I'm gonna go tomorrow. I'm gonna go tomorrow and get those. Also, I'm gonna order these…

Gacy: The '*First Hands*'.

Kasper: …the 'First Hands' for you. I've got the ad right here in my hand.

Gacy: Yeah, that I sent you.

Kasper: Now, it says here: "*Please allow 4 to 6 weeks for delivery*", just so you know.

Gacy: Yeah, well, that's why I was thinking, maybe not buy them there and maybe when you go up north you might find them right there in the store. I can't believe that the store doesn't handle those.

Kasper: You know what? That's a good idea. I'll tell you what, um, uh…Saturday…

Gacy: Certainly in 4 to 6 weeks you might find a store that might have them. I know there's a bookstore down there at Broadway and Diversey, and there's got to be some over by the Bijou.

Kasper: Broadway and Diversey. That's where I want to go. That's where I want to go. I couldn't remember what corner the place was on.

Gacy: It's about…not Surf Street. It's the block after Surf Street. But no, I told Jason Moss…of course, I asked him "*What time you gonna get here?*" He says he's gonna get here Sunday morning.

Kasper: Right.

Gacy: What the hell you gonna do all day Sunday?

Kasper: Well, I don't know. We'll find something to do. Well, I'll be driving all night, so I'll be taking a nap.

Gacy: Yeah, he said you'll be tired anyway when he gets in. But the thing of it is, you know, basically I don't think it's… Get him here at five minutes to eight.

Kasper: I will.

Gacy: Then you can take off and do some other little things or whatever you're gonna do.

Kasper: Right. I told him already. I told him to make sure he's got his picture I.D. He's got two alternative forms of identification.

Gacy: Well, if he's got a birth certificate, that's a good thing.

Kasper: Oh, that's good, too. First I said, *"Birth certificate, social security card, student I.D. – but your driver's license is very important."* He said, *"Okay, no problem."* So he's gonna have all that. I said, *"Don't forget it, now, because if you do…"*

Gacy: They won't let him in, no-how.

Kasper: *"…they won't let you in and it's gonna be…"*, um, you know. So let's see, what else?

Gacy: Well, he says he's got something to tell me, but he wouldn't tell me over the phone.

Kasper: Hm. I sent twenty-five dollars along with his ticket for any incidentals that he might have.

Gacy: The other day, obviously, Jurzak didn't get the money over to Greenlees. But I thought you guys knew Greenlees lived right in that building?

Kasper: No, I didn't. We didn't know that.

Gacy: Yeah, he lives with the partner of his, the one that looks like a boy.

Kasper: Who? Durante?

Gacy: Yeah! That broad there. They live together!

Kasper: Oh, I didn't know that. Well, we pounded on the door. We stood out there ten minutes pounding on the door.

Gacy: I would have gone around to the back door. Well, whatever it is, I know one thing – it hasn't been done. Also, I have to know if there's going to be any more canvases being sent in.

Kasper: Canvases? Yes.

[*JAMES JORZAK ENTERS CONVERSATION*]

Jorzak: What sizes do you want, John?

Gacy: I was thinking that you're gonna go sixteen by twenty, ten by fourteen. Ten by fourteen is a nice size for those…

Jorzak: I'm gonna have…I'll get those out tomorrow, um…ten by fourteen?

Gacy: Yeah, ten by fourteen… [*SOUND OF PHONE RINGING*]

[TAPE STOPS]

TAPE 5:

James Jorzak, John Wayne Gacy and Edward Kasper

Jorzak: Exclusive last interview?

Gacy: "*Exclusive last interview of G.G. Allin*". And that's why it was sent to me, cause my name was in there with G.G. Allin. 'Cause G.G. Allin talks about me being the real person and not the monster image. He's a nice guy.

Jorzak: Where is he?

Gacy: Well, he died last February…

Jorzak: Was he down in Menard?'

Gacy: He's been here twice. He was here.

Jorzak: Oh! That's right! That's right! But weren't you like a father figure to him?

Gacy: Yeah! Yeah!

Jorzak: I mean, you really, uh…

Gacy: I got some of his music.

Jorzak: Right.

Gacy: But you see, that's why I got the heavy metal and cult following that I do. Because everyone that was in love with him knew that he was close to me. Because, let's see, in this interview here it says…okay, here…they've got two pages of interviews and it says, *"Serial Killer John Wayne Gacy: I've been friends with Gacy for years and the main thing is that I did not get in touch with Gacy because I thought it was a so-called 'cool' thing to do like everybody else does. I looked to Gacy as a human being and I wrote to Gacy as a real person."* This is G.G.'s last interview.

Jorzak: No kidding.

Gacy: Yeah. You ready for this? See, what I got into an argument with the Superintendent about? After he said I lied about the visits and all this and that shit. Then he says, *"Let's get on to May 10th. Are you gonna make a statement at the end? I want you to stick it in writing what you're gonna say."* I says, *"Well, I got news for you. The going rate for that right now is two hundred thousand dollars. If you want to put a bid in for it then I'll give you a copy of it."*

Jorzak: John, why don't you just do this? We could agree to do whatever we want. If that's gonna make it easier, O.K. Just to make it easier on you, then we'll agree to it, O.K.? Because…and we'll structure it, we'll word it so that, uh, you don't obviously…

Gacy: It ain't a point of that. What I'm trying to tell them… I was pissed off. I says, *"I ain't gonna give you no statement about anything yet because,"* I says, *"May 10th is your date, not my date."* And I says, *"I'll decide when I'm gonna go."*

Jorzak: That's what I'm saying…

Gacy: So right away, *Whoa!* Then, *"He might be suicidal!"*

Jorzak: Right. That's why I'm saying. Go along. What the hell can they do at this point? I mean, there is a number of things that you can do. But what the hell can they do to enforce that agreement? That's why I'm saying, if it's going to make life easier on you, in a couple of weeks…

Gacy: What they're wondering is what they're gonna get out of it. That's all they're worrying. They're not concerned about John Gacy. They're worried about *"Cover your ass, so that we don't make headlines in the papers so we don't get heat put on us."*

Jorzak: Right. Exactly.

Gacy: Then exactly, just the opposite because when I get the room and board lawsuit I am going to be the chief witness and I'm also going to be the co-counsel. That's what I've been trying to get ahold of Adamski for.

Jorzak: Right. Exactly.

Gacy: I want him to call me back so that I can get all of them. Because I got to talk to him!

Jorzak: Do you know that they are having a powwow right now? At Greenlees office? Adamski, Ed, Greenlees, and Keefe are all at Greenlees office right now.

Gacy: I didn't even know it.

Jorzak: Okay, well, that's why I'm telling… Well, I didn't know that you weren't aware that they were meeting today. The purpose of it, as I said, um…Ed has been barking out orders over here, you know, since he's been back and he's been, you know… Oh! Ed just walked in. [*To Kasper*] *How did it go?* [*To Gacy*] John, in any case, one question before you get into it with Ed. Did, um, you get your three, um, packages that went out on the 14th from me?

Gacy: Uh, yeah. I believe so.

Jorzak: Okay. Well, did you have any problem because there were multiple shipments? On one day?

Gacy: God, no! God, I get three or four packages a day, anyway. There's no problem.

Jorzak: Oh, okay. I hope you enjoyed them.

Gacy: I appreciate that. Thank you.

Jorzak: We're sending you some others out today.

Gacy: Yeah, I just told him that I need an accounting on how many canvases you sent so I know where I stand with those canvases.

[ED KASPER ENTERS CONVERSATION]

Kasper: Okay, I've got, uh...

Jorzak: I got a wholesale account at, uh, Johnson's, where we're getting them. So don't worry about it. They're nothing...they're almost nothing.

Kasper: He wants to know how many were actually sent. That's what he...

Jorzak: Okay.

Gacy: So, I can make sure I'm getting them alright.

Kasper: Okay. I sent, I sent you...

Gacy: I can't hear you, Edward.

Kasper: I said I sent you, um, a list of how many canvases you've received, not including the 14th's shipment, so whatever is added to that... What I did was I just copied, uh...

Gacy: So, in other words, I'm not supposed to be expecting anything else, except...

Jorzak: No, no, you are. You should be.

Kasper: Expect more. Expect more.

Jorzak: We sent out the last one, um, there were some smaller canvas panels in it for some of the less important, um... *exhibits*. And, because that's all they had at the time.

Gacy: Well, that, in other words, I need to know the number and the sizes...

Jorzak: I think I've still got a copy.

Gacy: Just send it...drop the letter tonight.

Kasper: It's on the way already.

Jorzak: There is a letter enclosed in it, indicating how many, you know, there are. In any case...

Gacy: I need to get ahold of Adamski, but I don't know where he's at.

Kasper: Okay. Adamski should be in his office in about fifteen minutes, because he just dropped me off.

Gacy: How, how did the meeting go? [RECORDING STOPS]

[CALL RESUMES]

Kasper: *"I don't think he mentioned dates."* I said, *"I think he did."* So he found twenty-three dates [*on which Gacy was absent from Chicago during victim disappearances*], like, immediately.

Jorzak: Oh, my God!

Kasper: Immediately. I'm serious. It was just like that.

Gacy: Well, if you look in 'A Question of Doubt' you'll see some of the stuff that's…

Kasper: Right! Exactly! But we need it from the court records, from the transcripts. We needed those dates, and I was like…I…

Jorzak: You came up with a shortcut of how to find them.

Kasper: So he came up with twenty-three right away.

Gacy: If you look at the opening, if you look at the opening statements, too…

Kasper: I…that's the next set of things. All I did was get the closing right now.

Gacy: Yeah, 'cause all of that stuff is in there.

Kasper: Right. So, I've got, uh, we'll just have to make sure that it's on the record. That they said the exact dates of the disappearances… And there might be just a couple that are indispersed throughout the rest of the trial, but we know twenty-three we got already, so…So that's good, um, there's no, um…just so you know it's a complete team attitude. There's no…

Gacy: Well, I know Dave and John worked as a team. It was that they only wanted a watchdog on Adamski so they knew what he was doing.

Kasper: Right, well I think it's all understood now. You know?

Gacy: Well, see, there's some things that I'm unclear on, with Adamski, because again – and I'm going back to the master file. I got that one letter from you, Edward, and that upset me when I read it.

Kasper: Which letter?

Gacy: The letter from Roland Burris's office. Okay, this is the letter from March 10th. This from James Dodge. Now this is the letter that we discussed on the telephone yesterday. *"The sizes of your plans, master file, and Department of Corrections is enormous. It contains numerous items that have no relevance towards the present litigation."* They are not to decide what is relevant and...

Kasper: What is not...

Gacy: Damn right! We asked for Discovery.

Kasper: Alright. Okay. When you receive some of the stuff that I sent Friday...you should receive that today. There is mention in it, in the Motions... Oh, by the way, before I forget, I don't know if you know, um...the deposition was pushed up and the, uh...the court date was pushed to April 25th.

Jorzak: The Randolph...

Gacy: The Randolph County date was supposed to be set on the 25th. That was supposed to be done by...

Kasper: It's done. It was done last week.

Gacy: Okay, see I've got papers here that says that the meeting...here: *"You are hereby notified at 2 p.m. on March 22nd by telephone, telephonic conference. If it pleases the Court I will present attached defendant Motions to continue trial. Requests a ruling by the Court."*

Kasper: Did you get that from me already?

Gacy: Well, this is what I got.

Kasper: Okay, 'cause I sent that stuff already.

Gacy: Okay, but here's what's interesting to me, is that here, on March 10th, you see I have still not seen the Motions demanding that we get the entire

Master file from the Department of Corrections. The entire file. And I want the entire file. Here he's got a memorandum from the Attorney General's office to Jim Dodge from Greg Adamski: *"I understand that you are photo copying Mr. Gacy's master file. I understand that it is voluminous, and please make copies as quickly as possible so I may determine deposition, if needed. I was advised on Wednesday that D.O.C. intends to withhold certain documents."* No, you're not going to hold none of 'em. Fuck you! Not a fucking thing!

Kasper: Right.

Gacy: Because that's our fuckin' right. Because this idea here, it says on this March 10th letter from the A.G., it says, *"Department of...is enormous...contains numerous items which have no relevance towards the present litigation, i.e., i.e., letters to the Department by other inmates regarding Mr. Gacy..."*. Wait, other inmates are not supposed to be in my file. And if other inmates wrote about me, how do you know that they're not gonna be used to testify?

Kasper: Exactly.

Gacy: That's why we have to know the contents of those letters. See, this is bull — what they are is stool pigeons. If they're writing to the Department of Corrections and they're putting a copy in my file, then it's about me or something that I'm doing. So we have a right to see a copy of those letters.

Kasper: Right.

Gacy: That's what I want Adamski to understand. I not only want a copy of those letters, I want to know whose names they are.

Kasper: As I understand it, he's still fighting them for the complete master file. That's what I understand.

Gacy: Yeah, because how the hell...

Kasper: Not parts of it. Not pieces of it. Not what they want...

Gacy: Exactly. That way, see, you decide what is relevant...I gotta go.

Kasper: Alright. Hey, have a good dinner.

Gacy: I'll talk to you on Monday.

Kasper: Alright.

Gacy: [*To Prison Staff*] If that's Polish sausage, take it and shove it up somebody's ass.

Kasper: Ha! Ha! Ha! Polish sausage? You get that there?

Gacy: God! Whatever they call Polish sausage! Ugh! It is terrible. I'm serious. They'd run 'em out of a Polish neighborhood with this shit! Greasy sausage! You know, they forget that we're used to eating real Polish sausage.

Kasper: Well, they're basically just serving you old sausage, right?

Gacy: Okay. Everything else is kosher. [TAPE ENDS]

TAPE 6:

James Jorzak and John Wayne Gacy

[OPERATOR] *SAY 'YES' TO ACCEPT…*

[*SOUND OF BEEPING*]

Jorzak: John?

Gacy: Yeah.

Jorzak: Hey, how 'ya doing?

[OPERATOR] *THANK YOU FOR ACCEPTING THIS COLLECT CALL…*

Kasper: Why did you hang up on us?

Gacy: They pulled the plug down at the armory and had to turn it back on. [TAPE STOPS]

[TAPE RESUMES]

Jorzak: I don't know if you've seen this one, uh…

Gacy: She says, "*I need advice on how to take care of the kids.*"

Jorzak: That, that, uh, bitch who went on Geraldo a few years ago?

Gacy: Oh, that stupid Sue Terry. That fuckin' cow.

Jorzak: That fat broad with black hair?

Gacy: Yeah, that fuckin' Indian broad.

Jorzak: Right, I remember. I didn't know much about the case. I believed her!

Gacy: Yeah, well, she had love letters in the Sun-Times. Those assholes run that shit. But here's a broad that's been married twice, divorced twice, got eight kids – three of 'em on parole – and I'm gonna marry this? *Heh! Heh!*

Jorzak: Well, Jesus. Regardless of any of that. Still, take one look at the fuckin' woman. I'm sure you didn't meet her, you know. It's probably like a, you know, you guys were corresponding a lot…

Gacy: We were pen-palling, she was close by and wanted to know if she could visit. She wanted to know if she could bring the kids with her. I says, *"Yeah, I love kids. Bring the kids along."*

Jorzak: Sure.

Gacy: She asks me questions like, *"Well, how did you raise your kids?"* And I explained to her, *"Well, my kids were treated this way."* And so she released the letters to the Sun-Times and said *"This is how John is going to raise my kids."*

Jorzak: Oh, my God.

Gacy: I says, *"Wait a minute. I didn't fuckin' say that!"*

Jorzak: Right. Did she say that you were married or engaged? The two of you?

Gacy: We were engaged to be married. This was in '88. In '88 we were engaged to be married. Now, in '89 or in 1990, all of a sudden I confessed the crimes to her.

Jorzak: *Ha! Ha! Ha! Ha!*

Gacy: Then in '90, '91 she said the divorce, er…the engagement was off. Then in '92 she comes out and says that I threatened to kill her. I said, *"This fuckin' broad will say anything!"*

Jorzak: Well, sure…there's probably somebody advising her.

Gacy: Jimmy, here she is living in downstate Illinois – Mount Vernon at the time. Now she's in Carbondale. Okay, here's a woman who's never had no attention in her life. All of a sudden TV shows are picking her up in limousines, taking her to big hotels, buying her...

Jorzak: Buying her flowers...

Gacy: Fuckin' eh! Yeah. She's ready to swear on her life that she probably was present for the murders.

Jorzak: You probably had sex with her and everything else...

Gacy: Exactly.

Jorzak: I think that would make it sound a little...

Gacy: More bizarre.

Jorzak: ...more interesting. Right. Of course. Of course.

Gacy: She took a lot of heat, but she lied like a sonofabitch.

Jorzak: Well, that's what I'm saying, um...you can't...'cause I wasn't actually familiar with the case at that point and, um, just being someone in the general public observing her...I actually believed her! That's what I'm saying – I don't blame her for that as much as I blame fucking Geraldo for putting her on there and not, uh, clarifying it.

Gacy: And he knew it!

Jorzak: And you weren't able to defend yourself there. No, there wasn't anyone on the show who was, uh, able to contradict or ask her about what she was claiming. That was the...

Gacy: Well, I got Winona Smith up in Michigan, same thing. She's got a eight-year old son. I was gonna marry her. I've got Randy Powers up in Maine. I was supposed to be marrying her and I says, *"That's interesting, because I didn't know it."* And then...

Jorzak: Did you get a lot of marriage proposals?

Gacy: Five of them! I says, *"I only fuckin' write these women. I'm surprised, next they're gonna say we swapped spit and their next child is gonna be mine!"*

Jorzak: Right. That's what I was gonna say.

Gacy: Exactly.

Jorzak: Then you'd have to quit…well, actually, that might not be a bad idea, you know. They'd have to do the blood tests and everything else. Ha! Ha! Ha!

Gacy: It is just unreal. I'm surprised the younger ones don't come out and say, "*He's my father!*"

Jorzak: It's like the, uh, Edward was telling me about the woman who purchased the, uh…built the house on Summerdale Avenue…in the Enquirer a few years ago for saying the house was haunted. Did you…

Gacy: Oh yeah, the spirits. The spirits walked through the house on Summerdale.

Jorzak: Right. Right. Exactly. I mean, it doesn't surprise me a bit.

Gacy: She bought the lot for thirty grand, but the home, a two hundred fifty thousand dollar house on this lot which looks out of fuckin' place in the neighborhood 'cause the house is in a neighborhood in the hundred-seventy thousand dollar range. Here they put a quarter million-dollar brick bungalow there.

Jorzak: Well, they're losing money the first day that it's completed.

Gacy: Fuckin' eh! It looks like a monument! *Heh! Heh! Heh!*

Jorzak: Well, it's always better to buy the, uh, the worst house on a nice block than, uh, build something new or buying the nicest house on the block. Sure, it's nice to live in, but you're certainly not going to get your investment back on it. In any case, um, Edward's over at Greenlees office right now and I offered to go with him but he wanted to go there alone, and he went with Adamski…Adamski picked him up here and, um, they left around noon.

Gacy: Well, Edward don't trust nobody right now. He thinks that he is getting blamed for everything so he's going to have everybody put everything out. I says, "*Edward.*" I says, "*If they're gonna do it, they're gonna do it anyway.*" So I says, "*I don't want you tickin' people off but there's nothing wrong with you prodding them just so you know what's going on.*" But you know, he actually is not on the staff, so to speak.

Jorzak: Right. Well, that's for you and him to discuss.

Gacy: I have no problem with what he is doing, as long as he keeps me abreast of what he is doing.

Jorzak: Well, that's the whole thing. Actually, since Wednesday, the day after he met with you, he's just…he seems to have a much clearer head now about what his objectives are and how he's going to approach things instead of, um…it seems recently every little thing winds up turning into a big project. Um… [TAPE STOPS]

[CALL RESUMES]

Gacy: …just 'cause I blew up at the Superintendent when he came down here on Thursday, on my birthday, he comes down here and fuckin' aggravates the shit out of me so I blew up in his face. And they fuckin' turn around and put me on suicide watch.

Jorzak: Oh shit.

Gacy: And I figure, you know, you talk about stress and harassment. If that isn't what that is then I don't know what the hell it is.

Jorzak: That's fuckin' ridiculous. Does that mean you're being watched twenty-four hours a day?

Gacy: Every ten minutes the officer walks by to see if I'm still in the cell.

Jorzak: Well, that's…that's not as bad.

Gacy: But can I tell you something?

Jorzak: That sucks…

Gacy: No, but I mean, I just talked to the Superintendent yesterday. He come back here, he says, "*John, it ain't that hard in here. It's Leo Meyer.*" I says, "*Get out of here with that bullshit.*" I says, "*The fuckin' stress is caused by you people with your fuckin' game-playing.*"

Jorzak: Right. That's it. And then some.

Gacy: This Mickey Mouse shit, well…the guy sat across the table from me and he says, "*I don't know where you got the idea of unlimited visits.*" I says, *"You said it!"* I says, *"There was Warden Wilburn and Superintendent Caldwell sittin' right here."*

Jorzak: What about last month? They allowed it!

Gacy: Exactly. I says, *"How did I get those visits if you didn't say so?"* Then he says, *"Well, we're gonna have to bring you back to five visits."* I says, *"I've already had fucking nine visits this month!"*

Jorzak: Well, that's the whole thing, John. Um…they can't show that there's any, uh, urgency or any reason why your visits should be limited this month. All they're relying on is that – this is my understanding – is, uh, that they're going to strictly enforce this policy since there's a new guy in charge now, right?

Gacy: Yeah, well, the new Warden was sittin' there and the new Superintendent was sittin' there and they didn't even know what the fuck was goin' down.

Jorzak: But he was there last month when you were allowed…

Gacy: Yeah, well, the thing of it is, is Edward took a painting out of here because it had an address on it. You know, Dan Hancock, who is the one who gave us that information on Monroe, Wisconsin? Okay, so this guy, I sent him a painting, you know, for doing it and so I gave Edward the envelope. The envelope wasn't sealed, there was no letter in it, goes out the same way as all the other paintings that he ever picked up. And just because Edward was being served with papers, this bitch decides he's got to show him they're enforcing the rules. And so they took the painting away. So then I talked to him yesterday and I says, *"Look, I got a painting…"*

Jorzak: Which was it, by the way?

Gacy: Which?

Jorzak: You got the, uh, Adolf Hitler?

Gacy: Oh, oh, yeah. That…so they took the one away from me, 'cause I had it in an envelope.

Jorzak: Right.

Gacy: I said, *"That's a crock of shit."* 'Cause Dan Hancock did us a favor. We never would have found that Shotgun News ad, to know what…

Jorzak: Right, exactly.

Gacy: And I says, *"What the fuck. It's only a canvas."* See, I don't look at it as the value, it's that the guy gave us an invaluable service and he continues to watch and monitor art sales out there.

Jorzak: He shouldn't be jacked around because of the prison's fuckin' policy.

Gacy: But, you know, we can't show any in…*who the hell is showing any involvement?* I says, *"Warden Wilburn had worked it out."* By the painting going out on my visits, it shows the D.O.C. is not involved in my artwork.

Jorzak: Exactly. Not only that, John, but why change…why should this guy change anything? Because that's essentially what it is…he's changing the policy…

Gacy: Apparently, I got some eight track tapes. So the Superintendent come up here, he says…

Jorzak: He probably said cassette tapes.

Gacy: Cassette tapes, Okay. I'm sorry, not eight-track. Cassette tapes.

Jorzak: Right.

Gacy: Okay, and he says, *"I'll send 'em up to you tomorrow."* So now I get the message today, he says, *"The Warden says they all have to be returned."* I said, *"Now wait a minute! What the fuck is this? These are birthday presents to me and I'm gonna return birthday presents?"* You got other men in here that got 120, 150 cassette tapes. And I've got 40 or so, and I…

Jorzak: That's, that's a crock of shit. John, why do you have to deal with this shit?

Gacy: Well, I got news for you. It's always better for me to deal with it. You see, they feel threatened when an attorney comes. If an attorney contacts them, why can't… You say everybody's supposed to be treated the same, but then you don't do it.

Jorzak: No, exactly. That's the bottom line. You're not asking for anything more.

Gacy: No. In fact, twelve of the tapes come directly from Columbia Records, from, uh…Benjie Gordon, the Vice President of Columbia

99

Records. He sent me ten. They've been sittin' down there almost two fucking months now. See? Then all of a sudden, *"Oh! You can't have 'em!"* And the other one was a Yanni tape. You know, the concert pianist?

[TAPE ENDS]

Editor's Note: On May 10, 1994, shortly after Jorzak's last recording, Gacy was strapped to a gurney at Stateville Prison and asked for a final statement. His parting words were, not surprisingly: *"Kiss my ass."* Like his Yanni cassette, Gacy's lethal drugs weren't delivered on time. An IV solidified, prolonging the execution 18 minutes, but finally stopped Gacy's heart at 12:48 a.m. Gacy's sister claimed his body. His brain sits in a jar in the office of Dr. Helen Morrison, whom Gacy mentions in his confession. Today, Gacy's autobiography 'A Question of Doubt' can cost $2,000 a copy.

Grim Reader

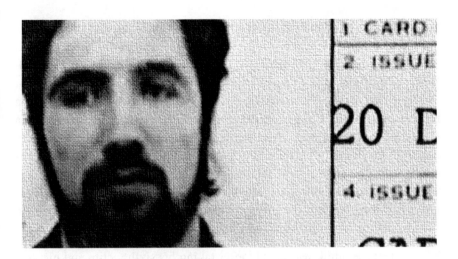

CELLAR OF SEVENTY-EIGHT:

GARY HEIDNIK'S CHAPEL OF HORROR

pril 1998: the Philadelphia Daily News carried the headline.

"KILLER'S CARS GO ON THE BLOCK".

But not just any old cars, nor just any old killer. *"These cars were owned by convicted sex slave-killer Gary Heidnik who drove them around North Philadelphia playing rock n' roll as he searched for victims"*, announced the manager of Associated Auctions, Ed Barkowitz, to eager reporters. A week later Barkowitz opened the floor to bids on one *"slightly weathered"* '71 Rolls Royce and an '87 custom Cadillac DeVille bearing the initials 'GMH' beneath each door's handle. And with, as the auctioneer shrewdly noted, just 2100 original clicks on its odometer. Yet it had been mileage enough for Heidnik to turn the streets of brotherly love into a serial sadist's playground, calculatedly preying on desperate sex workers; luring them in with cash and flash and briefly relishing the power it gave him until he'd had or seen enough. Then, 'Bishop' Heidnik, as his loyal parishioners knew him, would hang them by their wrists. Or zap them with electricity in a water-filled pit he dug beneath his skid-row Church of the United Ministers of God.

Heidnik first went subterranean a decade earlier, in 1978, when he kidnapped his girlfriend's sister, a hospitalized psychiatric patient, and trapped her for ten days in her sister's basement closet. Raped repeatedly,

102

the girl survived. Heidnik briefly served time in a hospital for mental defectives before his 'supervised' release, but the dungeon he then set about constructing beneath his North Marshall Street chapel was very different. When one of Heidnik's more defiant prisoners died there in February of 1987, surviving witnesses said, Heidnik mixed her boiled remains with dog food and forced them to eat. At other times, Heidnik would pretend to be a Police officer coming to free the women from their captivity in chains, only to beat them viciously for their betrayal if they called out to be saved. It was established by investigators that Heidnik continued to hold church services while collecting, torturing and attempting to impregnate the women. Gary Heidnik wasn't merely the inspiration for the character 'Buffalo Bill' in Silence of the Lambs. He *was* Buffalo Bill. And, arguably, he was far worse.

Gary Heidnik was caught after taking his sixth victim and just like that, following a trial at which jurors flatly rejected insanity claims, he went away to face execution. The world wouldn't hear very much from Heidnik beyond a small handful of opinionated letters published as curiosities by Philly newspapers. It was reported that, near the end, Heidnik refused to cooperate with volunteer attorneys working to postpone his lethal injection. Which finally came to pass one year after another man named Gary purchased Heidnik's cars in Ed Barkowitz's auction and pried loose the lock on the Rolls Royce's trunk. Waving off a putrefied odor the new owner reached in blindly, pulling back a set of screwdrivers identical to those Heidnik used to puncture victims' eardrums.

These candid, frenzied letters to a Pittsburgh musician moonlighting as a porn shop clerk who'd later change his name and himself become a lay evangelist – written on topics spanning race, religion, torture, sex, and the mentally handicapped then mailed for reasons only he knew – are as close to a dying declaration as we will ever hear from Gary Heidnik.

Gary M. Heidnik
#51398
P.O. Box 99901
Pittsburgh, Pa. 15233

March 22, 1989

Dear Mr. Beck Rosy,

Your letter of March 20 arrived and to that I'm replying. As for your peripatetic letter, no sign of it.

Your research at the library was impressive to say the least. I'm a bit of a diletante antiquarian, but the name Publius Syrus doesn't ring any bells with me. But thank you for your research.

My inquiries indicate that the only way you can get the desired books to me is via the post office. You'll have to mail them. That seems superfluous, especially since you live so close, but that is the regulations. I'm waiting with unbridled enthusiasm for their arrival.

Also thank you for the offer of stamps or writting paper, but my stocks are adequate. It's the books I mentioned that will be more than adequate. I don't want to put you to any other lengths. Thank you again.

Gratefully yours,

Gary

❖

March 31, 1989

Dear Mr. Beck Rosy,

Thank you, THANK YOU! THANK YOU! THANK YOU! THANK YOU! THANK YOU!

Christmas came early for me this year. Yesterday I got a present with three books from you. I didn't wait for Christmas morning though to open it. And having opened them, I dived right in, enjoying myself. I've been wanting to improve my memory, improve my reading for quite some time. Now I can, I hope. The memory part seems to be going well, and I'm hopefull I may soon accomplish my ultimate goal in life…. To memorize the BIBLE; at Least the NEW TESTAMENT. It sounds like I should be able to do that, but we'll see. It looks like the hardest part will be improving my reading speed. I'll have to first improve my comprehension. Memorizing is one thing, and improving my comprehension is one thing. I'm going to have to learn to ……… think. I'm trying but it's not going too well. However both books say the mind is like a muscle. You can do exercises and build it up. The best part of this cerebral muscle is it doesn't develop cramps, wear out, get tired and has no limits. WELL!! That sounds good, but we'll see. I've always been in favor of the exercising though and my bodies pretty well shot. Maybe, just maybe mental gymnastics will help.

I'd like to reciprocate in some way to show my gratitude for your beneficence, but I don't know how I can repay you, other than saying THANK YOU! You not only sent me some books, you sent HIGH quality books. These books were not written by some fly by night, get rich quick con artist. They were written by dedicated pundits. That means you took time to find decent books (or got lucky on first try…ho, ho). I prefer to think you invested time, as well as your money. That makes your present doubly valuable. THANK YOU again!

Perhaps you could tell me something about yourself. I know almost nothing, other than you've got a tremendous heart. In your letter you mentioned relatives in Ohio. That's interesting. I was born and raised in Cleveland myself. (Eastlake to be exact).

Also thank you for your offer of tape, but I don't have a radio, cassette or T.V. where I'm at. Not even a plug to plug them in at. I'm really in solitary. Almost like The Bird Man of Alcatraz, but not quite that bad. But thanks again. The books are just terrific and I look on the bright side. No distractions.

Well that's enough for now. I gotta do my "exercises".

Again: THANK YOU! THANK YOU! THANK YOU! THANK
YOU! THANK YOU! THANK YOU! THANK YOU! THANK YOU!

Gratefully yours,

Gary

❖

April 26, 1989

Dear Beck,

Hi. I got your slightly delayed letter and was glad to hear from you.
Hope you had a nice time in Ohio.

I'm keeping very busy myself. To handle both self-improvement
projects simultaneously (memory & speed reading) has proved impossible
so I've dropped the mnemonics only for the time being. That is going rather
well, so far. With memory it's retention that counts and we'll have to see
how much I retain after a couple of months. I'm really looking in the third
chapter, Book of John. Next I'll start on the 5, 6 & 7 chapters of Matthew
which is the sermon on the New Testament. At my present rate of speed that
may take me about three months, but it doesn't seem like work. It's very
enjoyable. It will take me years to memorize the whole New Testament but
it'll be worth it. When the lights are out and I'm in bed, I'll just open my
"mnemonic" Bible to such and such a chapter and "read"! It'll be a great
comfort. Thanks again for the books that will enable me to do this. And
thanks to the LORD also. Without HIS help, nothing would be possible.

It sounds like your life has been somewhat difficult. Especially the
facial scars. Do people ridicule you for that? Or is it none of my business. I
know how it feels to be ridiculed for being "different". It's not pleasant.

You didn't mention much about your schooling, but I'd bet you
graduated from high school and I'd put more money your having had a
"few" college courses. You seem pretty knowledgable and are certainly a
good "researcher." It's also possible that much of your education is "self"

education, since you seem to be a fellow book worm. What are some of your favorite books and subjects. I'm kind of an <u>antiquarian (history buff)</u> myself. I just hit literary gold several days ago. They got some new books in the inmates library and one of them was "I Claudius." It was an old, ripped apart paperback that didn't even have a title page. It didn't need one for me. Just the first couple of lines told me it was a book I've been looking for, for a long time. Ever since they have "I Claudius" on P.B.S. I've been enamored with the guy and story. I saw the series twice and could watch it several more times. It's really great. Claudius is mentioned in Acts a couple of times and his life is intertwined with other Biblical characters also. Unfortunately the book is only the second half, not the whole book. Mr. Robert Graves must have wrote several volumes, not just one, but still I'm happy.

Along this same vein I've been given a complete works of Shakespeare that unfortunately isn't complete. The only parts missing though are the last seven pages of Anthony & Cleopatra. I hate to impose on your <u>munificence</u> again but could you possibly get me a copy of Shakespeare's Anthony & Cleopatra. I'd like to be able to finish the play. It doesn't have to be a new book, as a matter of fact I think I'd prefer and be more comfortable with an older <u>used</u> copy. Maybe even you've got some other old books laying around. I'm really more interested in books now than T.V. It's not that I don't like T.V. I do. As a matter of I don't just like T.V... I LOVE T.V... T.V. with me is like an addiction. If I don't get my daily injections of news, P.B.S, sitcoms, and especially movies I get the shakes. When I was "outside" I had 5 color T.V.'s and several ancillary black & whites. It was so bad I had also one of those little watchmen T.V.'s. The reason was if I had to go to the bathroom during a show, I'd take this little jobby right into the bathroom and not miss any of the broadcast. I'd even watch T.V. in the tub, but it was difficult holding that little screen in one hand and scrubbing myself with the other. Would you say I was "hooked" or what? A regular "Boob Tubaholic." The trouble is that I'd spend so much time watching, my reading suffered. About the only thing I had time for was the newspaper and not quite enough of that. Well since being locked up I've gotten that "monkey" off my back and I'm back into reading again. Maybe later on I may consider a T.V. but not now. The "<u>may</u>" is <u>contingent</u> on my learning to speed read. If I can improve my memory and speed read, then

I'd consider T.V. again. It'd be like having my cake and eating it too. The key to this grandiose plan is to master speed first, not after. There is also that very large word "of." As of yet I can't even be sure of being able to do it. So far my prospects appear tenuous at best. But thanks for the offer. That was really nice of you to think of me like that.

You mentioned a little bit about your business and it sounds like you've got the best of both worlds there. You've got not only an income but it's tied in with something you enjoy. I assume anybody who had a band is a music lover. Considering you went to art school also, you seem to have strong penchant for artistic things rather than science and such, but I'm interested. Tell me more. What do you call your band, and what kind of music did you play. Also I'm interested in how you manage to make a living selling tapes by Mail order. Do you specialize or sell all kinds of tapes. To succeed, you probably advertise; in magazines. It'd fascinate me to know I've seen one of your ads, what do you call your business? I used to have a lot of tapes myself, but they were all "homemaders"! I'd go out and buy my favorite records and then record them on tape. They even gave me a write up in the paper on my wide range of taste in music. Philly must be desperate for news to find something like that newsworthy, but Philly's a strange city. By the way speaking of cities, what is it about Pittsburg you find so attractive?

Well enough for now, gotta go. Big date tonight.

P.S. You've probably noticed by now that I like to brighten my letters with colorfull metaphors and analogies.

Dottily Yours,

Gary

❖

May 16, 1989

Dear Beck,

Do you find my Little Tableau bemusing?

108

Well bare with me, everything will become pellucid as you slough though my syntax. (By the way, please don't be offended or think I'm being condescending when I write like this. At times I'm like a little kid with a new toy. I just learned all those bright, shiny, new, $10.00 words and I'm bursting to try them out. So please don't be upset, I'm just breaking them in. (When the novelty wears off, I'll start talking normally again.)

Yesterday the mailman brought me a package. It was of course from you and I found it delightful. It took me several minutes to realize that the one book (Claudius The GOD) was actually the same book I've been calling "I Claudius, part II." The reason for my temporary befuddlement is easy. My copy (library's) has no title page and no title --- period. That's all been ripped off, along with a couple of the last pages. While perusing your copy of "Claudius the GOD" I really had trouble accepting the fact they were the same book, since the prisoners copy is about 4 times bigger. The discrepancy occurs in that they simply used smaller type. But having two copies isn't really redundant, it's great, since I've only "borrowed" the library copy and it must be returned shortly. This is such a great book that I'll want to reread it several more times over the years. Now I can do so since I'll have a copy available. Thank you. Also, at long last I can find out how "Anthony & Cleopatra" turns out. But first things first.

You asked how my mnemonics is progressing and thats a great lead in to my main topic. So here goes. Great! TERRIFIC! FABULOUS! AMAZING! UNBELIEVEABLE! Now we'll take a brief rest while I stop jumping up and down and catch my breath ---------

The quantum leaps in my mnemonic skills have actually flabbergasted me. I'm now able to remember lots of things, even recondite things like numbers and dates. I've learned all the presidents – in order, dates of the Civil War battles, dates of the reigns of the 5 Caesars (which is useful right now). For instance when this picture comes to mind: a maypole vertically, with a cow suspended underneath, then the cow tries to moo but instead out of her mouth comes a crutch. All this farcical nonsense translates into May 8, 1963. Ring a bell? I'm on my way to developing a preeminent memory just as surely as my name is --- um --- uh --- Bill? --- Sam? --- Joe? Wait a minute. It'll come to me in a second. Oh --- oh yeah --- Tom. So anyways you can see I'm making great strides forward. But you will also recall my problem is twofold. My other problem was slow reading. Then about a week or so ago I was lying in my bed ruminating (ruminating is not a dirty word or dirty activity so stop laughing and look it up). A tid bit of a memory came to me, something I'd been taught about thirty or thirty – five years ago. The teacher pointed out that most people, when they read, actually form the words in their mouths and that takes time. One trick to reading faster is to stop forming the words in your mouth and just see them and use them in your mind. That's been something I've never been able to do. A habit impossible for me to break. Well, almost by accident I've cured it. What I'm now doing is plastering my tongue to the top of my mouth and when that doesn't work I also lightly bite the tip of my tongue holding it in my teeth. Ever try to form words when you tongue is pinned down. ITTHH P-P-PHT-RE ETY TO – U F - F! And guess what? It's worked. Oh sure it's not speed reading --- yet. But it has greatly improved my reading clarity. Now instead of taking 12 to 16 hours to read 2 newspapers every day, I can knock them off in just a couple of hours and have lots of time for fun things like ---- "I Claudius". The time spent in reading by forming the words in your mouth to reading just by eye movements is analogous to sending a letter though the mail and sending it by fax machine. Thus far that much has become fait accompli but there may be room for another improvement. Whenever I'm sitting around ruminating (stop laughing. It doesn't mean I'm sitting on the toilet either. I told you to look it up). It seems like that whenever I'm thinking, (having internal monologue) I do the same thing. Actually form the words in my mouth as well as in my head, thereby wasting all that time. SO now I clamp down on my tongue whenever I'm meditating (I had to switch to meditate since you keep laughing and won't look up ruminate). It should be interesting to see if I can also improve my thinking speed. Maybe I'm not as dumb as I've always thought, just slow. Even in writing it may help. Since I'm doing it now as I write to you. Of course, my handwriting speed is still dependent on the mechanical machinations of my arthritic hand. The actual speed won't increase, but perhaps the quality will, since I'll have more actual time to think as the thoughts are transposed into graphic transformations. (Writing). As of yet I don't know if this trick will also increase my thinking alacrity, but I'm going to find out. Some experiments are called for. For instance I want to see if I can memorize numbers --- faster. I can memorize numbers now quite well, but it takes time to do it. Perhaps I'll be able to do it almost as fast as a person calls one off. Stay tuned and I'll let you know in a couple of weeks. Of course, to achieve true speed reading status I must improve my rate of comprehension also. After all it takes just as long to send the same mistakes through a fax machine as through the mail. So I've still got to improve my comprehension but my prospects look bright and are becoming brighter.

Another thing I'm trying to figure out is if you're an extremely intelligent guy or one of those others. By others, I mean someone who, when he doesn't know something knows where to look to find it. (Fooled ya, huh?) Any ways I'd like to ask you to locate another quote for me, if you would be so kind. The quote is *"You are what you read as much as you are what you eat."* Have you ever heard it before?

Also you've been so nice to me and are always doing me favors. Is it possible I can do something in return? I'd really like to, but since I'm locked up, there doesn't seem to be much I can do, but I'm willing to try.

In closing a couple of more questions:

1) There's a dessert dish in which slicked bananas are mixed with milk and sugar. It has a name but I've forgotten. Do you happen to know it?

2) Do they get pearls from clams or oysters or both?

3) What is the genus for oyster bearing pearls?

Thanks again.

Your description of the type of music your band played "Industrial music" sounds like it had a predecessor in something from the late 50's, circa about 1958. Hi-Fi had just come out then and they were selling records (for a very brief time) of sounds like railroad trains, factory noises and such. Yours of course is different since you're trying for a more entertaining effect. On that same line a guy I think his name was "Spike Jones" used to create different sounds (circa 50's) but mostly for humor. He was rather popular for awhile.

Well, gotta go.

Dottily Yours,

Gary

Dear Beck,

Just a quick letter right now since maybe I can be of some real help, but time is of the essence.

About your father. I'm awfully sorry to hear he got cancer and will say a few prayers for him.

Also a couple years ago, a gentleman by the name of R. Block (the same Block in H&R Block) had cancer. They told him he didn't have a chance but by luck he heard of somebody working with his type of cancer (in Texas I believe). Any ways he went there for treatment and they saved him, Block then wrote a book about it AND started a non profit organization that monitors and disseminates all the latest cancer treatments and who is working on what. Quite frequently doctors themselves are not current on the latest treatments and people die just because the doctors didn't know about a cure somebody had just developed.

So if you were to contact this agency, maybe, just maybe they'll know something or somebody who can cure your fathers cancer. It can't hurt to ask and the way medical science is advancing new cures are developing constantly.

Unfortunately I don't know (remember) the name of this agency, but lots of people do. So if you were to ask at the library?? or somewhere else they'd know. Library of Congress would certainly know.

Sorry I'm not much more help than that, but hopefully it'll be enough. As long as there is life, there's a chance to save him, your father. You never mentioned, but I'm sure you love him very much (even if he is your adopted father??)

Sometimes the love of non-relatives or strangers can be stronger than relatives.

Best of luck to him, and my prayers are with you both.

Gary

P.S. Will write more later.

June 21, 1989

Dear Beck,

Hi, how's your father doing? I hope he's feeling better. You didn't mention anything in your last letter. Are the doctors able to do anything for him? I hope so. They keep coming up with new treatments and cures daily. They're even able to do somethings with A.I.D.S. People used to die in an average of 18 months, now they can keep them alive for five or more years.

I got the books and letter you sent. Thank you very much. The one book, "Battle Cry of Freedom" was one I've been trying to get for over 6 months. You must be a little preternatural to have knew I wanted it. I've also finished reading "I Claudius". That was very enjoyable. In another year or two, I'll re-read it. Can't get too much of a good thing you know.

Also, thanks to you (and Mr Harry Lorayne; <u>Super</u> <u>Power</u> <u>Memory</u>) I'm able to remember dates and such. It really WORKS!! For instance I learned all the dates of the Caesar's reigns, like Claudius's was 41 AD to 54 AD. When I start reading "Battle Cry of Freedom" I'll memorize some of the dates of the battles, and thus be able to keep the whole war in some kind of chronological order.

In spite of all these achievements, my mnemonic problems aren't solved. In the article I'm enclosing about Juke boxes, they mention the date of the first stereo juke box being 1959. It looks like I may have been the provider of false information. In a previous latter I mentioned '59 as being when they brought out Hi-Fi. It looks like I boo-booed. Sorry about that. Anyways you're interested in music, so you may enjoy reading about the history of juke boxes. Amazing! They've been around 100 years. (Almost as long as me, smile).

As I mentioned I tried to get in the same book club (Book of the Month??) as you, but they rejected me for some reason. They don't even answer. They've got another book I'd love to read ---- Steven Hawkings "A Brief History of Time." By the way Steven Hawking is crippled with <u>M.S.??</u> and is confined to a wheel chair. Sometimes he gets mentioned in magazines like National Geographic. You have to admire him. He refuses to let his mind be chained in a desiccated rotting body. He doesn't let his handicap restrain him any more than Claudius.

113

Well gotta go. I'll say a prayer tonight for your Dad and ---- you. Thanks, again. Your friend,

> Uh, um --- uh -- I'll
>
> Think of it in a second,
>
> uh --- oh yeah -- Gary!!

P.S. You may not be very religious, but you've got more kindness and understanding in you than any 10 Christians. You know the meaning of the "Golden Rule" without being taught from The Bible. Some of us "so called" Christians should be taking notice. Thanks again!

July 1, 1989

Dear Beck,

Hi buddy (Hope you won't be offended by my calling you Beck and buddy.)

I remember you said you went to art school for awhile so you might enjoy the article I'm enclosing about the art student earning literally her bread and butter.

Also I'm enclosing another article about Steven Hawking. Right after I wrote you, my July issue of Readers Digest arrived and this was in it. Apparently I was wrong when I said he had M.S. He's got Amyotrophic Lateral Sclerosis. But he's somewhat famous and gets mentions in different sources. He's also very interesting and should be considered a suitable role model for other handicapped people. It doesn't sound like he's got much time left though. Sad!

Another interesting person I've read about lately is a fellow named Jim Pietsch. What makes him doubly interesting to me is that he reminds me so much of you. For one thing he's a struggling musician with a strong interest in art. His art interest is mainly cartoons though. Also he's not doing

114

too well as a musician but he keeps trying. So to make ends meet he drives a New York Taxi cab. He has a superb sense of humor and is an aficionado of jokes. Whenever anybody would get into his cab, he'd ask them "heard any good jokes lately." When he'd hear a good one he'd remember it and write it down. So pretty soon he had a large compendium of jokes. What he did then was write a book. He called it The New York Cab Drivers Joke Book. Now he's famous and rich and can devote all his time to music, which is his real love. Neat story huh? I've got the book and it's pretty good. I highly reccomend it. The whole thing is sort of a modern Horatio Alger Story. Maybe you should write a book (he, he). But some artists really do make it. Sometimes they wind up coming through an entirely different door than the intended one.

By now you've probably noticed also that I've a rather keen interest in writters. Not only do I enjoy reading, but I've a vested interest. Yes! I'm writing a book too. Of course I'm not exactly a starving artist since my room and board are paid by the state (ha,ha,ha!) But don't worry, it's not a joke book. Neither is it about my um -- "miss adventures." None the less I's a true story, and it's mostly about my handicapped friends and my experiences with them in '84. A lot of very interesting and funny things happened to us that year. I got thrown out of a friends house and me and two other disabled friends set up house keeping in a camper on the streets of Philly for about a year. (You know me. I'm a very unconventanol type of person). Anyways the books name is "The 40th Street Soaps" or "Life in The Slow Lane." I started to write it in 1985 but stalled after only about ten pages. Now though, I seem to have a lot of time on my hands, so I started back on it. So far I've got almost 400 pages written, and am starting on the last chapter. It's a mostly humorous, true look at life with the handicapped and should be a big seller since I'm including lots of sex. Funniest thing about "normal" people. They don't see handicapped (especially mentally handicapped) as regular people and it never occurs to them that even though they're handicapped, that they have and do a lot of the same things as "normal" people do. We just do it at a different "pace" or "level." (The 'slow lane'… get it?). We have love affairs and romances, just like everybody else --- but --- sometimes they get pretty funny or tragic even. I'm not -- and never do -- poke or make fun of the disabled. I try to get people to laugh or cry with us, not at us. Hopefully, then people will see that we're all human beings and all in the same boat --- life. Sound interesting?

Well, I need a little help with some of the technical aspects. For one thing in the book "Claudius The God", Mr. Graves says some equivical lines about Claudius giving us the letters "J" & "Q" and sometimes "Y". Mr. Graves was rather vague on this point, and so I need to know for certain what the story is. I'll look like a real "boob" if I give Claudius credit for these letters and he didn't give them to us. So could you use some of your phenomenal research powers to find out for me? If you'll do this I'll be certain to mention your name in the acknowledgements (You and your band... he, he).

Look. I hope you're not offended at me. I'm playing again. I know damn well you'd do this for me without the offer. You're just that kind of nice guy, But I'd really like to thank you in some ways for all the nice things you've been doing for me. Thus by mentioning you in the acknowledgments, it would be a way for me to say thanks a million. Not only that, it'd be honest, since you would have really helped (he, he).

Also I need some other help with this book. I need to find a literary agent. One guy that might help is a guy in (I believe) New York. His name is Andrew Wylie. Could you look up his address and send it to me? Thanks.

Also if you're interested I could let you read some of the book --- a little at a time. If you're interested. I'd also like your opinion of it, and maybe a friend or two. What I could do is send you a couple of pages every couple of days. You could then read them (and maybe make few xerox copies) and send them back with the copies. You probably should keep one photo copy for yourself too, but that's your decision. I think the book is pretty good, but I'd like some other opinions, preferably objective. That's where your friend (or friends) come in. Let them read it without knowing who wrote it and see what they think.

The flyer you sent to me about the "Hope Organization" sounds very interesting. If some stranger sent or gave me that flyer with that message, I'd be extremely skeptical. But since it came from you it has the ring of truth. You do indeed seem to me a man of very HIGH ideals. So you've really piqued my interest on this. Would you mind telling me more about it?

Thanks again.   Your friend,

Gary

P.S. I'm considering they pseudonym of "Gary Claudius." Whats your opinion of this. Does it sound too hokey or campy??

P.S Who was the famous Greek author, who stammered a lot, and then trained himself by putting pebbles in his mouth, was that Aeschines??

P.P.S Hope your father is doing better. He's in my prayers every night!! That chemotherapy can be pretty rough sometimes.

July 11, 1989

Dear Beck,

I'm starting to send you some pages from my book but you'll probably notice that they start at page 300. I've got a little problem in that my book is scattered around a little bit. My wife has most of it, I think. I'm a little discombobulated after that "experience". My wife is someone whom I just don't understand. (And that's putting it mildly). She hasn't deceived me, like most women would have done, she writes me almost every day, but ---- ???? She also (and my son Jesse) has full financial rights to the book. When/if I can get her to return the xerox copies of the first five (??) chapters I'll forward them to you. Most books would be a problem trying to read them from page 300, but not mine. Since each chapter is almost a short story, albeit all are interconnected, one can read each chapter independently with little confusion, but a little preview can't hurt. The story is a true one. All events happened and the people are real. The dialogue isn't. I couldn't remember everything everybody said exactly, so I did the best I could. I also took some liberties with it to make key events relevant and bind things together. A conversation that might take place over a couple of days or weeks I'd often summarise at one setting. The dialogue is only maybe 25% to 50% accurate. Also I changed everybody's names but my first name. (I'm still trying to decide on a pseudonym). Also everybody's I.Q. went up about 50 points, (he he), including mine. Since I did have to change names I decided to have some fun with them. Almost every name has some ulterior meaning or relevance to it's character or some person in history or literature where apropos, or it gave me a chance for a pun. To wit Mona & Lisa! I'm sure you know who Montague and Capulet are.

The book is about the handicapped, especially the mentally handicapped including the retarded, but it's about them in the community and not inside of institutions. I was an integral part of such a community in 1984, and a lot of the things that happened were awful funny. but not to laugh at us but with us. I used to have one girl friend who would walk up to me and sucker punch me for no reason at all. Nowadays for a book to succeed it needs lot's of S E X!! So I did my best in the first 5 chapters. There isn't much sexy in the last two, but I do get in a little. Some of my sex experiences were so funny that my wife, when she read about them, laughed so hard the neighbors were pounding on her door wondering what was going on. The last two chapters, the one's you'll be reading first are a little more serious, especially the last chapter Antoenette, which involved a shooting. (All true, a real mystery). Also, please remember that this is only the rough draft. I'll have to rewrite it a couple of times to get it right. So please excuse all the grammatical errors and such.

Also make about (and keep) two photo copies of each page for yourself and your records and me. If you've got a record of the book, I'll be able to call on it, if something comes up on my end. Things do "come up" like transfers and such. In a transfer my property becomes separated from me and sometimes "lost".

So you can see how important it is that a copy of my book be with a reliable source. My wife isn't so reliable. I mean all the money from it will go to her, and our son Jesse. She has that in writting. But she has only a rough draft of the first five (??) chapters, and I need photo stat copies of it to rewrite it. She can keep the originals. Apparently I'll also need photo stat copies to send to a literary agent --- myself. I do have a sneaking suspicion she may have already sold the book for some unbelievably ridiculous figure like $10.00. If somebody offered her $1.00 for something she could be guaranteed of selling next week for $1,000, she'd go for the $1.00. She's a money "junkie." As such you'd think she'd be cooperating in this thing, but --- I just don't understand her. Anyways here's her address: [*address redacted*]. And I almost forgot her name is Betty Heidnik. Relax though, I'm not trying to set up a dialogue or anything between you and her. I'm trying to develop a safety factor, or backup.

As you know I'm living on the "edge" here. I may be here today and "gone" the next. I mean permanently gone --- dead! I just don't know, from one day to the next. I've been set up by the guards at Graterford one time and beaten up. I'll enclose two letters also that I've written and had published in newspapers, that will explain some of this. So if something does happen to me you'll have a partial copy of the book, and if part of it gets lost "in transit" or something you can send a copy to my wife. Maybe even intercede with a literary agent for me (if I'm no longer here). If a real literary agent gets involved and starts talking money, she'll probably listen then and cooperate. (If she hasn't already sold the thing. I don't know and can't find out. She LIES like a dog. But yet as tight as her money is she "blows" it on me by buying me subscriptions to Time and Readers Digest, and would buy me a T.V. if I'd let her. She writes me almost every day, wants to come out to see me (which could be dangerous to her and Jesse) and will accept any and all collect calls, from me. So she must love me, just to not divorce me BUT I'm confused! I can't figure her out. Do you know anything about women (he, he)? So "if" something happens to me, would you contact her and help with the book publishing?? AT least my kid/kids should get some benefit from it. Since it has absolutely NOTHING to do with my crimes, it should be exempt from that PA law.

Also I got distracted from telling you about it. It all occurred in 1984, and I had bought a new van then which I was customizing myself (covered in chapter two). But also my friend Jack (aka Dunn Ayle, a car repossessor), threw me out of his house and instead of looking for another apartment, I lived in the van for awhile. Then a couple of my handicapped friends, "Cyrano Montague" and "Juliet Capulet" also becomes homeless. So instead of getting another apartment together we bought a camper and lived on the street. (I'm kind of an "untraditional person"). Anyways there is a group of handicapped people that gather and hang out around "40th St" and we were part of that group. It was a lot like a T.V. soap opera, but at a slower pace. (Get it)? Every day somebody was going with somebody else or swapping partners or in some kind of problem. Some things were "strange," some "sad" but many often very funny. The only person I poke fun at though is me. I made plenty of mistakes and did some "strange" things myself. By the way the camper idea wasn't mine but "Cyranos". Hopefully though, through humor and an eyeball view, the readers will come to realize and see the "humanness" of the handicapped especially the retarded. A lot of people can't see them as human beings, but as "children" or even pets or something and lots of people take advantage of them like

119

"Livia Holiday." Also most people don't think the handicapped should have or need sex! Well we like sex as much as or maybe even better than "normal" people. Hows that for a "hot potato". Letting people in on the idea that handicapped can be sexy or need sex, (including marriage). Hopefully through this insight into their lives people will come to see that also. We're not <u>children</u>, we're not <u>pets</u> and we're not <u>angels</u> either. We're ALL human beings, with the same desires, goals etc. The handicapped (retarded included) can be just as in love as anybody else. That's the (leit - motiv) of chapter "Tony & Maria." Most of this chapter can be proven to be true too, since there was court records and city documents and such. IT REALLY HAPPENED!

Your friend,

Gary

P.S. Another letter to follow!

P.S.S If I tried to get this thing xeroxed here in prison, another inmate would wind up with copies. Thanks again.

"40th ST Soaps---"

Acknowledgments

At this point I'd like to take opportunity to extend my profound gratitude to Mr. Beck Rosy, without whose technical assistance and more importantly moral encouragement this book would have been impossible.

He restored my faith in the innate goodness of men. Thanks for all your help Beck and thanks most of all for being my friend.

(The mention of your technical help is now very accurate since you kept me from making a big faux pas "boo boo" with Claudius)

(Beck, I need a photo stat of this page too)

July 12, 1989

Dear Beck,

Hi buddy! How're things going. How haven't you been robbed yet. It does sound like you're next on somebodies list. One thing you can do that may help is to leave a T.V. or radio playing when you're in & out! That way burglars can be less sure if anybody's home. One trick burglars use to determine for certain if anybodys home is they go up to the front door and --- knock! Right. It's that easy. If nobody answers, they're likely to go to work. They also usually hit in daytime, when everybody's at work. Good looks help also. The more difficult you make it for them, the more likely they'll go rob somebody whose easier. Also it's tough to move anywhere you won't be robbed. Burglars like the suburbs too, since they're richer pickings and people are off guard. How ever; whatever you do --- GOOD LUCK!!

The two books and photo copies arrived. THANKS. As soon as I complete a certain civil war book I'm going to dive right into Mr Hawkings book. You're also a super researcher. In one shot you kept me from making two boo boo's You also zeroed in on my ignorance in getting my book published and finding a literary agent. You were right. I know next to nothing about it. My only information on it and Mr. Wylie's name come from reading a recent article in Time Mag, So the information is very much needed and very much appreciated.

Also by now you should have received the first 16 pages of chapter 6. Will follow with more pages in a couple of days. It's a shame you can't get the whole thing at once, but I'm doing my best. I'm also EXTREMLY Interested in your and your friends opinions. Again you're right on target. What's needed are unbiased objective opinions and critiques. I can't get candid opinions from my wife. Thanks again.

Now I'm having a crises of consciousness. You're always helping me, including with material things. I'm feeling guilty. As a matter of fact I feel like --- a --- parasite. If I didn't have any money, that would be one thing, but I do have some limited funds. I'd like to send you some money to help with your expenses. Your time is also valuable. However I've got a sinking feeling you're going to refuse. Please don't! Let me send you some, say a hundred dollars. If you won't take it for yourself, will you at least take it for me. Then at least I won't feel quite like a parasite. Also you know how money is, here today, gone tomorrow. At least now I can help reimburse you for your time and expenses, especially in the matter of this book. Your time is worth lots more than $100 of course, your kind of help is priceless, but if you don't take the money, I'm going to feel bad. So how about? You'd me doing me a favor, and maybe you could even use the money.

Enclosed also are my two articles printed in the Daily News. They should help give a broader spectrum to judge my writting or lack of writting ability. Good luck again on your apartment hunt. Gotta go! Big date tonight.

Gary

❖

July 25, 1989

Dear Beck

Hi buddy! Well only 5 months till Xmas. First some good news. In another week or two you should be getting a check for $100. This money is perfectly legal and such, but to send it to you isn't like sending money from the outside. Ergo, I can't just sit down and write out a check or something. It'll be coming from my account here at Western and thus there are a few regulations and red tape. I sent in the forms last week for the money. Those forms have to be approved (they will be) and then the administration will make out a check after checking a few things like my balance and then when they get around to it, they'll send it out. That usually takes a minimum of two weeks, but frequently longer. Once it took me three months to send out a check. So hopefully you'll get it soon, but don't hold your breath. I have to obey the rules or I'd get in trouble. The money comes from my V.A check, so it's perfectly legal. Speaking of V.A checks, maybe you heard I used to have a church. It was a legimate church and there was nothing illegal or susspatious or "tax" dodging about it. This is very easy to prove too, since everything was documented and on paper. There's a "paper trail" that shows all the moneys went from my pocket (V.A. checks and S.S. checks) into the church, not from the church into my pocket. Usually when they declare a church a phoney or something like Jim Bakker, they always show that the money goes from the church into the ministers pocket. So that automatically shows I wasn't a crook or stealing or anything since I not only didn't take money from the church, I only added to it. Also I wasn't avoiding taxes since my V.A and S.S was already tax exempt. Also I had my own car (a 1972 Dodge) and was buying my own house (V.A loan). I worked entirely for the church on a gratis basis. No pay, salary, benefits --- NOTHING! We also held services regularly and there was NO collections or collection plate or nothing. As a matter of fact, I often used my own car, house, etc to hold or use for services. Also I'd often pay for the expenses of our fellowships out of my own pocket. Etc, etc, etc.

So the church was legimate and for real. The problem is that I can't get fair or honest Treatment from the legal system. (For instance I was framed and put in jail for 5 years for a crime that weren't even committed. I was framed delibareily, on purpose, and because a crooked cop and others wanted to steal the churches money, and NOBODY cares. But that is another story). The church is also as helpless as I am. Since all the members were handicapped, they are all helpless too. If they weren't helpless, or if I'd had some political connections or had donated to some politicians P.A.C., it wouldn't have been so helpless. So irregardles of the MYTH that we live in a just and loyal society, neither I nor the church can get fair or honest treatment from the courts, legal system or society even. You may have heard they had a real attack on the churches assets. Everybody and their brother sued he church even though it had NOTHING to do with my crimes. But NOBODY cares. They'd rather line their own pockets and steel including the I.R.S. Ironicaly, I just found out the church has a lawyer representing it. HAH! BULLSHIT! This putative lawyer has never even contacted me or anybody else in the church. If he's supposed to represent the church how can he do that and present any kind of defense without contacting me. He's NEVER contacted me or anything. How's that for the American judicial system or fair play. But that's how the law works, when you're a NOBODY and have NO political connections or support groups to back you up. I have no family, political connections, zip. Nobody. To make it worse I crossed color lines, so even most (all) white people have no

123

interest in seeing I'm at least treated fairly. But that's how America REALLY works. If you're a nobody and have no political base or friends, you're a NOBODY and will be misused and abused by the system, etc.

What's bothering me though is that not only is GOD being robbed here, but also the handicapped, the disabled veterans, and the poor of other countries. This statement may confuse you, so let me eloburate. Part of the churches Constitution states that when the church is dissolved then all it's assets are to be divided amongst the V.A., Veterans Administration and the Peace Corps. Without me the church can really no longer function in it's original function of serving GOD and helping the handicapped. However now that it's being divided up amongst the various taxing agencies and "victims", there is nothing going to the disabled veterans or Peace Corps. The victims, two in particular are only going to blow the money on illegal drugs. That is really sad. BUT does anybody care! I doubt it. Anyways I wonder if I should protest, challenge the courts or something and attach the stipulations that the church be dissolved in accordance to it's constitution and all monies go to the handicapped veterans and Peace Corps. But of course even if I tried this, it wouldn't happen, because neither I nor my church can get fair, or honest treatment from society or the legal system. So the poor and starving people of the world lose, and the drug problems win. How's that for justice? Sorry to drop all these problems on you, but I need some advice and probably quick. What do you think?? Also my wife is useless in this. She's not only not a member of the church but is trying to "ROB" it also. You can't blame her though. Since it's being carved up, she might as well get some too. Also, she'd never carry out the tenets of the church even if she were running it. The biggest problem with my wife is something that just occurred to me as I was writing you these last letters. I think I've figured out what the problem is with her. Why I, or nobody else understands her. She's having a nervous breakdown. She's cracking up. When you're very close to something, in almost daily contact with it or them, some things can be hard to see until they become patent. She's been under a lot of pressure, LOTS and it seems to be taking it's toll. She's getting more and more erratic and unstable and illogical. I've only just come to recognize the symptoms, and unfortunately can't help. I wish I could help, but there's little I can do. But everybody's got there problems. You put people under enough pressure, ANYBODY and they'll crack, sooner or later. Including you with your father being severely ill and sued lately, you're under great pressure too. I hope it doesn't affect you too much, since you obviously care and love him very, very much. If there's anything I can

124

do, let me know. In the meantime, be reassured that you and you're father are in my prayers every night, Good luck to both of you.

As for the xerox copies, I need two of each page and the manuscript back. I want the original back, to keep everything in order. Also it is only the rough draft and all has to be rewritten. But if (who knows) something happens to me, or my files, they're be a copy (or couple of copies) will a reliable source. I consider you reliable, much more so than my wife. So if something happens to me, I know you'll send her a copy of whatever she doesn't have. But she's so unreliable that even though she and my son Jesse, are to get all the proceeds she'll blow it or screw it up. I like to think that this book can really do a lot to foster understanding of the mentally handicapped. It would be nice if my legacy to the world was an increased understanding and tolerance of the handicapped instead of what it is likely to be ("an evil genius, etc.) so it's important to me, to all the handicapped that it be published. You, with you're "disfigurement" know what it is like to be discriminated and persecuted against for being different. People probably tore at you, and snigger at you and such, and thus you know what it feels like to be laughed at and ridiculed for being different. Society treats us as nerds and never really accepts us. But like I point out in my book, we do have and can find comfort with each other. So called "normal" people would <u>not</u>, <u>never</u>, and <u>still</u> do not accept me, or socialize with me or any other handicapped people. They laugh and avoid us and we can get pretty lonely. But at least we have each other. We truly know the meaning of that old Indian cliche "you can't know what a man feels, till you've walked a mile in his mocasins." So thanks for everything, but most of all thank you for your friendship.

Gary

[Enclosed articles: "Alcohol's Young Victim" & "A Long and Painful Search for Answers about his Son"]

July 28, 1989

Dear Beck,

Hi buddy. How's things going? First of all some real good news. Today they gave me a receipt notifying me that your check went out today so by the time this letter reaches you, you should have received it. For the administration here, to send a check out that quickly is some kind of record. So things are looking up.

Another piece of good news is something I just read in the July 31 issue of Newsweek. The hardest or next to the hardest problem I've had all my life is trying to understand how my mind works. You're peripherally aware of some of my problems! Ergo my abject failure to master speed reading. Let me elaborate. Essentially I'm moderately retarded, or at least learning disabled. REALLY! Only the people who are very close to me are aware of this.

Of course when you encounter somebody with a putative I.Q score of 148 this sounds like quintessential paltering, but I'm telling you the truth. I've learned to compensate and overcome it in many ways, but I haven't totally overcome it. When I was a little kid I had flunked 2nd grade once and was flunking it a second time. At the time my brother and I were living with our mother. Then my father (who was divorced from mom and had remarried) got custody of us. The schools were giving us special tests and were preparing to send us to what my father pejoratively dubbed "dumb school." He really worked with us, hours every day, and it worked. By the time I reached 4th grade the school administration thought I was some kind of genius. The greatest gift from my father (other than life) was the mental "spark" he lit in my mind. He caused me to learn a love of learning & knowledge. It was a "spark" that never went out. As you personally know in my requests for such self-help books on things like mnemonics and speed reading. Just consider that book on memory. It really, really helped. For instance I've mastered some mental tricks for remembering things like fates and numbers , So if they gave me one of those I.Q tests that often contain a portion on remembering 6 or 8 digit numbers, I can do it and recite them backwards and forwards. So now, if they gave me another I.Q. test my result, would improve in that area. But does that make me smarter, being able to get a higher score -- hmmm? Also I work everyday on my vocabulary, about two hours everyday. You're the beneficiary of some of this, since I've used you for a Guinea pig even in this letter. My use of such words as "pejorative, paltering etc" is nascent. I've only just learned them and hit you with them. After all what's the use of learning them if I can't use them. BUT --- does that mean I'm smarter?? NOT really. You see when they give I.Q tests or try to measure intelligence they factor in a little element called --- time. All or almost all I.Q. tests are timed. Also matter of fact here's my vetting on I.Q. tests and more importantly intellagence expressed algebraically.

$$I.Q = A + E + T$$

I.Q = Intellagence

A = Ability

E = Effort

T = Time

In my case, I'm a bit weak in the A department, but that is compensated with larger amounts of time and effort. The effort is expressed in the fact I'm always reading or watching educational shows etc. and trying to improve my database (knowledge) and even learning techniques. I'm always trying to improve myself. What distinguishes me from other people is it just takes me longer. No matter. If it takes me longer, then I willingly devote more time to the effort. That "spark" my father lit in me is a powerful one, and drives me on to always keep learning, and keep improving myself. You don't actually know me personaly, only through letters. But if you did meet me in person, at times you would soon discover that I'm as they say in the street argot, "slow on my feet." This isn't always immediately apparent. You've got to really look for it to find it, since I've learned to compensate and hide it. For instance if I know ahead of time what the conversations is going to be about, I've probably prepared myself for it. Kind of like taking a test or something. Know what I mean? I've probably reviewed the topic in my mind several times, so I'm prepared and usually do quite well. But if and when the conversation goes into virgin territory or requires heavy cogitation, then my "slowness" becomes potent. Believe it or not a [illegible] example of this slowness has actually been documented. Read chapter 16 in Cellar of Horror. What judge Levin characterized as equivocating was actually my "slowness" and unpreparedness.

When I found I had to appear in court on June 14, I prepared my brief to oppose my wife's claim, and discredit her. I'd have really embarrassed her if I'd have remained resolute, but before the court hearing started she let me hold my son Jesse (she actually named him Jesse which was my choice of names), and completely won my heart. So when we went before Judge Levin, I no longer wanted to oppose her and was thus unprepared to present it.

Anyways, by now you're asking yourself, what has all this got to do with the Newsweek article. Well the article told me WHY I have this problem. I always knew I had a problem, but now I know WHY! It's a terrific revelation. The article told about some recent discoveries in Fetal Alcohol Syndrome and more apropos Fetal Alcohol Effect. When the mother drinks during the first couple of months, then the unborn child suffers. Let me quote a paragraph *"Research in this area has just begun in earnest. but drinking during pregnancy ranks as one of the major causes of mental retardation in America. Last year, one to three in every 1,000 newborns were diagnosed as having full-blown F.A.S."* And Dr. Kenneth Lyons-Jones, a leading researcher in the field estimates that 10 percent of babies born to "moderate drinkers" my have alcohol-related problems. A recent study by University of Washington psychologist Ann Streissguth found that women who averaged one or two drinks a day during the first two months of pregnancy had children with slow reaction times and difficulty paying attention. I haven't mentioned the other anomaly "difficulty paying attention" but that is also a problem with me. Apparently it can be overcome with training though. When I first started to drive a motor bike and cars, I had trouble maintaining my concentration but with lots of practice, I no longer have problems concentrating on my driving. There are lots more details I can give you on all this but they'd probably put you to sleep. You probably got the nexus of all this. I always knew my ability was lacking, but now I know why. My mother was always an alcoholic and she always drank every day. That's why my father divorced her. So my deficient inability is probably organic since I wasn't born with a full load of brain cells. I don't hold any condemnation towards mom though. She didn't do it on purpose, she didn't even know she was damaging her sons. As a matter of fact this knowledge about drinking is only coming to light recently, and thanks to my father, it hasn't been crippling in my case. Also thanks to my father I've got the wherewhithall to be able to understand and appreciate this information. So I've got a little greater understanding of that greatest mystery of all --- myself. There's still much more to be learned though. The mind is a genuine conundrum. BUT you can learn from this too. When you get married don't let your wife drink, while she's pregnant. MAKE SURE SHE DOESN'T DRINK! If she does drink and the child comes out retarded, you'll know you failed your son, since you now KNOW this danger. Believe me, you don't want to bear that guilt feeling. That your child is retarded because you failed him. You sure as hell don't want your child turning out like me or my brother.

The xerox copies of "40th St. Soaps" arrived yesterday (Wendsday). You did it <u>exactly</u> right. The two copies and the original. Perfect. Thank you! Their also legible. I can read them. That's very important. As for the typewritter. It's a good idea, especially since the final draft must be typewritten --- but, they don't allow inmates on death row to have type writters. So regretfully I'll have to turn down your offer. Later though, when I've finished my final draft, we'll have to type it up and make more copies. Maybe you know someone who could do this, or you could do it yourself. (The person would be paid, of course). I'm going to include in this letter the next 16 pages also. By the way, as long as you're "playing" with a xerox machine here's an idea for you. How to make customized stationary --- CHEAP!

Take a sheet of paper and one or two photos of yourself, etc and put them in each corner. As for the name and address, Kinkos rents I.B.M typewritters with real fancy typing. (looks just like printing) and it only costs about 2 ½ ¢ (??). Anyways, you get the idea and it only costs about 2 ½ ¢ a copy at Kinkos. You can hardly buy plain paper for that, let alone "customized" stationary. Is that fun or what? Hows that for "creative" thinking. Let me know how it comes out??

Your creative friend,

Gary

September 20, 1989

Dear Beck,

A truly amazing thing has been happening: Consider:

1) First you start with a super abundance of idle time and few distractions.
2) You stir in some self-help books and techniques like "Super Power Memory" and "Speed Reading".

3) You season with several hours a day of enhancing and improving your vocabulary.
4) You sweeten this porridge with ticklers like "Mensa" and crossword puzzles.
5) Then you slowly cook the whole concoction together for several years and VOILA! You serve a delectable dish of improved mentation.

Yes indeed! My mental powers appear to have made a quantum leap ---- forward. I <u>seem</u> to now be able to think, comprehend, and remember things at an unprecedented rate. Peripherally it has also created a few problems. That's where you come in. I need to draw on your spectacular research ability again. The aphorism "Expect the worst; Anything else can only be an improvement." I'd like to use this adage in my book, but I'm not sure if its an original creation or something I recycled out of my memory. Could you please check? Thank you. Also I'd like to impose on you for another book. It's called "Body Language, the Secret Language of Success", by David Lewis. This book could be a real revelation and help to me. I've an awful problem of interpersonal relationships, getting along with people. It's possible, just possible that the reason hasn't been with what I've said, but in the way in which I talk, and the manner I have purported myself. Consider that usually, whenever I'm talking to people I invariably fail to make eye contact. This trait surely creates a very negative impression. I'm a very forthright person, but this failing probably creates an aura of duplicity about me, even when I'm telling the absolute truth. It's entirely possible that a lifetime of personality problems may have been connected to not what I've said, but the way I've said it. This is a likely a simplified observation on my part, but any improvement in my ability interface is a step up. My personality is so poisonous that, in all my contacts, I "Expect the worst and anything else is an improvement." (I couldn't help sneaking that in again).

I also got the book you sent, "The Broken Card" and am extremely grateful. Thank you. I noticed the pages were unthumbed so I assume you didn't pre-read it, before sending it to me. SHAME ON YOU! [Just kidding] Anyways, after I've devoured it and added it to my cerebral potpourri, I'll share any delicious insights with you that may develop.

Now I'm happy to be the harbinger of some good news for a change. All the forms have been filled out and you should be receiving another check of $100 in a couple of weeks. You're a very classy guy, and have too much class to ask for money, but I hope it will help and be accepted. If you factor in the cost of all the books, photo copies and such, you're not even breaking even on costs, not mentioning labor. In a purely <u>material</u> sense, it looks like being my friend isn't going to be a profitable endeavor. Sorry I'm not much financial help to you, but I suspect money's not a primary ambition of yours. The prevailing myth is that I'm some kind of financial genius (not true) but if you ever need any advice on the stock market or something, I'm yours to command, and it's gratis. Also any stock market advice from me is probably worth whats paid for it -- worthless. Oh, well, none of us are what we used to be.

I haven't yet finished my final chapter, but one problem I'm having is developing a pseudonym. I keep coming up with and rejecting one idea after another. Could you help? Do you have any suggestions?

Also don't think I take your advice lightly. You and your friends exegesis on "40th St. Soaps" hasn't fallen on deaf ears and gone unhearded. I'm reigning in some of my flamboyance, but not all. You'll find fewer sesquipedalian words but still plenty of my "unique" style. For instance there is a unique ending to chapter Tony & Marie. Your opinions on it will be greatly valued.

Well enough for new, or this letter will never reach the post office.

Dottily yours,

Gary

Gary Robert Stroud

(Jail house Shakespeare)

P.S Thanks again for all your help.

❖

October 22, 1989

Dear Beck,

　　Great review! Despite my "reviewers" critical remarks, he ended with the words "more". That's the best news an aspiring author could hear. Also, after he reads the rest of this chapter, some of his remarks will be ameliorated. Also he'll be surprised. Each chapter, as a matter of fact has a surprise ending. This is a true story and life can be much more unexpected and unpredictable than fiction. My narration is as unpredictable as life itself. Add to this the torturous writting techniques of an unconventional person (some people say 'crazy'), you get a very unique novel. Like my use of pseudonyms for everybody. As your friend mentioned, that hasn't been done for a long time aka Pilgrims Progress. Well why not? It can be fun and enjoyable reading. Some of the names are really inspired. Did you/he catch Tony & Maria (Check West Side Story). (An updated version of Romeo & Juliet). There is a connection. You'll see it when you read the end of this chapter. Also the girls real name is --- Mary. And when he completes the chapter his opinion of me as a social worker may change considerably. The whole book is a "feeler". In a diagram it would look a bit like this

　　Comedy ----------------------------------> Pathos

Chapter　1　　2　　3　　4　　5　　6　　7

And it advances in stages. From very funny or lugubrious (sad). And to keep it interesting I sprinkle it through-out with generous doses of SEX! Sex amongst the handicapped can be something of a unique experience. My wife on reading the first couple of chapters laughed so hard, the neighbors knocked on her door to see if she was all right. Also I'm including part of the prologue in which I advertise my status as a mental patient, instead of hiding it. (This helps give me a greater license in writting, and covers up my boo boo's.

　　Also my wife has finally gotten off her tush and is sending me some - not all - of the book. I'm rewriting chapter 5, and your friend will get the improved version rather than the rough draft. He'll also see that this book, which at first looks like a mish mash potpourri is in reality well connected. The stories are in reality all connected, although chapter seven seems a bit distant in some ways, but the ending ties it all together. As a matter of fact chapter seven seems to depart into a crime drama, but in reality is one very incisive view into the ranks of the disabled, with a surprise twist. And it's

132

all TRUE. When I lived this stuff in '84, I actually felt like I was in a novel or something.

Well enough about me. So sorry to hear about your father. Your both in my prayers though, and the MAN upstairs is the final arbiter. After all is said and done, we're all in his hands.

Anyways I'm glad you got your gas turned on. Christmas is coming up shortly and you're on my Christmas list. Best of luck to everybody. Gotta go, and THANKS!

Your friend,

Gary

P.S. How do you like my pseudonym?? Do you know who Robert Stroud was?? Hint = Birds.

P.S.S. When I said "40th St. Soaps" has lots of sex, it isn't the prurient type but a candid humorous type. "Normal" people have a lot of trouble thinking of the disabled participating in and enjoying sex. Hopefully that is something my book will open their eyes to, that the disabled (physically & mentally) need, like, and enjoy sex just as much as "normal" people. NOT to mention things like "true" love, and marriage and etc. You know what I mean. That the disabled are human too.

"40th Street Soaps---"

Pete! Be sure to return this please!

(Addition To Prologue)

My most difficult chapter in this book is my last chapter, "Antoinette." This chapter I find myself trying to characterize and fathom a "normal" person. Such creatures are alien to me and difficult if not impossible to comprehend. It is as difficult for me to write about them as it is for me to deal with them in real life. Real life people, and not those of fiction are very complicated. It was a tough nut to crack and I may not have been equal to the task, but I gave it my best effort.

Another salient point that will stir criticism is that even though it's a book about the disabled, you'll soon realize I seldom mention or dwell on mentioning or describing those malfunctions. The reason is quite simple, a matter of perception. This text is being written by a member of the group and not as an outsider. Thus I hardly see/think of them as disabled, but as people.

This is a novel unlike any you've read before. It's written in a way as only one living on the edge could write it, and in the end only book sales reception will be the determinant of whether I'm creative or crazy.

I.N.R.I

November 19, 1989

Dear Beck,

Hi! Your letter arrived several day ago, and although I was glad to hear from you, I was saddened to hear of your tragedy. It has taken me several days to respond since I wanted to think up something nice to say to you, to comfort you in your hour of pain. I know you truly loved your father, so your pain must be immense. Watching him suffer and deteriorate before your eyes must have scared your very heart.

You see you're one of those very rare individuals in our society who cares about others. You really care. So when they feel pain, you feel pain. Only someone who cares about others can feel another man's pain.

I could write volumes about how JESUS suffered for us, but I know you're not religious and specifically asked me not to. I will honor your request.

When my own mother died many years ago, I knew such pain, I thought I couldn't bear it. As you loved your father, I loved my mother. They say time heals all wounds, but not always. I still feel that ache in my heart as if she just died yesterday.

I suspect that with you it will be as it was with me. You will always feel that pain. It will never go away. You just sort of learn to live with it. Life is like that. Full of joy and pain. We can't escape it. We just born to live with sadness and look forward to the joy life offers us.

As I said, I spent several days trying to formulate some things to say, that would give you comfort and ease your grief. As you can see, I've failed miserably. I'm sorry. I really did so want to help.

So take your time. There's nothing that has to be done today, that can't be put off till tomorrow. Take a look outside. See the clouds scudding overhead. Look at the trees with their changing leaves. See the birds singing. Perhaps you've never really seen them before. This is maybe the first time you've ever really seen them.

When you do you'll realize that there is a beauty there, a power there, forces at work more powerfull than us, perhaps beyond our comprehension. Certainly beyond our domination.

These forces we cannot totally dominate. We are in effect a part of this cycle, not its masters. With this recognition comes acceptance of our own mortality and some measure of peace.

Your friend,

Gary

[Enclosed article: "A Tale of Two Smut Merchants"]

December 8, 1989

Dear Beck,

Hi buddy! Welcome back. And welcome to the working world. I've been pretty worried about you. You've been under a lot of strain lately and you've been taking things pretty hard. Some people can handle stress better than others, but everybody had their limits, the breaking point. The point when they can't take anymore, and they go off the deep end. When it happened to soldiers in wartime, they used to call it being "shell shocked." You sound like you're over the rough part though and you're on your way back. GOOD FOR YOU! I'm glad you didn't do anything stupid! I'd miss you! And a lot of other people would miss you too!

You've been under pressure from two sources. You lost a loved one, and you've had to get a job. A real job! Nothing but time will ease your loss of your father, a pain that will always be with you. And a job is the only thing that's going to solve your lack of bread. It sounds like you've found an interesting one too. Working in a newsstand. That sounds like something straight out of the movies. The pay isn't bad either! $4.00 an hour? That's pretty good! Especially for a job that one likes. I know I'd enjoy a job like that. The work isn't too hard and the fringe benefits are good too. You laugh! You say what fringe benefits?

You've got lots of them! Probably lots of pretty women come in, not to buy newspapers, but to chit chat with the new sales man (Well, I tried, he, he). Also you've got all those nice papers and mags to read --- free!

Here's a piece of "interesting news, you can't use." Isaac Asimov (have you heard of him??) got his start in a newsstand. When he was a kid his father (??) used to own one and he used to borrow some of the magazines, books, and papers to read. He learned to read them in such a neat, nice, clean fashion, nobody knew they had been read and then when he was done, he'd put them back in the rack to be sold. Nobody ever knew they were buying "used" mags. Asimov still brags about it and as a matter of fact he still reads things like that. He's still such a "neat" reader, you can't tell he read the thing, whatever it is. And this guy reads one HELL of a lot. He is either the first or second all-time most prolific writer in the world. I'm not sure if he's first or Barbra Cartland is. She's a tough act. I think she's not only written almost 500 books, but is about 50 books ahead of her publisher. Boy! Talk about scriveners palsy! (By the way scriveners palsy is the egg head phrase for writters cramp).

So enjoy your new job and by the way, how about telling me more about it? It sounds interesting! Did you know one of my characters in "The 40th St. Soaps" winds up working in a newsstand (a real minor character, Joan Wolfe). I forgot to put her in the chapter you just read, "Tony + Maria". Speaking of that chapter, thanks for returning it. By the way, what did your friend (and you) think of it? Your friend may think I'm not following his advise, because what he doesn't realize is I wrote the whole rough draft long before he ever gave me the advise about too many "big" words and a "stuck" capital letter key. I haven't been ignoring his advice it's just that that whole chapter has already been written. Since then he (you'll) find I've "reined in" the use of the "big" words, but I haven't "killed" the beast with the capital letters. Although I quit capitalizing whole words, I'm still trying To Capitalize The First Letter Of Each Word Like This (could you ask if that's permissible?? Somehow I think I already know the answer is No, But I'll Ask Anyways).

My wife finally got around to sending me the original copy of chapter 5 (For some reason she won't send me Chapters 1 - 4) but anyways I rewrote it. (Using your friends advice). I changed it from "Tony and Gail" to "Cyrano & Juliet" and also wound up lengthening it to chapters 5 & 6. So of course that created a problem. So I'm making chapter 6 chapter 7 (Tony & Maria).

When I told my lawyer about it, he got so excited. He wanted to read it and mentioned he was willing to help me get it published. So I sent him a copy of chapters 5 & 6 and I'm waiting to see what his response is. I'll keep you posted.

You asked me for a little dissertation, exegesis on the word "Hope." I'm flattered that you asked me. It's also a curious thing. My book is going to close with an interesting 8 (??) page epilogue, and although I never once mention the word "Hope" the word is implied throughout the 8 pages. Originally when you asked me, I planned to send you a copy of the 8 pages but then I thought maybe you should read chapter 8 first. The epilogue makes more sense after you've read it. But it's not necessary. So that's where I'm at, right now, this dichotomy. When I make up my mind, I'll let you know. But thanks for asking my opinion, and don't think I'm stalling or putting you off.

You also asked about that book I wanted. I'm going to write a whole, complete letter on that one. You should get it in another week or so. My reasons for wanting the book are so meaningfull (to me and maybe you) and numerous, it will take a whole letter to explain them.

Unfortunatly I've got a little bad news for you. You know how I've been sending those nice fat checks? Well I won't be able to do that anymore. They cut off my V.A. checks and social security awhile back. I still get $73 a month on a V.A. but that's all. Anyways I had managed to save a little of it, but I've blown most of that now and so I won't be able to send money anymore. Unless I get lucky and hit the lottery or something (just kidding). So I hope you won't be upset or offended if there are no more checks forthcoming.

Well so much for the bad news. Let me see if I can find some good news to wrap up this letter.

Yes! I think I've got it. In a recent newspaper article in The Pittsburgh Press they wrote about how to make homemade pizza, how about that? Homemade pizza! I assume you like pizza?

Anyways, what interested me was to find out how easy it is! Can you believe making homemade pizza is easy? It is!

The whole secret to it is the dough. You go to the supermarket, where they sell frozen bread dough. That's how easy it is. Just buy a batch of ready made frozen bread dough (also a roll of aluminum foil, bottle of olive oil, a couple of cans of boiled tomatoes, some mozzarella and parmesion cheese), that's all you need. (Oops! You might want to buy some oregano and garlic too if you don't already have them).

Then when you get home roll out a sheet of aluminum foil and spread it on the table. Cover it with a film of oil (so the dough doesn't stick).

Then rub a little flour on your hands (so the bread dough doesn't stick). Then take a chunk of your dough (of course you've defrosted it) and plop it down on the foil. Then work it into the shape of a pizza pie. You don't have to get fancy and throw it up in the air like the pros do (unless you want to of course). But if you do throw it up, let me know how you get it off the ceiling (or floor) as the case may be.

If you tear the dough, just pinch the tear back together or patch it with another piece. Also be sure to raise the edges slightly to keep the sauce from running out (but of course, you know that).

The sauce is really easy. You just take a couple of cans of boiled tomatoes and dump them into the blender. Turn it on and *whiizz*, you've got tomato sauce. As simple as this sounds, it was a revelation to me. I didn't know it was so easy.

Now you pour a table spoon or two in the pie shell and rub it around. Then pour on a layer of your homemade sauce.

Then sprinkle on some grated mozzarella and parmession cheese. You put on as much or you like. You're the chef. Then sprinkle on some oregano, garlic and salt to your tastes. Now the coup de grace. Another tablespoon of olive oil.

Also you can get real creative here and add your own toppings, like pepperoni, olives, onions, hamburger, sausage etc. Whatever turns you on. That's the beauty of making your own pizzas, you can do your own thing and it's so easy. Like my wife is absolutely nuts about rice, so I'd put some fried rice on it for her. Most kids I know LOVE cheeseburgers, so when I've got kids over I'd let them make their own cheeseburger pizza. Yum! Yum! (I'd substitute American cheese for the mozzarella, of course). Wouldn't that be fun!

Then you pop the pizza (on aluminum foil) into the middle shelf of your oven (set at 450°) and bake for 25 to 30min.

That's all there is to it. After you bake you take it out and enjoy, enjoy, enjoy. If you get one of those pizza cutters, you'd look and feel like a real pro.

Boy! Do I wish I were outside, so I could make my own pizzas. I love pizza, and it'd be fun to make my own, but I can't. So I'll make them vicariously through you. Let me know if you try this. O.K? Also let me know if you try any innovations. I'll give them a taste test (in my imagination).

When I was locked up in Philly, they had a guy there who used to work in a pizza shop and he loved pizzas too (he weighed about 300 lb). This guy was really brilliant too. He figured out how to make pizza, using bread slices, and sauce from our dinners. He even managed to get cheese and spices from somewhere too. And you know what? It was delicious! Really! The guy was an absolute genuine pizza genius!

Well gotta go.

Your chummy friend,

Gary

❖

[Enclosed article: "Indictment May Mean Life for OK Corral Drug Dealers"]

December 18, 1989

Dear Beck,

Shame! Shame! Shame!

Don't be mad. I'm just having a little fun. When you told me you were working in an X-rated book store, I laughed for about ten minutes. And no I'm not mad or disillusioned or anything. As a matter of fact I'd like to thank you for being candid and honest with me. When it comes to morality and things like sex and pornography, I try not to cast any judgements or criticisms. Hypocrisy is what upsets me and often times it can be dangerous. Often times the biggest hypocrites are the ones preaching the most morality. Jim Bakker and Jessica Hahn are two of the most current examples. And if anybody believes Hahn was a virgin at the time, they probably still believe in Santa Claus and the Easter bunny. Lots of people preaching morality especially sexual morals, probably have loads of pornography stashed in their cellars, and cheat on their wives with their secretaries or alter boys. It's probably the hypocrisy that make it / them so dangerous. Either for reasons of guilt or fear of discovery they're the first to condemn someone else for what they're doing.

I've recently gotten caught in this hypocrisy myself. I went to one of the black inmates and asked for the address of Playboy Magazine. He gladly supplied some and I ordered not one, but two subscriptions. Then I asked him for the address of another magazine, Players. (That magazine specializes in nude photos of black women). He really got mad at me then! He not only wouldn't help, he got almost violently hostile. The reason of course was he didn't mind a white man admiring naked white women, but he couldn't tolerate a white man gawking at naked black women. Now hold it! Don't jump to any conclusions. Theres more. This same black inmate has pictures of naked white women tacked up all over his cell. You see the hypocrisy in all of this. He certainly doesn't, and I don't waste my time trying to explain it either. He'd not only not change, but probably only become more hostile. As if that weren't enough, there's even more. Those two subscriptions of Playboy never arrived, or at least never reached my cell. I know the subscriptions did go out, but only one magazine ever reached me. More than likely the guards are intercepting them and reading them, themselves. Those same guards who profess the highest morality are thus not only stealing but indulging their own latent sexual fantasies. And they'll condemn everyone else for doing what they're doing. Is that hypocrisy or what?? They don't see it, because they don't want to see it.

Again, I'm not casting judgements or condemnations. I'm only being objective. Now please don't think I'm launching into a lecture, but I've got a very serious purpose in all this: your safety!

If you pull back and try to get the big picture, read things like the Bible or history books, you get a very interesting view. Even the Bible is loaded with sex and pornography (In a sense, they didn't have cameras then). Take the Garden of Eden. They were running around nude, till they chomped on that apple. After that they took a different view on nudity. Later Noah got caught naked and Sham and his descendants (?) are still cursed. Moving up into the New Testament we have Solomen and the dance of the seven veils (the 7 veils not actually mentioned, but there's probably some truth there). And that dance was never condemned either. And how about those paragons of virtue like Abraham, Judah, David, and Solomen. All of them kept concubines and/or messed around with other females than their wives. There's a scent of hypocrisy here, too.

Now lets look at history, etc. What one notices if one takes the long (big view) is that morality (including pornography) not only varies from one society to another, but it always changes. That's the only constant, it's always changing. It's like a wheel that keeps turning. Sometimes morality can be set by just one man. Caesar (Julius) and Antony were a couple of lechers. Then along comes Augustus (27 B.C. to 14 A.D), who was a prude and he clamped down on everybodies morality. He even exiled his son for a putative bout of adultery. And yet his loving wife used to fix him up with the choicest slave girls. After him came Tiberius. His love of pornography is legendary. Caligula gained favor with him by smuggling him the ancient world's version of it. Check out the

movie "Caligula." It's not very accurate, but they dramatize effectively his love of naked females.

But so it goes through the ages. When Michelangelo painted the Sistine Chapel, he hid some nudes in it, but they were painted over by somebody else. Also some of those old religious paintings have lots of nudes in them, including cherubs. You paint a naked child today (cherub) and you'll wind up in jail. In the late 19 century along came Queen Victoria (Prude in "40th St. Soaps"). Even Mark Twain, a 19th century liberal, condemned one of his political heroes (I forgot his name) when he found out the guy was traveling with a woman he wasn't married to. Washington D.C. also had a whole red light district with oodles of whore houses about this time. (earlier actually). Things get a little more interesting with the invention of the camera. Now they could actually take pictures of nudes, not just paint them. You've heard of Lewis Carroll (Alice in Wonderland). He had a penchant for photos of little nude girls (and maybe something else too, I'm not sure). Imagine what they'd do to him if he took those pictures today in America!

Let's consider child pornography and sex for a minute. In The Bible, you were a man or woman at the tender age of 13. You could even marry them. And in frontier times you could marry at age 13. Edgar Allen Poe married his cousin at age 13, and was condemned not for her age, but only because she was his cousin. Back in the Byzantine Empire we had a woman who used to dance naked on table tops before the soldiers. She was very popular and only 11 or 12. She also became the wife of Justin the I (the Great). Nowadays if she tried that, they'd lock up the whole army. Currently they're down on child pornography, but when does a female child become an adult. Some states it's 16 and others it's 18. A girl can have a boyfriend, but only until he turns 18. Then he's a child molester. Of course, in America it's only one sided. If an older woman has an underaged boyfriend, she's NOT a rapist. They've even got an unusual twist to this thing they call statutory rape. You may not have heard of it. It involves retarded women. Remind me to tell you about it. I'd never even heard of it, till they caught my butt in it and ground me up. Nudity and pornography have been constantly changing. When I grew up, the late 40's and 50's, pornography was a NO NO! You had a tough time even seeing a topless woman, let alone bottomless. Let me digress for a minute. Have you ever heard of "Little Egypt"? She was a belly dancer around the turn of the century and you should see her. There are actually a kind of moving pictures of her still surviving. You'd laugh if you saw what passed for pornography in those days. The only thing they show is a naked stomach. No breasts even, just a pudgy naked stomach, and she was considered vulgar. But in my later childhood things started to loosen up, when Hefner published Playboys with Marilyn Monroe, but only topless. Playboy didn't go bottomless until the late 60's. We also had the sexual revolution, which got a big boost with the birth control pill. In 1965, my brother got ahold of a "smoker" and I saw my first porno movie. But they were still illegal even then. Can you believe we could have been arrested for watching such a movie in 1965? Things have loosened up a lot since then. Boy! Have they loosened up. In 1984 I went to a dirty bookstore in Philly, right in Center City. And they had graduated from movies to live sex shows. And I mean live. One guy would do two or three women at the same time, right there in front of everyone, and it'd only cost a quarter to watch. And this was at noon, right in the heart of the city. What's more, no police raids or anything. This of course was illegal, and I'm pretty sure the Philly cops were paid off. One thing about Philly cops, they're the best you can buy. If the price is right, they'll do anything or let you do anything, like sell drugs even. In some other societies like Japan and Sweden they still take baths together, whole families. Mother, father, and children. If they did that here, they'd all be in jail, but over there it's considered normal. And yet in China there having a crack down, and the children are being forced to turn in their baby pictures even. Why some dedicated parents are even going out and buying porno pictures to give their kids, so they can turn them in at school. Hows that for an anti-porn program. Ever watch Geraldo Rivera? There's hypocrisy for you. He and everyone who comes on puts down sex outside of marriage, but the only reason he's there and anybody watches is to be titillated.

By now you may be wondering what my point is? Well when it comes to pornography, sex or morality, it's all a matter of where you are and when. It's not consistent, and the only thing it does is change. It's like a wheel that keeps turning, and turning, and turning. Which is what it's doing now, and you could be one of those to get ground up in it. As the baby boomer generation ages, they're getting more conservative and they're starting to crack down on pornography. As a matter of fact, I'm not sure, but you're very own boss, may have been the latest victim. Really. I don't actually know who he is but there's been a lot of press about a PORN KING out of Cleveland, (who also owns a few stores in Pittsburg) (Small world isn't it) who just got convicted and got a heavy sentence. I

143

don't know his name, but he's also the same guy who owns "Doc Johnson's Products". So what may happen is you may get caught in this crackdown eventually. It's a complicated thing, and in the big cities you're safer since somebodies paying off the cops, and politicians so they can operate. Eventually as the wheel turns, they're going to close your store and make a few arrests. When they do it's the little guy (you) whose going to get the biggest sentence. Of course they won't stomp out pornography just drive it underground.

I think the Dutch have the most enlightened view on things. They figure morality is a personal thing. That every person should set his own moral standards, and they quit trying to control or legislate everyone else's. For instance in the Netherlands, you can buy pornography without being arrested. Also prostitution is legal and they only make the girls (or guys) visit the doctor for exams. I LIKE the Dutch's ideas. No hypocrisy there. If you don't believe in something, you set your own standards, not someone elses. As a result, they have much less crime, and you can walk the streets at night. Nobody standing in soup lines either. They have very little organized crime, crooked cops, or crooked politicians. No profit in it! The Dutch were such dedicated people they risked their lives to hide Jews from the Nazis (Remember Anne Frank?) My step-father was Dutch (Vanderoart??) and he was one of the first people in the late 40's to hire blacks as truck drivers for his business. He treated me decently too. The Dutch aren't perfect though. Who is? Look at the terror they created in Indonesia. Anyways they realized you can't regulate or control someone else's morality, so why try?

That's pretty much my outlook too, you set your standards and I'll set mine. You read The Bible the way you want, and I'll read it the way I want. I won't cast aspersions on you, or tell you how to live your life, and I'd appreciate it if you don't tell me how to live mine. If and when I feel like crusading for something, I'll go out and feed the hungry, open my house to the homeless, or try to help the handicapped. As a matter of fact that's my goal in writing my book. To get the idea across to people that the handicapped, even the mentally handicapped are sexual beings and should be allowed to go to bed with anyone they want to (and who wants them), whether they be black, white, yellow, man or women. I had problems (LOTS) accepting that homosexuals were also human beings, but I've reached that conclusion. I'm NOT a homo, but I won't blame them for the lifestyle they've chosen.

144

Just because I'm liberal, doesn't mean everyone else will accept my ideas and leave me in peace. So it becomes necessary to see how that "wheel" of morality is turning and be carefull not to get caught in it. You too! So be carefull, and don't think I think anything less of you, because you work there. Just be carefull not to get arrested. Take it from me. Jail's not a pleasant place, no matter why you're here. Well buddy, I've got to go. I'm running out of paper.

Your friend,

Gary

P.S. And thanks for being honest with me.

P.S.S. If you'd slip a couple nice "pictures" into my letters I'd be grateful, especially if they were of colored woman, but NO children or men either please. Thank you. Don't bother sending whole magazines. I'll never get them.

December 20, 1989

Dear Beck,

Hi! I got your card today and was glad to hear from you as usual. I just wrote you an 8 page letter yesterday and here I am with another letter. I'm liable to develop an acute case of scrivener's palsy. (writters cramp).

I was reassured by your response and wasn't the least bit surprised. You seem like a nice person, the kind one can trust. I wouldn't like the things I'm going to tell you to become public. It would get awful embarressing. Also I'm having problems with my outgoing mail (some of it). I'd appreciate it if you could identify each letter received by dates, so I'll know I'm getting through to you, and you're not missing any letters. This letter is in response to your card and note of December 18. Also I like to seal my letters with scotch tape to keep them from "accidently" popping open. So if you ever get one that looks tampered with or with a different handwriting on the envelope, I'd appreciate it if you'd tell me.

Okay enough of the cautionary chit chat. Let me get down to cases.

Today, everybody talks about child abuse. Well I was abused as a child too. But not by my parents but by my peers. When I'd go to school, all the other kids would pick on me, pick on me, and pick on me. Even as an adult in the Army and in civilian life, everybody always keeps harrassing me, persecuting me, and hating me. My parents loved me but everybody else made my life miserable, especially the other kids. I was a square peg that didn't fit into a round hole. The perennial nerd: The abuse was so bad, and the stress so bad that when I was in military school I developed a nervous tic of my head. My head would keep twitching and I couldn't make it stop. As if my problems weren't bad enough, now the kids had something else to rag me about. The names they used to call me! Like "shakey" for instance. I don't want to bore you with a lot of details, but you can see the problem. One thing I noticed was they didn't pick on the little guys, so I started lifting weights with a passion. Also my father told me to fight back. I did. For awhile I averaged about a fight a day, got pretty good at it. Being big and a good fighter doesn't solve the main problem, but it helped. After awhile they quit picking on me, at least not openly. (I was raised in the suburbs and the white middle class kids had ethics, and a sense of fair play. The fights were always one on one. Try it today in the city and you got beat up by about a gang of 10 or more. What's more city kids think 10 on one is fair fighting). Later, in adult life, you can't solve many problems with your fists. But with kids what happens, is sometimes the strongest kids are the most popular. That didn't happen to me. Being stronger just got me some peace. Nobody wanted to fight with me (and I never really enjoyed it either). It didn't get me any friends, but at least they tended to back off me. Still I wanted friends but couldn't get any and was never accepted. You can relax a little bit. This isn't one of your typical 'The weird other vs. the them, oppressors' tale exactly. But it may be something you can relate to. You don't talk about it much, but those facial scars you have, I suspect (??) have brought you some grief. People sometimes stare at you or look askance at you, and people sometimes misjudge you by your face, rather than what's in your heart (you obviously have a good heart).

But you see my point? It's kind of like the Indian aphorism of "you've walked in my moccasins" so you know my pain. (I think??) Nobody likes being sidelined and hated, especially when they haven't done anything. In your case though your problem is pretty much physical. You don't have a personality problem. In my case it was a double whammy. My head kept twitching (physical) and there was something in my personality people despised. You see my point? It wasn't them! The problem was in me. As Shakespeare might say "The problem, dear Brutus isn't in the stars ---". So recognizing this I decided to try and do something about it. What I did was a BIG mistake. In Staunton Military Academy I made the mistake of asking some of the other cadets, "What's wrong with me? Why don't you guys like me? Will you help me?"

Boy was that a mistake! They only laughed at me and ostracized me more. So I made sure I didn't do that again. The problem though has lasted all my life and continues today. But I have made progress (some). For one thing back in 82 & 83, when I was in prison at Graterford, they put me in solitary confinement. They did it NOT to help me but to try and drive me to suicide, so they could steal the $350,000 that the church was worth then, but that's another story. What happened is pretty fascinating. It deals with stress. You know what stress is? In war time, when soldiers are under stress, they often crack up. They used to call it "shell shocked". So when they put me in solitary confinement, what they actually did was reduce my stress level. By separating me from the other people, who were causing all my stress, they removed me from my problem. So (and it surprised me) the tensions lightened and nobody could see my head twitching, my head stopped twitching. (This is an abridged explanation). So eventually when I got back out into the public, the physical aspect of my distastefull personality was removed. The other part was still there though, but it was somewhat better. The less stress I'm under, the better I can perform, and my self esteem goes up. All very positive things.

Well as I say, I still don't know what my problem is, but I do know it's ME, not other people. And I do know I can possibly, eventually cure it.

Also (I hope) by talking about it to you, you aren't going to laugh, belittle, or think less of me. I've got a problem and I need help. But I've got to be very careful who I talk to etc. Can't you just see me going up to a guard or inmate and explaining this? They'd laugh their asses off at me!

So a couple of months ago, I was listening to a talk show and they started talking about "body language." I then realized that "body language" is a large part of my problem. For instance when I talk to people I have a habit of not looking them in the face, especially the eyes. That apparently creates some bad impressions. You're supposed to look people in the eyes when you talk to them, at least part of the time. I'm trying to do that now, but it's difficult For instance there is one guard here who acts nice and cheerful, and then sometimes when I look into his eyes I get the distinct impression I'm looking into the barrel of a gun. If the expression is true, that looks can kill, then I'd have been dead a long time ago. When I catch that look on his face it sends chills up my spine.

Also another technique of body language is when I'm telling a joke, I should smile. Some comedians can carry off a joke with a deadpan demeanor, but not me. And some of my jokes can be kind of weird and easily misunderstood. So now when I crack a joke I try to smile.

But you can see, I can improve. But I need help. I'm asking you for it.

There's a book out called "Body Language, The Secret Language of Success" by a David Lewis. I'm not naïve enough to think one book can resolve a lifetime of personality disorders, but every little improvement helps.

There's also another book out, I'm not exactly sure of the title or author, but it sounds like "How to get your point across in 30 seconds or less." That book could be a big help to me too. Maybe I can learn to make my points without writing all those rambling, long winded letters.

So if you could get me those books, I'd be very grateful. Also you can see their importance to me.

It'd be nice, that when they executed me, they were only killing me and hating me for what I have done and didn't also hate me for having a bizarre personality.

Your friend, Gary

❖

Dear Beck,

Hi. Merry Xmas. How's your Christmas going? I hope you're enjoying your new job too. By the way theres something I'd like to explain to you, but I'd like to have your promise that you won't laugh at me, think I'm crazy or tell anyone. Not that you're the type to do anything like that, but it's something very personal, and it would make me feel better, Okay?

Well don't eat too much turkey and have a great Xmas.

Your friend,

Gary

❖

January 26, 1990

Dear Beck (Music Man),

Hi buddy. I hope you're laughing. As for your idea of cutting a record, I don't know if we'll make dime one, but it sure as hell sounds like FUN!! And I need a little fun.

I don't know what kind of musician you are since I've never heard you play, but I know one thing. You're a <u>genius</u>!! A true GENIUS! But not the ordinary kind. You're what in college we'd have called a "marketing genius." You know how to market a product. In the music business one needs a "gimmic" or a hook to make it. Maybe (??) this is it. No matter, it'll still be FUN!!

When the public and maybe the news media here's about a death row inmate making a record, it could (??) just make it. There are no guarantees in this life, but it's sure worth a shot.

I know you're the artistic director, but we're working on two different tracks. You're looking for a record with lots of pathos. (maudlin or Lugubrious even) I'm thinking of humor and satire. Actually I'm

149

against the death penalty, but I think we can accomplish more with satire than looking for pity. NOBODY has pity for me.

You asked about some of my ideas. Well I've got an idea for a title or subtitle. How about

"LIVE - FROM DEATH ROW."

is that catchy or what???

Sometimes I wonder if you can't read my mind. When you suggested I might write a song or two… well I did!

The very night you first suggested we make a record I sat down and wrote two songs (after I stopped laughing) after and as I wrote the songs I kept laughing. I could only write the lyrics though, You'll have to write the music. Hows this for a title:

"SEND ME A BIG RUBBER DOLLY"

Or how about

"GIVE ME A CALL GOVERNOR - PLEASE"

As I say I've actually written the lyrics to those songs. Are you interested?

A couple of other possible titles I came up with (but no lyrics) are

"I, Electrified"

"I Got The HOT'S For You"

"What's Cookin'"

"I'll Get a Jolt Out of You"

"Alcatraz Stomp"

"I'm Gonna Do the Rockview Rock"

"Did you pay the Light Bill Governor"

etc, etc.

Any of those tickle you?

Also believe it or not I can make music. My singing ability sucks, but I can play a musical instrument, behind bars. That's right! Are you ready for this?

"Gary Heidnik plays ---- Handcuffs!"

When you tape me, even through the phone, they'd have me in handcuffs, so I can just kind of tap them together. With your friend's electronic devices, you can give them a beat or whatever. Is that catchy or what?

And as for that big subject of money. Well I don't want any! All of my share (if there is any) can be given to charity. Preferably the Salvation Army. (I Like them). That's only my share of the profits. What you all do with yours is up to you. But you might advertise that ALL my profits are going to charity. That would short circuit most of the criticism you'll face (and short circuit lawsuits). Also it'd be nice knowing some good might come out of all this. That we might (??) wind up feeding some of the hungry. Give them HOPE!

Well moving right along. This mail problem of mine, frankly, has me confused. I can't quite get a "handle" on it.

I've gotten your letters, the book "How To Get Your Point Across in 30 Seconds", the ripped out pictures and the Pictorial Magazine from Players. Then today the Players calendar arrived. So, so far so good.

Now for the confusion. Before when I tried to order my own subscription to Players I couldn't even get their address, let alone send out a subscription. But I did order Playboy and a doctor friend (Makenzie) ordered me a subscription. I only got 1 issue. What happened to the rest?? Probably some sanctimonious guard is enjoying them. So imagine my surprise when you got the Players mags and calendar to me. I'd have thought that would be the stuff they'd intercept.

Also it's only some of my mail that disappears, not all, and it's slightly inconsistent. But it does appear that ALL mail going to the news media, journalists, judges and F.B.I. gets "Lost." That seems to be constant.

I've always been a great admirer of the Peace Corps. That is a group that not only feeds the hungry and starving of the world, it

<u>TEACHES</u> them to feed themselves. And it does it, not by teaching them the superiority of the American way but works within each culture's infrastructure. In other words it teaches them to feed themselves and doesn't destroy their cultures.

You've read that newspaper article (and returned it). The nice thing about it, is it summarizes the whole situation. Now even at best, if the Peace Corps only gets a couple of hundred thousand dollars, what they can do with such a small amount of money is truly miraculous. Some church organizations can feed whole families (and teach) them for only $20 or $30 a month. So that couple hundred thousand might save (and make independent) a whole village or two. Also, since the Peace Corps is an agency of the Federal government, they couldn't object too hard to my plan. The money would still be going into their pockets, just a different pocket. One that doesn't buy guns or bombs, or fatten already fat politicians. So if in the <u>very</u> <u>unlikely</u> <u>event</u> everybody dropped their claims it's the starving of the world who'll benefit. People who really need help. Everybody claims the "victims" are entitled to something. Well you read the article. They tried it that way. Under the present course of events the "victims" aren't going to get ZIP! NIL! What's more some of them like Rivera, Askins, and Adams are junkies. So they're only going to spend what little they do get on DRUGS. It's all going into their arms or up their noses. Personally I'd rather see the hungry of the world eat, than some junkie get a high, some drug dealer get more assets to buy guns or crooked cops.

So I'm very grateful for your help in this. You're a person who is concerned about the helpless of this world and wants to give them HOPE. You've even shown a little incentive in this. By sending a copy to the Pittsburgh Press, that wasn't a good idea. It was a GREAT idea! I laud you for your initiative! And thank you!

Enclosed is another copy of the letter since it was written before Christmas, the line about holiday season is getting a bit dated, but "oh well." If anybody wants I'll rewrite it and bring it up to date.

Thanks again for all your help

Deferentially yours, and Grateful,

Gary

152

P.S. I need the phone number of the Federal court house in Philly and/or the phone number of a Judge Scholl who operates out of the courthouse (federal) in Philly.

IMPORTANT!

(Holographic Copy of Letter Written December 16, 1989)

Jan 26, 1990

This Letter is for Publication

I am deeply saddened in watching all this squabbling over my churches funds. For all the world it sounds as if nature is being imitated by men. Have you ever watched a nature film of a shark's feeding frenzy. You toss a piece of "meat" out to a bunch of shark's and they go absolutely crazy struggling for a bigger bite. Often they even turn on each other, chewing up their rivals.

That's whats happening here. And as in nature, it's the little ones who are being pushed aside, getting little or nothing. They are weak and powerless, so nobody fights or speaks for them.

In all of this nobody, and I mean <u>NOBODY</u> has asked me my opinion. But I am going to give it anyways. The money was collected in GOD'S name and GOD'S money should never, ever be used to buy guns and bullets, give politicians fat pay raises, line lawyers already deep pockets, or put dope in a junkies needles. HIS money shouldn't be used to by fancy cars for would-be ministers either. It should be used to clothe and feed the hungry, to buy wheelchairs for the disabled.

The only thing I agree with in this embroglio is that the church as a functional entity is finished and therefore it's assets should be divided up and given to the truly needy. There is a provision in the church's constitution that in the matter of dissolution all the moneys should go to the Peace Corps and the Veterans Administration. Have you ever seen a poor starving child in a foreign country? Have you ever seen a paralyzed veteran in a wheelchair?

Of course you have! They are the weak and helpless and as usual they have been pushed aside.

In this holiday season, I call upon everyone to stop fighting for a bigger bite and to allow the money to go where it'll save lives or ease some misery.

This is America! Such things can't happen here! I know the American people won't forsake the truly needy and helpless of the world. The ones who can't fight for themselves.

Hopefully,

Gary M. Heidnik

❖

February 5, 1990

Dear Beck,

Something that had me wondering when you first wrote me about the record was, "Is this guy serious? Can I trust him?"

Upon reading your letter of February 1, 1990, I believe you are. If you're not, you're putting on one hell of an act, and for what purpose? Also there seems to be a concerted effort by the prison authorities to keep me incognito. They seem (??) to be trying to keep me from the news media, judges and F.B.I. The last thing they'd go for is to have me make a record. As to why (??) they're opposing me I don't know, I'm not trying to make problems for them. I'm trying to expose a crooked big time drug dealer and extremely crooked Philly cop (desperate too). Also I'm trying to divert the money I accumulated in GOD'S name to feed the hungry and help disabled veterans. How could any law abiding citizen object to that?

Anyways the embargo (??) on my mail may have been at least partially lifted. I've been trying to write a Judge McCruddan 3 times and my 2nd letter may have finally gotten through. We'll have to wait though and see if others like Judge Scholl responds. If he does it could lead to big developments in my case.

I'm going to send you <u>copies</u> of Judge Scholl's letter and a letter to Judge Mirurchi. They explain considerable.

If you have a copy of "Cellar of Horrors" by Ken Englade, read pages 49 & 50. When you do ask yourself 2 questions. 1) Why didn't they arrest Mr. Rogers, who even admits publicaly to house breaking. 2) If I had really wanted to kill him, WHY? didn't I? I had a loaded rifle and pistol.

This was the start of many of my legal difficulties and lead to me being framed in '78. (which is explained in other letters)

So I want to get the F.B.I. to investigate <u>and</u> also institute law suits against, among others, Merrill Lynch. I'm trying to get my wife to conduct the suits on my behalf, but she seems reticent to say the least. If she won't do it, I'll go to some public attorney like Kunstler. Since this involves a crooked policemen etc., he'll have it (and ALL proceeds to go to charity, of course).

As for the F.B.I., I've got to get them to take me seriously. When they do, I can support many of my accusations via a polygraph also <u>if</u> (??) Mr. Kirkpatrick has committed perjury and is in collusion with Patrick Devlin, I can prove I was framed in '78, and unjustly spent 5 years in jail. Devlin is a professional and nobody can crack him anymore than you can break or get a mafia member to talk. His weak spot is all the "amateurs" he would have enlisted to help him. Kirkpatrick seems to be his weakest point. It would only take one honest accountant ten minutes to verify my accusation via church records.

So I'm really "HOT" for that interview you mentioned (and record). If the request for an F.B.I. investigation comes from the news media then they'll have to take it seriously (or Judge Scholl). Kirkpatrick may have really put his foot in his mouth via the bankruptecy trick. I'm trying to find out.

This whole thing is extremely complicated. There's a HELL of a lot more involved, like they take my second daughter Maxine away from me for reasons of pure racism. They key to that is a Mrs. Maxine Johnson. If she cooperates, (the bigots confided in her, but I think Devlin has threatened her too. He's already threatened another investigator, Dr. Apsche, and a lawyer Mr. Jack Bulkin). Also I can now prove I didn't kill one victim, but I don't want to (Yet). So you've got a teensy peek into how complicated everything is. I don't think you're in any Danger from Devlin since you live in Pittsburg, out of his jurisdiction. He is VERY dangerous, and even tried to kill me in '78. (Legally of course). BUT once the F.B.I. gets involved, they'll clip his horns. Even he won't be intimidating people when they're involved.

So your idea of a news interview can be genuine and maybe just what we need to get the F.B.I involved.

Also I'm glad you liked my song ideas. I'm also enclosing copies of the lyrics. You'll have to add the music etc., maybe have me repeat each chorus or something. You're the boss!

You also suggested I read or recite a statement. I concur. I'm working on a statement to follow the song "Give Me a Call Governor - Please". I'm trying to use the techniques from "How to Get Your Point Across in 30 Seconds" (I got a big laugh out of chapter 8, "Paint a Picture". He was speaking of doing it with words (imagery). Hell, I even drew pictures to get my points across (he, he).

What do you call your record? Do you like my idea of "Live-From Death Row"? (Maybe as a sub-title)

The idea of my statement is to ask not for mercy, but a dignified death. To have your head shaved, wear rubber pants and have cotton stuffed up your ass before being killed is DEMEANING! At least they can let me die with some modicum of dignity. That's not asking much. I'd much prefer lethal injection to electrical "barbecuing".

I'll put you and John on my visitors list but I need both your addresses. I don't think they'll settle for just box numbers. I could maybe use your phone number too. In case of emergencies or something.

Also thank you for the "Players Pictorial," I got it and was delighted to see that women are still built the same way I remember. It's been over 3 years since I last checked.

Also, thanks for Judge Scholls number. I sent him a letter last week, and will give him another week or two to answer. If not I'm going

156

to call. As you can see from your copy of his letter, he can't not answer, (If he gets the letter registered). So take care till I hear from you.

Your buddy,

Gary

(Holographic Copy of Letter to Judge Charles Mirarchi Jr.)

January 4, 1990

Dear Sir,

Do you remember me? I appeared before you in November 1988.

I am assuming you're an honest man. That you hate crime and justice with a passion.

I'm also assuming that you were lied to and duped. That you were made an unknowing partner in the type of crime that violates your sensibilities. I think it's time you know the truth.

In 1978 I controlled a church with assets of $115,000. In the book "Cellar of Horror," Mr. Kirkpatrick says on page 238 that the church was worth only $21,000 in Oct '79. That's not true! I don't recall the exact distribution in '78, but there was approximately $30,000 in Provident Savings and Loan at 40th & Chestnut and approximately $85,000 in Merrill Lynch's account. I don't remember the exact figures, but I do know the church's whole balance for most of '78 was approximately $115,000. Why Mr. Kirkpatrick claimed it was only $21,000 in '79 I don't know. But by '79 it would have been even higher than $115,000.

Anyways, that money is the crux of my problems and the real reason I appeared before you on trumped up charges in '78. A very crooked cop named Patrick Devlin was after that money! He found out that it was very accessible if he could just eliminate me. So he not only framed me, but even arranged an "incident" so he could shoot me legally.

157

He was unable to shoot me legally because I'm not a hot head and didn't attack him like he thought I would!

I'm almost positive he duped people like Mrs. Snauffer and the others into lying in court by convincing them I was some kind of evil pervert that the police had been trying to get off the street for a long time. I'm almost positive he didn't get them to lie for him by offering them a "piece of the action."

I'm also almost positive he influenced you into giving me a heavy sentence. He did it, <u>not</u> by offering you a "piece of the action" but by also lying to you and convincing you that I was some kind of pervert.

The reason I feel certain you're an honest man is going to surprise you. During the trial your aid would sneak up behind my brother and I and listen to our private conversations. I noticed him one time hiding behind a pole listening. What this tells me is that you are an honest man who wants to know the truth and do the right thing. A dishonest man wouldn't care what I said to my brother. Also Devlin was doing lots of illegal and unethical things trying to influence yours and everyone else's decisions. Such "enthusiasm" by a white cop over the <u>putative</u> injustices done retarded black women, stretches ones credulity to the breaking point. If he was so interested in justice for downtrodden blacks he could show it in many ways. I'm betting he hasn't.

The real reason for his "zeal" in prosecuting was to steal the $115,000 the church was worth at the time.

Don't feel bad about being duped by him. It took me over 5 years to figure out the real reason he was framing me. Oh, I know he was framing me, but I always thought it was because of racism and an incident that occurred on pages 49 & 50 of "Cellar of Horror". I suggest you read those two pages and ask yourself two questions.

1) Why didn't the police arrest Mr. Rogers who is openly bragging about breaking into my house. House breaking is illegal so why didn't the police arrest him, instead of me.

2) Also if you'll notice I had a loaded pistol and rifle. So if I wanted to shoot him why didn't I? I certainly had the means to do so, didn't I?

Detective Patrick Devlin was involved in this mess! If you want to know why they didn't arrest Mr. Rogers, go ahead ask me. I'll tell you.

Also we live in a very small world. Believe it or not you are involved in this '76 incident in a peripheral way. Really! I'm not making this up. Several months later, I don't recall the exact date, I appeared before you for a short time. The police had confiscated my weapons and I wanted them back. You gave them to me.

Check your records and your extremely adequate sources of information and you'll find out I'm telling you the truth.

When you do, you'll know something else too. That Devlin duped you! Used you! He tricked you and I assume you'll be outraged to find this out. NOT because he didn't offer you a "piece of the action" but because he made you an unwilling participant in a crime.

I'm trying to expose this crook. Everytime I find a weak spot he plugs it up. He's going around threatening people, like my former lawyer Bulkin and a Dr. Apsche and others. If he can't suborn people, he threatens them. But I'm still finding leaks and weak spots, so he's getting desperate and overstretched.

I'm the one who is trying to get an investigation started. He's trying to stop it. Common sense tells you that a man who has something to hide tries to stop one.

Devlin is dangerous, to protect himself he's even willing to kill (legally if possible). He's also using all kinds of dirty tricks to hamper me from getting an investigation going and has stopped several.

So if you could do anything to help, I'd be grateful.

For instance there "seems" to be a problem with my mail. Both outgoing and incoming (here in prison). It "seems" that all mail I write to the news media and letters to the F.B.I just simply "disappear". Quite possibly this letter will disappear also. We'll see.

But hopefully this entire letter will get through to you.

Consider John 3:20, 21

Isn't it time for fiat lux?

Differentially yours,

Gary M. Heidnik

P.S. I know you to be an educated man so I hope you won't find me pretentious or pedantic.

(Holographic Copy of Letter sent to Judge Scholl Jan 26, 1990)

Dear Judge Scholl,

I've been following the progress of the case against my former church with some misgivings.

I'm enclosing a copy of a letter that I've tried to send to Mr. Chuck Stone at the Philadelphia Daily News for some time. I'm uncertain if he ever got it, but it certainly hasn't been published. It outlines some of my hopes for the church's assets.

These are some points I'd like to elaborate on.

1) How can you have a trial when only one side is being represented. I have not been contacted by anybody and have not been given the chance to defend the church.

2) If I had been consulted I could prove that the church was a legitimate entity, operating towards the extension of GOD'S word and not for anybody's personal gain, especially mine. Since all the church's monies were documented, this can be proved. Consider

a) No collections, so the members (and there were members) were not contributors.

b) All donations were made from my V.A. and S.S. checks which were already tax exempt, So I couldn't be seeking a tax dodge.

c) ALL board members, especially me, served gratis. We were not paid.

ETC, ETC, ETC.

3) So how can you have a trial without any representation of the opposing side?

4) Also there may be other problems. I was framed in '78, by a crooked policeman seeking to steal the church's assets which in '78 were $115,000 NOT the $21,000 declared by Mr. Kirkpatrick on page 238 of "Cellar of Horror". Mr. Kirkpatrick may have committed perjury and been in collusion with the crooked policeman (Patrick Devlin) I'm very desirous of getting the F.B.I to investigate. Could you help me?

5) Rivera, Askins and Adams are drug abusers and junkies. Whatever money they got will only be used to buy more illegal drugs. I feel sorry for them, they were wronged, but to give them any money is equivellent to throwing gas on a fire. I'd rather see the starving fed, than a junkie get another high.

   I'm having problems with my mail and would appreciate it if you'd at least acknowledge my letter. I'd appreciate even more, any other help you can give me. Thank you.

        Respectfully,

        Gary M. Heidnik

P.S. I don't think my children or my wife are deserving of the church's money either. They are well provided for, and the starving of the world are not. Besides the money is not and was not mine. It was GOD'S money.

     (Addendum To Judge Scholl)

1) Eddie Antar of Crazy Eddie has been found with 64 million he stole. Shouldn't we be suing him for the $100,000.

2) Rivera will agree with my plan. The last thing she wants to explain is why she waited a week to turn me in.

[Undated]

Dear Beck + Jack,

I would like to practice singing the two songs I wrote, but to sing out loud where I'm at would be too embarrassing. If the guards heard me singing they'd probably hurt themselves, laughing so hard. So I tried humming them under my breath. That proved beneficial. I realized the lyrics were too "rough", so I "streamlined" them a little. Here's the new, improved (??) product.

GIVE ME A CALL GOVERNOR – PLEASE

(Chorus) Give me a call governor

Say you remember

Give me a call governor

Say I'm not alone

Give me a call governor

Say you still care

Here I sit, nobody around

I'm all tied down, no where to roam

The clock on the wall says, only ten minutes to go

My times running out, I'm so all alone

My heads all shaved and covered with goo

The clock on the wall says only five minutes to go

My rectum is packed, my rubber pantys in place

The electrodes are all hooked, I'm ready to glow

I'll have to go now, my time is run out.

Repeat chorus ending with

"Give me a call governor - Please."

SEND ME A BIG RUBBER DOLLY

(Chorus) Send me a big rubber dolly

Someone to appease

Send me a big rubber dolly

Someone to squeeze

I'll take you to bed nightly

Where we can tease

I get so lonely

I need someone to hold

I need someone to love me

I'm so all alone

I'll blow you up at night

And give you the love that you need

I'll hug you and hold you

And play with your hair

I'll unfold you

and fill you with air

I'll love you and please you

and whisper sweet things in your ear

So send me a big rubber dolly

If you love me and care

Repeat chorus

When we record, I'll need a couple practise rounds, maybe you can help me add a little rhythm to it. When I hum it, it puts me to sleep.

❖

Dear Beck,

I got your letter of February 17, 1990. I must say, it's good to know that at least one person in this outfit has a set of functioning brain cells (you - not me). You sound like you really know what you're doing!

For one thing I'm very happy you guys et al. are desirous of giving all profits to charity (after expenses, of course). Your hearts are in the right place. I also concur that some kind of "contract" or written understanding is advisable, to prevent misunderstandings later. Actually I've kind of already involved my lawyer in an informal way. I told him in abstract terms of our project last week. He should be giving me an opinion any day now.

You really showed perspicacity in suggesting I write out the questions ahead of time to conduct an "interview." Believe it or not, that common sense thought never occurred to me. So I'm working on some questions (and answers) for you to ask me. Another intelligent thing is if I were to use some of your perspective. You have a more "tuned in" attitude to what the public may want to know. SO why not send me a couple of questions you think the public will want answered and I'll decide which ones I want to answer. By the way, in a true sense, you and your friend John have scored a "news scoop." Ever since my arrest, I've never granted a news release! And I've been asked. Last year I was contacted by C.B.S. (Ch. 10 in Philly) and turned them down flat! So you and your friend are in a privileged position. I'm extending to you the trust I have never felt in any other new organizations and I hope there won't be any "surprises." The very fact you proposed asking me prearranged questions has <u>vastly</u> increased that trust. Anybody planning a "surprise," or dirty trick, or "knife in the back" wouldn't be so overt.

Extending the same kindness to you, it's necessary for me to do a lot of filling in. Even though we've been communicating for over a year, there are many things you're not aware of, or only peripherally aware of. For you (us) to conduct a good interview I plan to fill you in and bring you up to date. You already know a little about my trying to get the bankruptcy court, lawyers, etc., to enforce the church's constitution so all the money that was collected and earned in GOD'S name will go for its intended purposes; the Veteran's Administration and Peace Corps, not for bombs, politicians fat salaries, lawyers even fatter fees or supply junkies with an illicit high.

By sending you some copies of letters I've written to involved individuals, it will save us both lots of time. I highly recommend you xerox each letter a couple of times and add them to your files. Then I'd like you to return the letters (along with a couple of copies). Well on the subject of xerox copies I need another copy of page 238 and pages 43 & 44. I tried to get more copies of page 238 and ripped out the page and sent it to the xerox department in prison. Guess what? No response yet and it's been almost two weeks. But this little episode highlights our problem. We do have a problem! Exactly what it is or WHY confounds me. I don't understand it! I'm not in any ways trying to make trouble for the prison officials, I'm not trying to do anything illegal, and I'm not even trying to save my life. I'm only trying to do good for society. I'm trying to expose a corrupt Philadelphia policeman and feed some of the world's hungry. How could any civic minded person object to that!

But we do have a problem! Part of it seems to be to isolate me from the news media (??) and legal authorities like F.B.I. (?) and judges?

As for the problem of the news media, that puzzles me. Not too long ago, an inmate was granted and gave an interview to the media. I actually saw it on T.V. the guys name was Roland Steele. I know him. I was in the cell next to him and he's not only a true misanthropic but a slimey, devious character. But they let him give a news interview with camera, etc. So at least we know it's allowed.

Maybe the best way to short circuit all our problems is to make the prison authorities privy to our whole project. If we did that it may expedite everything and ease everybody's mind. I'm positing that we allow a guard to be present during the entire interview, and even submitting all questions to the prison authorities for their approval. Even, yes, our musical lyrics that I'm going to sing. I will make one request of the guards though. I'm going to ask them not to laugh when I sing. The fact is that the songs I wrote are not exactly for entertainment. That they are satire and intended to make very valid points in a pithy fashion, they may be entirely acceptable.

That is my proposal, but you and Jack are the experts, not me. So I'd like your opinion on this and will probably follow your judgement to the letter. Any further ideas on your part will be greatly appreciated.

By the way have you added the melody to my lyrics yet? I'm kind of curious to know what kind of beat, instruments etc. you're planning to use of course everything is in the planning stage, and I feel excited, like a ten-year-old. I never, even envisaged myself as a musician, in fact my singing has never even been recorded. If they play any of our songs on the radio, people will probably be breaking their radios by the thousands. We may even do for radio what T.V. almost did, drive it off the air.

Your friend,

Gary

P.S. Your friend Jack is in touch with and part of the news media, so heres an idea he may want to exploit. The American people like to worry, so let's give them something to worry about. This one's a real bone chiller.

In all the jubilation over apartheid's demise in South Africa, people have forgotten something. S.A. almost certainly has the atom bomb. And remember Idi Amin? Suppose somebody like him seized power in S.A? Can you see what he could do with an atom bomb? Look at all the terror he commited without modern technology. I'm not suggesting we save the white regime. What I think we should go in there and get control of those bombs, before it's too late. You know what happens when it's too late? A nuke cloud. That's what!

February 20, 1990

Dear Beck,

As you already know I've been rewriting chapter 7 (Maria & Tony) and I need your opinion! By the way I've renamed the chapter "Sisyphus Rides A White Horse". (Does that make sense to you?)

I got through pages 369 to 375 and realized that it sounded too much like a lecture and also was too long. SO I've spent about three weeks rewriting those pages. I had a very important point to make. Also it gave me a chance to incorporate some of the ideas I learned from "How to Get Your Point Across in 30 Seconds".

So I'd appreciate your opinion, okay??

"But why won't they leave Tony and Maria alone." Juliet asked?

"The way I see it, it's a matter of power," I replied.

"Power," everyone asked uncomprehendingly?

"Yes! Mixed with liberal doses of hypocrisy and blindness."

They stared at me with rapt attention.

"Remember Tony's former landlady Livia? Well she was more than just his landlady. She actually controlled his life for seven years. She not only fed and housed him but made sure he got off to work every day."

"Yeah, especially paydays," Cyrano commented sardonically.

"Right. Whenever one person controls another's life, it beggars for abuse. She stole almost every cent he made for those seven years. And when Tony found a girlfriend, Livia became morally indignant and outraged. She couldn't stand to see her charge committing sin. The real irony is she probably died thinking of herself as a morally righteous woman."

"Do you mean Victoria is robbing Maria" Juliet probed.

"Frankly, I don't know. But she does control Maria's life and that invites abuse. That's where the blindness comes in. Social workers, society, just don't see us as grown-ups. Even if we stood before them completely naked, they would deny us our adulthood. They call us children with the bodies of adults. So they use that rationale to control us and force their moralities on us. They say we're really only children, so we don't know what we're doing, that we shouldn't be allowed to marry or have sex even."

When I used the word sex, they leaned forward to hear my every word.

167

"They don't see us as sexual beings. They don't realize we are adults and need sex as much as everyone else. When they enjoy sex with abandon, they're uninhibited. When we enjoy sex we don't know what we're doing."

Amazingly the next statement emanated from Juliet, "But isn't sex a sin?"

"Only outside of marriage if you believe in The Bible. And if you believe in The Bible you know GOD gave us all free will; To the healthy, as well as the sick. We were all evicted from Eden."

"They're afraid some of us would just go around screwing everybody in sight," Lisa interjected.

"That's a possibility. Some of us might. But if one of them does it, nobody tries to stop them. Victoria and Livia would never allow someone to tell them they can't have sex; even outside of marriage. But since they control us they try to force their sense of morality on us."

"Sort of do as I say, not as I do," quipped Cyrano.

"Right! History is replete with examples of one group forcing their morality on others. It also usually leads to blood, wars and rebellion. The Dutch recognized the futility and hypocrisy of it all and stopped."

"Let's all move to the Netherlands," Juliet said enthusiastically.

Ignoring her, I continued. "Can you imagine their surprise if they knew _____ was a homosexual? They can't conceive anything so complicated in us."

"And _____ is a lesbian," Lisa added.

"Not exactly," Cyrano emended. "She goes both ways."

Nobody challenged him. We just smiled in admiration. He probably had firsthand knowledge of what he was saying.

"My point being, I'm not defending gays, but I'm not condemning them either. They have the right to make a choice, just like everyone else. And as long as they don't force themselves on us, we accept them as people. It's time society removed their blindfolds and realized we're people too; not children, but adults."

"Sooner or later all parents have to let go," Juliet glossed sagely.

"Right," I said, my voice rising in intensity, "They talk about a 'sexual revolution' and every social group gained it's freedom; gays, feminists, heterosexuals, blacks, etc. Every group but one, the handicapped, were granted the same sexual rights as everyone else. It's time we had our own 'Declaration of Independence' or our own 'Bill of Right's'"

Is it my imagination or did I hear fire crackers going off and a distant band playing 'The Star Spangled Banner?'

So Beck, what's your opinion? Did I make my point?

You can ask your friend too. I'd like his opinion.

Your friend,

Gary

❖

February 27, 1990

Dear Beck,

Wow! Your letter of Feb 25, 1990 was a DOOZY! You touched on so many things I'll probably be up all night.

First let me write about the social issues. A lot of things you wrote about, I can identify with since I've experienced some of them myself. You never met my mother, but she was fascinating person and light years ahead of her time. She had 5 husbands and the last two were black. Also, unfortunately, she was an alcoholic. As a matter of fact her third and fourth husbands were also alcoholics. My dad was husband No. 2. The third husbands name was Larry Vandervoart (Dutch if I ever heard it). The guy was what I think they call a "binge" alcoholic. (Like Spencer Tracy). Back in the 40s I was living with him from about the age of 2 to 8. He was also a fascinating person and light years ahead of his time. Apparently most Dutch are! He (Larry) would start out with almost nothing and <u>build</u> himself, or buy, a big truck (semi). Then pretty soon he'd have two, three etc trucks. The money would be rolling in. Then he'd start binge drinking and pretty soon everything was gone. Then he'd "dry" out and start all over again. I remember one such time. He went out into the yard, set up a couple of wood "saw" horses and started actually building a truck. He was a wiz with a welding torch. When he couldn't afford welding rods, he'd use coat hangers. Not very many welders are skilled enough to be able to use coat hangers. We kids use to go through the house, finding him more hangers to weld with. Well pretty soon he'd have built another truck and then he was rolling, doing hauling jobs. I'm not sure if they had 18 wheelers in those days. I think they were only 14 or 16. Then he'd start celebrating and "binging" out and the cycle repeated itself, over and over. He didn't drink alone either. My mom could match him almost glass for glass. As a matter of fact, when he'd have two or three trucks rolling and needed a driver, he'd use my mother as a driver. Can you visualize a 100 lb red headed woman man-handling a big rig? Well she did! And she was proud of it. She could shift gears with the best of many and drink the most of them under the table. Another way in which Larry was ahead of his time. He was one of the first white man who would hire colored drivers. He'd give them good jobs driving trucks when nobody else would. And they weren't just employees either. There were his friends. He'd take them into the bars with him when he was drinking. These guys were us kids friends too. They'd spend a little time playing with us and always give us quarters. A quarter then is like $5.00 today.

When mom eventually divorced Larry, she married one of these former drivers. At the age of 8, my father got custody of me and my brother, and my life got a lot tamer and academic. Dad would try to teach me bigotry but it was too late. By then I knew blacks were people too, and couldn't understand why I was supposed to hate them. I still don't. I never felt ashamed of mom for having married two colored husbands. My father wanted me to hate her for it, but I couldn't. Unfortunately most people did. Mom was pretty lonely. She was discriminated against for marrying blacks. She got it from both whites and blacks. But she had her ideals and hung in there.

She also kept drinking and kept getting sicker and sicker. She developed osteoporosis, etc. (No cancer!) Soon she couldn't take the pain any longer and on Memorial Day, killed herself. (1970) Hardly anybody came to mom's funeral. Most people and relatives couldn't forgive her for marrying a black man. But there was one interesting person. I'm kicking myself in the butt for forgetting his name. He was the scion of some large grocery chain store and was loaded! He showed up at the funeral in a brand new Lincoln for instance. He was nice to mom too. He liked her and used to call her his adopted mother. He'd always be nice to her, giving her money and helping out. He was also gay. Mom was so far ahead of everyone else, that she could only see he was just another person. NOT a pervert or sociopath, but a human being! And when my brother and I weren't around, he took our place, as her son. And when mom died, he didn't abandon her. He was one of the few people who showed up. He really cared for her.

You mentioned the word "gay [illegible]" in your letter. I don't know what that is, but when I went to nursing school, we had something like 130 female students and 6 male students. I was the only "straight" male in my class. All of the rest were gay. They kept chasing each other around. That was fine with me. That meant I had all 130 women to myself. With odds like that even a "boob" like myself could score, and I did. At the tender age of almost 21, I finally lost my cherry. I always liked women, but with all my personality problems, I just couldn't "make" it with any. But with the odds of 1 to 130, even I could get "lucky".

Anyways I realized that mental patients, gays, etc. had something in common. It's called discrimination. We all know what it means to be discriminated against. Me, I had a double curse. Not only did I have mental problems, but I felt the colored were human beings too. When I was young and stupid, I used to go around telling everyone that discrimination was wrong. That segregation was wrong. That we should have integration and live together as equal human beings. Then a funny thing happened. I kept getting fired from jobs. Even as an extremely qualified nurse, I couldn't keep a job. As soon as I'd mention integration, I'd get fired. In the book "Cellar of Horror," when they mention I was about to be fired from my job at Coatesville Veterans Hospital, that was the real reason they were going to fire me. I was preaching integration again. Well sometimes we learn from our mistakes. I learned to keep my mouth shut on the job, about blacks and whites being equal, and living together. After that I had no problem keeping jobs. I just did my integrating away from the job as much as possible.

But do you see my point? Do you see the connection with gays? They do much the same things. They've even got a name for it. They call it being in the "closet." They don't like it and some actually come out in the open. The ones who do catch living hell! So they adopted a defensive mechanism of staying hidden as much as possible. If they want to survive they have to. Blacks aren't so lucky. They can't hide the color of their skin, even if they wanted to. So they catch hell too, and have no where to hide. But in a way we all have one skin, one thing in common. We all know the pain of discrimination!

My book "40th St. Soaps" is a kind of symbolic coming out of the closet for the mentally ill. I'm trying to convince people that the mentally ill are sexual beings, too, and should have the same rights as everyone else. We're people too!

When I discovered this whole group of the mentally ill meeting and socializing at 40th Street it was, for me, heaven. At last I found a group of people who would accept me and treat me as a friend. They didn't care if I was a little "strange" or "different." I found real friends amongst them. I was no longer lonely. Do you know what it's like to be lonely? No friends! We all need friends! We all need a place to belong to. I found mine in that little group on 40th Street.

Gays need a place to belong to also. For instance, they're not welcome in most churches. I planned to do something about that. I was planning on eventually, getting a regular church building, ordaining a gay minister and allowing him to hold services in our church. A couple of hours, my group of mentally handicapped would hold services and then the gays could have theirs. And anybody who wanted to join the others service would be fine with us. The mentally handicapped do NOT discriminate. We only know too well the pain of persecution. We also come in all shapes, sizes, colors, and sexual preferences. But in our church, we could all get to know GOD and each other better. We'd all have a place to belong too!

Well enough social history, time to get down to business. About the matter of a lawyer, my lawyer. I'm going to be honest with you. I think I've got a problem there, a big problem. A big RAT in fact. I'm only guessing. I don't know all the facts, yet; may never know them. But from what you've read in my letter about being framed by Detective Devlin and all, you've got a generic picture of what's going on. This creep Devlin may be pulling some of my lawyer's strings. I'm not sure yet, but a little "birdy" keeps whispering in my ear. (Figuratively speaking, of course) He acts very strange and suspicious at times. It's like he's trying to hinder me, or protect some people. I've got a handle on things yet when I mention things like a big time drug pusher I know, Devlin etc. he gets cagey. I've started asking him about the transcripts from the trial etc., as well as hinting I might cut a record. He doesn't answer. He seems to be avoiding my questions all of a sudden, and I'm beginning to smell a BIG RAT! If my stock broker Mr. Kirkpatrick did commit perjury, I may finally be able to prove I was set up and framed in '78. Just mentioning page 238 and transcripts and all of a sudden his "Line goes dead." He has also gone to great lengths to keep me out of the bankruptecy trial. If Kirkpatrick lied at my criminal trial, he's also probably lied at the bankruptcy trial. I've even written the judge, but he has also suddenly "clammed" up.

I'm right now trying to fire the three lawyers who are supposed (??) to be representing the church, but who are actually only trying to carve out a chunk for themselves.

What I'm going to need and pretty soon is a lawyer to help me with the bankruptecy case, etc. Someone who's GOOD, and not part of the Philadelphia "Old Boy Network." Know what I mean?

I've seen this guy Devlin operate for more than 12 years. He's amazing, and scary. He has almost magical powers to talk honest people (suborn) into lying, perjury, and all kinds of illegal acts.

All these things are apparently interconnected. I'm going for the news interview in an effort to get the F.B.I. into this thing. It looks like the recommendation by judge Scholl dried up. I can't get him to talk or commit. Myself I'm almost positive that there's some real "interesting" stuff going on with the bankruptcy trial.

That looks like a tough fight, but a fight worth fighting. The possibility of feeding some of the starving, helping my fellow disabled veterans and maybe of finally exposing a crooked cop are all goals worth going after.

The real irony is that after 12 years, I may have finally gotten my big break. But it came, not when I was looking for revenge, but when I was seeking to help the less fortunate. There's an important moral in that for me.

So if you can recommend or hook me up with a good lawyer for both enterprises I'd be tremendously grateful. (Record, and bankruptcy case). If I'm able to prove I was framed and Kirkpatrick was in collusion with Devlin we're talking a megamillion dollar lawsuit against, amongst others, Merrill Lynch. Do you think somebody like Kunstler would be interested? My wife is not! I tried to talk he into it but she seems afraid or something. Anyways I did the right thing. I gave her first crack at it. I don't want any of the money for myself. Again in the event of a lawsuit, all my share (after lawyers expenses) goes to charity. I'm real partial to the Peace Corps, Salvation Army etc.

By now you can see how complicated and interconnected everything is. And remember I was framed in '78, by a crooked cop, NOT because he thought I was guilty, but so he could steal $115,000. We prove that, and you sell a couple of million records.

I may be paranoid, but I do not suspect blindly. I've usually good reasons to be suspicious. When people like my lawyer try to keep me from exposing a crooked cop and drug dealer, try to keep me from the press and the bankruptcy trial, I get suspicious. Even my wife, who I should be able to get to, is frustrating me at every turn. She's even hindering my book "40th Street Soaps". Why?? That's why maybe I'm suspicious there's a bottom denominator in all this and that is a creep named Devlin.

But you and Jack are doing everything to help me go public, etc. That tells me I can trust you both! If Devlin had got to you, you'd be trying to shut me up, not help me go public!

But if I can back up page 238 with verification from the transcripts, then we've really got something to talk to the F.B.I. about. Imagine if we can give an interview in which I show verifications of such things like page 238 & the break in and non-arrest of Mr. Rogers, then the F.B.I. can't ignore me.

The biggest problem is NOT proving I've been framed and shafted so many times you can't count but getting people to care.

That's the thing that discourages me about the law, and American judicial system. It's NOT what they tell you in the papers and news. It's very confusing.

There are some consistencies though.

1) If I break any of the "known" rules or laws, even the slightest infraction, the law punishes me severely.

2) Whenever somebody does something to me, the law does not protect me. People can rob me, beat me, discriminate against me, frame me and put me in jail for 5 years, take my kids away from me for purely racial reasons, even break into my house and the law does NOT protect me. Just the opposite. It's used to persecute me, not protect me. I don't want much from the law, only equal treatment. I want the <u>same</u> <u>protection</u> <u>everyone</u> else has, <u>nothing</u> <u>else</u>.

Many of the abuses are very public. Like Mr. Rogers bragging in public how he broke into my house. I've pointed this out to hundreds of people and you know what?

Nobody, but NOBODY CARES!

ANON

Your Friend,

Gary

P.S. I made a slight addition to "The 40th St. Soaps". That section I sent you. It's just possible it's my best line in the whole book. In one sentence it sums up and states my whole goal in writing the book. It also seems apropos to this letter. Here goes

"Well its time the handicapped were granted the same sexual rights as everyone else."

Cyrano suddenly leaped to his feet, affected a serious posture and dramatically intoned:

"*To screw, or not to be screwed, that is our right!*"

Shakespeare's probably turning over in his grave.

❖

March 8, 1990

Dear Beck,

Hi buddy. Sorry to hear you're not feeling well. That's a shame. And to think you're working 12 hours a day on a part time job. Thats a lot of strain. I hope you don't overdo it and really injure yourself. Offhand it sounds as if you've got a case of that virus that's been hitting everyone. I hear it's pretty nasty too! It makes you feel like crap for almost two weeks. Well I hope you're finely feeling better by the time this letter reaches you. Being sick is no fun. Take care of yourself, get lots of rest if possible and drink plenty of fluids. If it's the flue there really isn't much else you can do for it.

Maybe this will cheer you up a little. On this mornings news they were talking about how the Federal government is finally going to improve all the roads etc., but the cost is going to be exorbinant. Bryant Gumbel said that Bush wasn't going to raise taxes, only "user fees". He said Bush was going to keep his promise of no new taxes but that the taxpayers could "read between his lips."

And yes, I did get the book you sent, "Prisoners Rights", but consider this:

1) I'm a mental patient

2) I have no family and virtualy no friends (so called "normal," that is)

3) I belong to no support group, (ex, blacks can belong to orgs like N.A.A.C.P.)

4) I have no political connections

5) I am essentialy a white man who has lived with and had children by black women and other nationality. What all that translates into is that in America I have NO rights... not social, legal or anything else.

Also, my biggest mistake was in accumulating a large sum of money. What that did was make me an attractive target for greedy individuals who recognized my "vulnerability". Even though the money was in GOD's name, and intended for HIS use it was NO protection. The church was made up almost entirely of other mentally handicapped so it too was "vulnerable." Devlin and others recognized this and went after it.

176

Currently it's being carved up to <u>mostly</u> satisfy the greed of lawyers and help staunch the Federal deficit, buy bombs, and fill junkies needles.

<u>Nobody</u> is considering the needs or rights of the starving of the world or of the disabled veterans.

It's easy to say "Yeah, yeah, he's just crying because he's locked in prison."

No! NOT really. I'm just stating facts. For instance look at pages 49 & 50. There is a perfect example of "NO RIGHTS". Here is a guy, Mr. Rogers, not only admitting but bragging about how he broke into my house. Even if you accept his version verbatum as totally true, then <u>how come he didn't get arrested</u>? He not only admits to this crime, he brags about it in public. Hows that for hubris? If he had broken into ANYBODY else's house, the police would have arrested him! BUT he can break into my house and not only get away with it, but brag about it in public. He's lucky I didn't shoot him. I could have shot him, but didn't. I should get a medal for not shooting the bastard, but instead I am the one who gets arrested, NOT him. And remember this book and incident are nationwide and in the public domain, and this happened in '76, ten years before I went "off". So how come nobody is saying anything, or raising any protests or questions? Nobody cares that's why. In America, people like me have NO legal rights, and nobody cares! Do you care?

But it's only one example of the MANY abuses I've experienced. Some of the other more stellar examples.

1) They (boarding home owners) kidnapped my common law wife of 10 years, not once but twice, and I couldn't even get the police to help me find her, ever after <u>repeated</u> attempts. Eventualy they did find her, in about 10 seconds, but only when they thought there was some "glory" in it for them and that I had committed a crime.

2) They took my daughter away and broke up my family, for greed and bigotry! The saddest part of all this is that I wasn't the only victim. My daughter was victimised and so was my 2nd wife (girlfriend), and the happy life we had together, not to mention the lives of several "planned" children were lost. Also I spent 5 years in jail for a crime that was NOT even committed. The only good thing to come out of this misery, is that all Devlin's conniving and dirty tricks availed him nothing materially. He still didn't manage to steal one red cent.

3) My wife framed me for a rape I didn't commit. I don't entirely blame her though and will not make trouble for her. She became fearful when I threatened to have her sent back to the Philippines if she didn't come back to me, so she framed me and had me arrested. She was real clever. She went and cleaned (for free) one of Mayor Wilson Coode's relatives homes. The woman I believe is his niece or cousin, named Janice something or other and lived in Powelton Village. She used her connections on Betty's behalf and then, only a little later I was arrested. My wife delayed dropping the charges, because she wanted $1,000 to, as she put it, go back to the Phillippines. She didn't get the money but eventually dropped charges and came back to me anyways. But I bear her no grudges and wish her no evil.

4) I was subjected to an organized plan of harassment for almost two years, by my drug dealing, Puerto Rican neighbors. When I moved into 3520 N. Marshall they moved in next door, etc. Then they tried to drive me out because I wasn't a P.R., wasn't a customer, and their leader wanted my garage for his own car. They kept filling my yard with trash, knocked my fence down with their cars, broke the windows in my house and car, repeatedly vandalized my car when I parked it on the street, destroyed my mail box, and threatened my wife on several occasions. Actually, that in a perverse way was useful since she didn't want my house. She could have had me thrown out, but she didn't want to live there by herself. You should have seen the number they did on my '72 Dodge. They broke into it, dented it in many places, painted graffiti all over it, broke the back window, etc. They put rat traps in my mail box hoping we'd get our hand caught (when I had a mail box) and the grand climax they shot up my garage and car with something like nine bullets. I made complaint after complaint to the police department. If they came out and took a report, I was lucky. They never did anything else. I went to various city agencies screaming civil rights violations. They did nothing. The commission on human relations barely took notes. They had a special section for my neighborhood. The agent was a Puerto Rican too. I thought selling drugs was illegal. So I complained to the Philly police dept and even worked as a spotter for them, particularly one officer named Boucher. I helped get one guy arrested even and the police found a big cache, because I saw and told them where he hid it. But I soon realized the police really weren't interested in catching the leaders, or stopping the traffic. I was risking my life for nothing.

5) I went to the Federal government, I.R.S., D.E.A., Senator Arlene Spector's office, and something called R.I.C.O. It looks like they have finally done something after 3 years, and 4 years. But in the meantime, those Puerto Rican's made my life hell. Does anybody care?? NO! There was no public outcry, even after I was arrested. I never heard of all those police reports, and complaints to the commission on human relations etc. They only mentioned (barely) all the bullet holes and trash in my yard. Like maybe I put that trash there or shot up my own garage.

I can go on and on and on, and I will, but in future letters. It will take many.

In the meantime, to survive in America, I find the best way is to envision myself living in some third world country, like Cuba or Nicaragua, or the Phillippines even. I remember I really have no rights. When I get in trouble is when I believe all those nice things they teach you in school or put in the newspapers. You know, like racism is wrong and illegal, that we all have rights and are equal under the law, that you can trust a policeman. If you get in trouble, if somebody is doing something to you like robbing you or breaking into your house or kidnapping your wife, you can go to the police and they will arrest the perpetrator and protect you. B_ _ _ S_ _ _! Maybe for other people, but not for me! At least not the local or state level. But maybe I can get some rights at the Federal level, like the F.B.I. Actually I'm not looking so much for my rights, but the rights of others. I believe the church's money should go to the people who need it most, not some shyster lawyers or fat politicians or drug pushers. I believe I owe it to my family as well as society to expose a crooked cop. Do you agree??

That's why I'm trying to get the F.B.I. to investigate. There are some things I know and some I do not know. You went right to the core of the matter when you said "proof". Many of the things came down to my word against Devlin's and of course nobody's going to take my word, at least not at first. The F.B.I. usually gives a person a lie detector test first, to check his veracity. Once I pass that, we'll be getting places, and I will pass it. Devlin's weak point is he would have needed the help of amateurs to steal that money. He's too tricky and experienced to get caught, or be broken down, but his helpers are not. To get his hands on that money her needed some other people, like the church's board of directors. They will talk to the F.B.I. and Devlin can't coerce them or suborn them like he had others.

I have run into some bad news though. I heard from my lawyer, Mr. Peruto Jr and he even sent me a copy of Kirkpatrick's testimony. Mr. Kirkpatrick did say the church was worth $121,000, not the $21,000 reported by Mr. Englede. Mr. Englede screwed up. Damn! I was so sure after 12 years I had that crook.

Anyways my lawyer had some good news too. He's in favor of me making a record, but warns me not to sign anything until he checks it out. Right now he's on vacation, but I can work through him, record wise.

I'm still going to need a lawyer for the church though and I do not want to go through him. I need a good lawyer, someone not afraid to stand up against the "establishment" and hopefully won't charge the church too much if anything at all. It would be pointless to bring in even one lawyer, if his fees are going to eat up all the church's money. There would be nothing left for the hungry and needy. Hows that for a tall order? Do you think you can help? We may have to include that request in the news release.

I don't plan to make any public condemnations on that news release, only point out Mr. Rogers crime (and NO punishment) and say that there are many other crimes that need to be investigated by the F.B.I., things like official corruption, perjury, civil rights violations and big time drug dealing. And mention my willingness to prove my allegations with a lie detector test.

I may have had a brilliant idea, or maybe another dud. I sent in a request form to a prison official named Mr. Sieverling, asking for a conference with the F.B.I. That was three days ago, but it's still way too early yet. Maybe if I work through the prison authorities instead of around them, I'll have better luck. We'll see? This is such a sensible logical approach, I wonder why I didn't think of it sooner. Probably because it was so OBVIOUS!

Guess what? You're not going to believe this. The guard laid a note on my door, about a ½ hour ago. I thought it was just a receipt. It was instead my answer from Mr. Sieverling. He writes "I cannot contact the F.B.I for you. You may write directly to them if you wish."

Well, I wish! So I'm going to close this letter for now. I've got another important letter to compose.

Keep your fingers crossed and for goodness sake take care of yourself.

ANON. Your friend,

Gary

❖

March 21, 1990

Dear Beck,

I just got your letter yesterday and was very glad to hear from you. I was really beginning to worry. I knew you had the flu and that's bad enough. It makes you feel like shit for about two weeks and there's not much anyone can do to help. It's also possible something happened in your job. You're working a dangerous job and on the worst shift. Late at night like that, who knows when somebody's going to try and rob you, and drunks etc., will be coming in there and causing trouble. It's not a matter of what's going to happen, it's a matter of when. The odds are against you. The more I think about it, the more I worry. It'd be nice if you could get a job somewhere's else, or didn't need a job. At least not such a dangerous one.

Well enough depressing news. Let me see if I can cheer you up a little with an anecdote. You mentioned a mouse running across the floor. Speaking of mice, you should have seen the mouse problem I had when I bought 3520 N. Marshall. I bought a few mouse traps, but they weren't doing much good. I used to spread them 5 deep across the mouses paths but it still didn't do much good. So when I found them actually moving into my stove I got mad! I opened the oven door one time and found one of the little buggers looking back at me. So I closed the oven door and turned the gas on, very slightly. Then I got my friend Tony to stand with a lighted match. On the word go I opened the over door and he tossed in the match. Then I closed the over door and held it shut. You can guess what happened next. BOOM! That's what! Blew one hinge off the door, and a lot of porcelain off the oven. It also scared the HELL out of me and Tony.

I assumed it scared the hell out of the mouse too. I never saw him in the stove again.

Later I tried some of that stuff they sell in the supermarkets. It takes a week or two to work, but when it does it really works. It got rid of all of those wee beasties. You may want to buy a couple of them and put them around where you work. Pretty soon no more mice. Of course, after hearing my story about the oven you may not want to follow my advise -- - on anything.

If you've got mice, who you gonna call!

Mouse busters, that's who.

If this doesn't have you laughing, then you have no sense of humor. Either that or it's time for you to go back to work.

In your letter you said you felt a certain kinship towards me. That we had something in common. Well I think I know what it is, maybe. We're both aspiring would-be artists, looking for our big break. Bohemians if you will. You're forte is music. Mine is literature, book writing, I also have a strong penchant towards other arts too, like music and art itself. (I just have no talent in that direction). It's just a pity we didn't know each other sooner and under happier circumstances. We'd have had some good times together. In a way we're anachronisms, from a previous age, the 1960's. We'd have fit right in with the old beatniks and hippies. That was before your time, unfortunately. But you'd have fit right in. Sitting in coffee shops, listening to poetry and playing our music to an appreciative audience. Well maybe I'd better stop, before we get too teary eyed for the "good old days."

Speaking of music. I'd like very, very much to hear some of your creations. The trouble is they won't let us have any tapes or tape players in here. That's been jail policy for a long time and I often wondered why? When I'd ask the guards they'd give me the answer of "because the inmates would smuggle drugs in them." I never quite accepted that. Well I finally found out the real reason. One of the guards finally told me the truth. The reason is the guards are afraid some of the inmates will "tape" them.

Anyways the only way I think I could enjoy some of your music is over the telephone. If you were willing I could call and you could play

182

something for me. Something else I wish I could collaborate with you on ---- music video. I've got a suppressed desire to make one myself. I don't know much about how they're made but making them sounds like fun. I also like drawing and painting too. I'm not very good at it, but that never stopped me from trying. Imagine the fun we could have with a camcorder.

Now I'd like to ask a favor of you. I need your help! And it's important too! I may finally be able to prove definitely (??) that I didn't kill the second victim, Debbie Johnson either. It comes down to a matter of basic high school science. Let me start at the beginning. This past Saturday night I was talking with a guard about the way the second girl died. I explained how they were all sitting in the pit together etc. and then the electrode was applied. Then the guard asked "Why didn't the other girls get shocked. Weren't they all hooked together?" Well that really got me to thinking. Consider that if, as often happens, a person is sitting in a bath tub and drops and electrical appliance into the tub. Well we had three people, sitting, so to speak, in the same tub. Also they were even touching each other. So why didn't they get shocked too? It should happen when the appliance drops into the water, right? Well in this case was a little different.

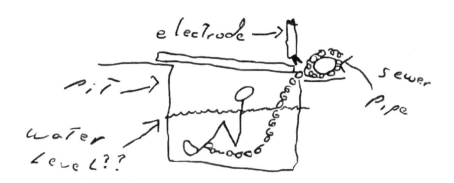

Do you see? The chains were also connected at the sewer pipe. Also they were all connected by being in the water together and touching. So why didn't the others get shocked too?

Well on watching T.V. on Monday they had a show called Universe and it was about electricity. They said that "iron and steal are notoriously bad conductors of electricity." Do you see? The electricity was only ONE electrode, and it (the amps) had to pass through about 8 to 10 feet of steal chain. The chain would act as a resistor or brake. Very likely Debbie didn't get a jolt big enough to kill a canary. And that can be proved. Do you know any high school science teachers, etc. Ask them just how much the "juice" would be reduced. That can be figured out scientifically. The current was 115 volts, regular house current. Also the chain was steal, 8 to 10 feet of it. Here's something else to consider. If you think of electricity flowing, like water through a pipe, it would look like this

The linking would be like narrowings in a pipe, which would further reduce the flow. What all this means is that Debbie probably didn't get enough of a jolt to harm a bird, let enough to kill her. The others didn't get any shock at all. I'm not an electrical engineer, so I'm only guessing on this. I need some help. If I'm right, I've got a lot of other ideas on this matter. So if you could check, I'd be very grateful. Thank you.

Also, about the letter to the F.B.I. I'm willing to sign a notorized copy of whatever you need. Just tell me what it should say. I'll write it out and have it notorized, or at least I'll try. I have a feeling it is just going to "disappear" or get "lost." I'm enclosing a copy of the letter I sent to the F.B.I almost two weeks ago. I sent it via registered letter and as of yet the green receipt hasn't come back. Other receipted letters have come back though. So it's possible this letter "disappeared." It's still early yet, but I'll know better in a couple of more weeks. In the meantime I'd appreciate it if you'd xerox the F.B.I. letter for your files and return the copy to me, and maybe two xerox copies.

Well it's 3am and I'm tired. Gotta get some sleep.

Thanks for everything.

ANON,

Gary

P.S. When the DCon eliminated all my mice, I didn't throw away all those useless mouse traps. I found a new use for them. Guess how I used them? Ask me if you dare.

❖

[Undated]

Dear Beck,

Hello, it's been a long time since I heard from you. I'm starting to get worried. I tried to get a Get Well card, but this is the best I could do. I know you were sick, but I hope you didn't get too sick! Did you get my last letter about two weeks ago? The one about electricity, etc? I had asked some very important questions.

Anyways, I hope everything is fine with you and you are well. Happy Easter & GET WELL SOON

Your friend,

Gary

❖

April 7, 1990

Dear Beck,

I was disappointed by your last two letters. I was disappointed at your reticence in wanting to help me. Up to now you've been more than a friend, you've almost been like a brother. Then I mention I need some help and that I may (??) be able to prove I didn't kill anyone, and you don't seem interested. You stonewall me. Well perhaps you can't see the importance of what I'm asking. For instance you don't know that I did NOT kill the first woman Sandy and can prove it, mostly by a process of elimination. To make a long story short, you can't "dangle" someone 5'6" or (5'8") from a 6 foot celling. The one thing I don't know, nor anybody else does, is how Sandy died. We do know I didn't kill her, since 3 hostile

185

witnesses watched her die. But nobody knows (??) how she died (or do they?).

Now in Debbie's case I'm pretty certain, but not positive, she didn't die of electrocution. The fact the other two didn't die is very important. I'm also certain she didn't get a full charge of 115 volts which can be fatal. She may not have gotten a big enough charge to kill a canary. So if she didn't die of electrocution, how did she die?? We know she didn't die of drowning since if she had water in her lungs the coroner would have said so. He's not much of a pathologist, but even he'd see something like that. So do you see what I'm saying?

We have NOT one mysterious death, BUT two! Now one death may be an accident, but two?? So now do you see the importance of my request. I'm talking about possible murder!! "<u>Murder</u>" you say?? "That's crazy" you say. Maybe not so crazy! At first I had trouble believing it possible myself, but the more I thought about it the more possible it becomes. First of all I asked "how"?

I'll tell you how! By the sleeper hold, that's how! A wrestling hold they are all intimately familiar with since I used it on all of them! They're fully aware of it's power.

Have you been watching the news lately. One college (high school) wrestler named Ty Moore is in trouble for using it. They even showed one of his victims collapsing on camera. You know, that collapse reminded me of something. It reminded me of Sandy collapsing and wallowing about the first time I went down into the cellar. She was groggy like that. Then in a couple of seconds she was standing up but didn't seem entirely all there. Then I went back upstairs. Do you see, they may have used the hold on her but didn't use it long enough and she either came back or I interrupted them. So they may have used it long enough the second time. Sandy was "mysteriously" dead the second time I came downstairs. Maybe her death wasn't so mysterious after all.

The second death, Debbie's, I had more trouble with.

The reason is if they used the sleeper hold on her, "How"?? All three girls were handcuffed together.

Let me explain.

Do you see how (?) I used only two pairs of handcuffs. I'm not certain which sides Lisa and Jackie were on, but Debbie was positively in the middle. So I asked myself how could one of the other girls get behind her, if her arm was handcuffed. Well it is possible! Try this hypothesis. Lisa tells Debbie to lean back against her. When Debbie does so (say Debbie's right arm is cuffed to Lisa's left), Lisa puts her left arm over Debbie's head. In the process Debbie would only have to raise her right arm up to accommodate Lisa, and would lean back against her, expecting nothing. Can you visualize this. Just hold your right arm close to your right shoulder and imagine you're leaning back against someone. Can you now see that the person behind you could now apply the "sleeper hold" on you? What's more your left arm is also out of action since it's attached to Jackie. She could easily hold it down. So you can now see it's possible, VERY possible!

But the next question is WHY?? At first I thought it may have been because Sandy was a lesbian. Yes! Sandy is a lesbian! That's why she slept apart from the others, when we found out. Nobody knew at first, till finally she told us. She asked me in front of the others, "When are you going to get any weal women?" I asked her what a "weal" was (she talks with a lisp). So she explained. She meant lesbians.

Well upon doing some heavy thinking, that may have been a contributing cause. But they may have had more basic motive. They know the police were searching for Sandy, and if her body turned up, it'd be traced immedeatly back to me. Rivera was street wise enough to know this. But of course Sandy's body didn't turn up, so maybe they decided to burden me with a second body. Or maybe Debbie was threatening to tell me what was going on. So the others got desperate. They knew I'd be pissed if I knew they'd killed Sandy.

So you see we now have a possible "how", and a very slimy "why".

Slimy is the right word for it. Sure they were in a tight spot, but it wasn't tight enough to justify killing two other people. Actually we're talking <u>three</u> murders. Two down and one to go!

At first it all sounds sort of fantastic, like something out of a mystery novel, but it is possible. A "good" cop could find out for certain if he were leaking too. He could break Jackie down in about 10 minutes. Lisa might take one hour or two to break. No cop could break Rivera though. She's too street wise. The cop that did break this case (if murder did happen) would be absolutly famous! He's be the biggest thing since Sherlock Holmes or Columbo. Everybody would be talking about how smart this cop was and be making movies about him, etc! You've got to admit that if there was a murder here, it's the kind of plot that would again make national headlines. But before we jump off half cocked, lets do some work. Like figure out how big a "jolt" Debbie got. If it's as small as I believe, we've got them on the ropes.

Also I'm trying to get ahold of the autopsy report, as well as the transcripts. If I remember right the coroner didn't give any positive answers about cause of death. He just said things like "it could have been electrocution." But I want to check his statements and reports. If in the meantime you did some "electrical" research, we could find out if I'm really onto something or off in left field. Also I need to know how they can tell in autopsies how a person dies of low voltage electrocution. If it was high voltage, of course there'd be burning. The sores on her ankles were identical to the sores on Jackie's ankles. Rivera's had already healed.

So if you want to help, this is where I need help. Are you willing to help?? You want to be famous?? Here's your chance. Everybody'd be buying your records after this.

Your friend, Gary

April 9, 1990

Dear Beck,

Contrary to popular belief the greatest works of art, literature and music are just that: work. Lots of it. Oh sure, sometimes artists got lucky and in the space of ten minutes or maybe a short cab ride turn out masterpieces. Unfortunatly you're not one of the lucky ones, at least not this time.

Don't missunderstand me. Your poem (a.k.a. future song) does have a certin something that can make it successful, but it needs work. Don't give up on it. Stick with it and take your time. Keep thinking about it from time to time. Then when you least expect it, like maybe when your sitting on the john (that's where I get my best ideas) you came up with another improvement or refinement. But you've got the hardest part done already. You've got the "hook." That's the main thing. Now just add some bait, a line, and reel and you're rolling.

I hope none of this has upset you, but if it has, here's your chance to get even. I'm enclosing <u>the</u> revised last three pages of chapter 7. Give me your honest opinion! Really tear the hell out of me if you wish. I want honesty! O.K?

Candidly yours,

Gary

P.S. Tell the truth! Does the vision of a knight on a rocking horse make you smile??

P.S.S. Your record label InGreats is GREAT! Don't change a thing.

SISSYPHUS RIDES A WHITE HORSE

Chapter 7 (formerly Tony & Maria)

389

"Stupid!"

"Don't call me that," he screamed! Don't ever call me that"! Then he turned on his heel and stormed off.

Slowly the curtain descents on a small stage, and the house lights flicker on. Readers begin stomping their feet and hurling catcalls. Timorously I sidle out to center stage.

One irate reader screams, "What happened next"?

"Nothing much," I reply. "The next chapter starts in a moment. May I recommend our refreshment stand. We have hot popcorn and ---

W-h-i-z-z! A bright red object tears past my head and splatters on the back wall.

"Hey! Watch those tomatoes"!

W-h-i-z-z! Another one sails by.

"ALL right! ALL right! I'll talk! But stop throwing tomatoes!"

An uneasy stillness settles over the audience. One reader hefts an egg and eyes me threateningly.

"Please try to remember that this is a true story, not fiction. As much as I'd like I can't just make up a happy ending. In fiction money seems to fall out of the sky, nobody ever works for it, and happiness grows on trees. In fiction love always triumphs. In our story life does imitate fiction --- kind of.

After a few weeks, exactly as predicted, Ms. Prude bounced Tony out. He reverted to his old custom of using the back door and sneaking through windows. Sad as all this was it shows the indomitability of the human spirit, even among the handicapped. Even the efforts of a whole platoon of social workers couldn't keep those two apart. What those social workers failed to realize is that they opened the doors of the institutions, they gave us a taste of freedom. Ingrates that we are, instead of being grateful, we wanted all our rights, not just some of them. The same rights everyone else had. People are like that, all people, even the handicapped.

Thus even in the topsy turvy world of 40th Street, love and the human spirit can triumph --- kind of.

And what about me? How about me, you ask?

Like some modern day paladin, with the best of intentions, a white knight in rusty armor, and flying the tricolors of romantic love and the rights of the handicapped, I climbed upon my rocking horse and blundered off to the rescue, and kept right on blundering. With every charge made, society toppled me from my steed but gamely I climbed back aboard, selected a new lance and galloped back into the fray. The heat of combat was so intense, my cause actually took on a life of its own and I lost sight of my real purpose. Then in a fit of rage, having again been knocked off from my high horse, and blinded by my own self-righteousness, I delivered the heaviest blow of all. Not on the enemy, but on my friend.

By insulting him, I shed his blood, only causing him more pain.

The unkindest cut of all came not from the foe, but from a friend.

To the mainstream my insult may have seemed little more than a faux pas, a social gaffe, but in the world of the handicapped I committed a mortal sin. A "normal" person cannot know the depth of our pain. A "normal" person has never spent a lifetime being laughed at, demeaned, being treated like a sub-species: an untouchable. Tony had spent his whole life hearing insults like "*hey retard*", or "*hey stupid*", and "*here comes the dummy.*" But finally he found a refuge, a refuge in the company of friends. People he could trust. A place where he could let down his guard. Then when his guard is down, what happens? He gets stabbed in the back with an insult. A thrust delivered, not by one of those "others", but by a friend. Then compounding my sin, what does this "friend" do? He never apologizes!

So Tony ---- if you're out there ---- if you can hear my voice --- "I'm sorry"!

April 17, 1990

Dear Beck,

Hi. I got your letter of April 15 (yikes) and was glad to hear from you as always. When you said you were back at work, I started to worry about you. Remember when I wrote you about "cycles" of history and the wheel turning? Well it looks as if Pennsylvania and most of America is becoming much more restrictive, conservative, and are cracking down and tightening up on sexual freedom. Pittsburgh is naturally in the vanguard. I'm worried you'll get caught up and crushed by that wheel. That big raid you got caught in was basically a <u>warning</u> (if I read the signs right). The state wants everybody to know that they're tightening the screws. Even though there were no arrests <u>this time</u>, they will not be so generous the next time. The next time (and there will be NEXT times) you will probably be arrested, especially since they will figure they WARNED you this time. I know you need a job, but couldn't you maybe find a "safer" job. Take it from me jail is no fun, even if they give you a friend like me as a cellmate.

I not only foresaw the coming crackdown on porno stores in PA, but I think I've spotted something else. Remember the [illegible] of several years back? Well they're tracing it to Iran and it looks like a government cover up. It's also tied to Colonel North and the missels we were supposed to give to Iran for the release of some hostages. Well about the time the Iran Contra affair broke and everybody found out, Iraq found out too! Shortly thereafter or in the time frame Iraq accidently (???) attacked our ship Stark and killed something like 21 (??) Sailors. If somebody would check, I'll bet dollars to doughnuts that Hussein did it deliberetly!! He's not the kind of dictator to take our sending missels to Iran sitting down. He wants revenge and I'll bet he took it, on the Stark! Remember you heard it here first!

But back to you. You say you're getting married?? I don't know whether to be happy for you or to hold a funeral. Marriage can be a terrific thing or it can be hell. IT ALL depends on the woman you're getting. I don't know Joyce, but for you're sake I'll pray she's a great woman and will give you only lots of happiness (and LOTS of children). Good luck!

Also thank you for the information on electricity. It's been a big help. Whereas before I thought this matter of electrocution was simple, it is NOT! It's very complicated and is becoming more so. But I'm SURE I'm on to something. And if I'm right, then we have not one but two suspicious deaths. In that case the possibility that these two women were murdered becomes a very real possibility and worth checking out! I can appreciate that Rivera et al were under tremendous strain and wanted to be free, but I don't see where they would be justified in killing <u>two</u> other people, (innocent people too).

Lots of "homework" needs to be done though. Your information is a big help, but eventually I believe I'll need the help of an expert! A good place to start is with a lawyer. I'd like very much to contact Mr. William Kunstler, who I believe practises in New York or I'd like to contact Mr. William Costopoulos who does practise in PA. He is Mr. Jay Smith's attorney. I asked the prision to help me get his address but they say he isn't listed as a member at the PA bar. That seems <u>curious</u> since he is representing Mr. Smith who is in PA!

So could you get me

1) Mr. William Kunstler's address and phone no??

2) Mr. William Costopoulos address and phone no.

Another good person to contact on electricity might be a Mr. Robert Allen Stratbucker from Nebraska.

The books you recomended that may help, I'd like No 4 QC522, C5x / Basic electricity & beginning eL * 1973 Clifford Martin.

Or, 37(37 - T86) Basic electricity by Turner, Rufus or 38(537-T86a)

You made a good start! When it comes to electricity, I'm really DUMB! and so the best place to start is with the basic of the basics. Some things I've got to figure out and calculate are ergs, Joules, and Hz.

There are two very BASIC questions though and <u>No. 1</u> is: House current is supposed to be A.C. right?

Okay, now my understanding of AC, is that it alternates, goes back and forth through the wire --- but, when I played around with it, it acts more like D.C. If you take a standard outlet and connect only one side to a grounded appliance, it won't work. But you take the other side and ground it and electricity flows I don't understand that and it makes NO sense to me. I'm frankly confused, but it's NOT a rhetorical question. It's DAMNED important. If you touched only one wire to Debbie's chain, electricity would flow. But if you attached the other wire to her chain --- nothing. As I pointed out in my other letter only one wire was used, NOT two. And it passed through her chain first. But this whole A.C. thing confuses me. When only one wire is used, and run to a ground, does it become D.C.?? or become weaker?? Or stronger?? Or what??

Eventually one question we're going to come down to and can't be avoided, but must be answered, is just how strong a jolt did Debbie get??

I think the only way we can answer this is with an experiment.

Do you have the time and can you get hold of a galvanometer and voltmeter (ammeter)???

Do you have some friends interested and knowledgeable in electricity?? Here is what I propose, in the most basic form.

First you buy about 10 feet of steel chain. The links need to be about this thick

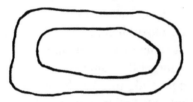

Then you take the chain and hook a galvanometer to it and wire one end. The other and hooks onto the chain. It would look like this

Then about every foot of the chain you touch the galvanometer to see how strong the current is. Of course you'd repeat the experiment with an ammeter. You see then we'd get an idea of how strong the current is through each foot of steel chain and could calculate exactly how strong a charge Debbie got. Let me give you some insight on steel and what a lousy conductor of electricity it is. You come into an example every day. That's right, and you don't even know it. It's your car. The whole car body is ---

194

- negatively grounded. True it's only 12V not 115 but have you ever heard of anyone getting shocked by touching a car?? Even it they're standing in a foot of water? No! But if they touch both poles of the battery, they'll get a tingle.

The more I thought about the example the more my curiosity burned, so I decided on an experiment. The toilet in my cell is steel and filled with water. So I took a small piece of metal and inserted it into one side of an electrical outlet. Then I touched it to my LEFT arm and touched the toilet with my right foot, thus the current would pass over my heart. I was POSITIVE this wouldn't be fatal too! I wasn't trying to commit suicide. Guess what? Nothing! Not even a tingle. So if you remember my piece of info in the first part of this letter, about A.C., I stuck the piece of metal into the other side of the outlet and repeated my experiment. Well I got a pretty good tingle that time. Just to be sure I repeated it a couple of times. As you can see I'm still here, (and no skin burns either, not even a red spot). When I first came to Western an inmate named Roland Steele passed me a book -- I forgot the name -- about a convict who committed suicide by standing in his sink, filled with water and sticking his finger in a light socket. The book was fiction, but Mr. Steele kind of suggested that an inmate could kill himself by standing in his toilet and holding on to an electric cord. Well, so much for fiction. It sounds plausible, but it's fiction. It doesn't work with a steel toilet, not even when the "juice" passes over the heart region.

But back to our experiment. The charge that would have reached the girls would have been even less than in your experiment. The reason is the ground. Because the chains were ground to the iron sewer pipe, that would have drained off some of the charge also. But how much? I don't know. In houses they use grounds to prevent dangerous electrical shocks. That's that third hole in all outlets. It's the ground. So my guess is that the actual charge reaching Debbie would have been less than the one I got off my toilet. For one thing the ground would have drained off some of it and it had to pass through 8 to 10 feet of narrow steel chain, not 2 or three feet of solid steal. Something else....

You couldn't know this because it never appeared in the newspapers even, but I sometimes watched Rivera give Lisa jolts (??)

Picture this:

Well Rivera would touch the wire to Lisa and sometimes Lisa didn't even react, she didn't so much as say ouch! Other times, Lisa would sometimes say ouch, but it didn't seem right to me. I've been shocked by 115 V and I am scared of it. I know! I've been shocked and don't want any more. Lisa didn't act like that. My guess is that the reason is the shock, if any, was so small. Of course if you felt really currious you could try this through 10 feet of steal chain, but you don't have too. I've already done the hard part. The easy part is to wire an end of the chain to the hot side of the wire and touch the voltmeter/ammeter to the chain at every foot. Of course wire the opposite end of the voltmeter/ammeter to a ground, like the cold water pipe of your sink or that third hole in the outlets. What I need to know is just how big a jolt Debbie and the others got. It can be figured out exactly. Maybe you know a science teacher or someone who could calculate it.

One thing your information shows me is that the sore on Debbie's ankles can be shown NOT to have been caused by the shocks they got. Nobody ever got burned or had blisters (vesicular nuclei) and I'm sure they didn't find any metal in Debbie's sores. But much work needs to be done.

I appreciate any help you can give me. I know you're very busy, with a life of your own to lead, but I appreciate any and all help you can give me. It's also extremely possible you may be helping expose a murder nobody even knew about. That's something you could really be proud of.

HOT NEWS FLASH! Boy did I get lucky. One of the guards I just talked to really knew his beans (electricity). I went over most of the things I just talked about and he was helpful. One problem though. He reminded me that if an electrical appliance falls into the water, it will make such a good connection it will cause a short circuit, blow the circuit breaker or fuse too! He said what he didn't understand is why the fuse didn't blow. My answer, easy! Because the steal chain AND steal sewer pipe provided resistance to the current flow. A resistance I feel can be calculated! He says it can't. I'm puzzled by that and it's going to be the first question I ask him the next time I see him. He also explained that the pool of water would have drained some of the current off also. The fact the wire didn't melt or even spark on contact with chain shows a very reduced flow. So I think I'm really onto something here, BUT I need to do my homework!

I'm trying to get Peruto (my lawyer) to send me a copy of the trial transcripts AND autopsy reports. He so far hasn't done it. I'm going to have to badger him more.

Further thought! When you scuff your feet on a carpet you get a spark. When Rivera was shocking (?) Lisa: NO sparks! No fuse's blown either! As I said, she barely reacted.

Boy! So I want to get ahold of that autopsy report. Thanks to your information you sent me, electrocution causes tissue damage, burns, calcification in collagen tissue etc. I'll bet the autopsy report doesn't substantiate that…it couldn't. I'm betting the actual jolt Debbie got was too weak to cause tissue damage, and he's lying if he says it did!

So it's beginning to look more and more like we have TWO mysterious deaths! But maybe they're NOT so mysterious.

Thanks for any help you can give me old buddy and good luck. I hope you don't get arrested too!

Your friend,

Sir Gary

❖

April 18, 1990

Dear Beck,

Well here I am back already. I'm making progress on this electrical thing but still have a ways to go. The best things I have going for me right now is you, and a stroke of luck, a guard who really knows about electricity. This guard not only has some answers to my questions, but he takes nothing for granted. He asks questions that make me think. That's the kind of work that gets answers. For instance he explained the "useless" wire. Why only one wire carries electricity. He also explained that that single wire hooked to a ground is still A.C. and not D.C. That's important. (I'm not taking his explanation for granted, though, I'm going to check on it). This is where you've been helpfull, in the info you sent me. Let me quote: "This confirms our previous suggestion that a higher energy dose is required of A.C. than D.C. to produce alterations specific for electrical damage."

This is important to know, since it indicates that A.C. (the type of charge Debbie got) is less dangerous than D.C. It may also answer another question I've been wondering about: the electric chair. They recently publicised an electrocution in which the guard switched the electrodes, and instead of killing the patient, it only stunned him. I suspect they use D.C. for the electric chairs, now I'm pretty certain.

Now another quote. "Transfer of low amounts of electrical energy by A.C. (40 - 285 Joules's) and D.C. (6 - 100 Joules) as described above produced necrotic zones of the shape of cones with their base at the epidermal surface, the A.C. lesions being more acute than the D.C. lesions." One reason this is important is that it shows the actual amount of "jolt" needed to produce tissue damage. I'm almost positive that Debbie did NOT get enough "jolt" to cause lesions, "vesicular nuclei" etc. Her sores were caused by bad fitting muffler clamps. Also if Debbie did NOT get enough "jolt" to cause tissue damage I can show POSITIVELY incompetence on the pathologists part. One thing I have to do is figure out and calculate what the hell a joule is! If it's less than 40 then I've made a part of my case.

That brings up a question that the guard raised. He doesn't believe that "iron and steal are notoriously bad conductors." So the next time he shows up I'm going to ask him this question - "What do you think would happen if the sewer pipe and chains were made of copper." (??) Obviously when the wire electrode made contact we'd have a short circuit/breaker blow so that proves (I think) just how poor a conductor steal is. That's one up for public television. I'd like you to do a little research here for me though. I'd like you to find a chart or whatever that tells us just what the difference is. For instance the chart might list gold and silver or maybe 95%, and copper 80% (??) and then iron and steal 35% (??) You see I'm only guessing at my %, but I think you get my point. All metals are conductors, but I really need to know the % difference between copper and iron and steal. That kind of info will be useful in calculating ohms. Something I'm going to have to figure out, so I can tell just how big a jolt Debbie got.

The guard (Bless his heart) raised another question. I explained that Debbie had been handcuffed to the other two girls and thus they would have gotten the same shock. Not so, he told me, and he went into parallel and series circuits.

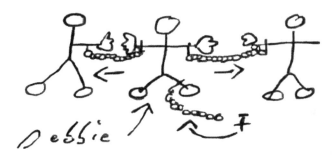

He explained that Debbie being in the middle would have got the biggest shock, and then the other two would have received lesser shocks. Well! That got me to thinking. Here's my next question for him.

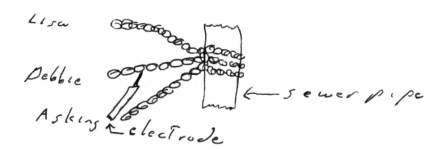

Do you see my question? Since all the chains were connected and wrapped around the same sewer pipe, wouldn't the juice travel equally through all three chains, via the connection? Not to mention the sewer pipe would act as a ground and drain off part of the charge. Even better it would drain off some of the charge going to Debbie --- I think. That would reduce her charge even more, making it less likely she got a deadly jolt. Now here's an interesting piece of info. There were actually 5 people (kind of) in that water filled pit, not 3. Lisa and Askins were pregnant, Debbie was not! Also if they got a big enough charge to kill Debbie, isn't it conceivable that kind of charge would have killed one of the fetuses? Also, being pregnant, wouldn't that have weakened Lisa and Askins??

Still everything seems to boil down to the main question --- just how big a "jolt" did Debbie get?? I can't see why, eventually, we can't set up the exact same sequence. and attach meters and gauges and find out. It may develop that Debbie only got 10 or 20 joule (whatever the hell a joule is) and that would not kill a canary, in the best/worse of circumstances. The guard said they couldn't reconstruct the situation and I'd sure like to know why!

Also further reducing Debbie's jolt (I think), wouldn't the water filled pit conduct current away from her?? Also does body size affect anything? If so, Askins was smaller than Debbie.

And here's a goodie. You've heard of phasers and stun guns? I've never read of them killing, but they do incapacitate. How come?? They use electricity. Something I need to know positively, when electricity does kill --- why?? My guess is it stops the heart, and to do so does it have to pass over the heart?? So many questions, but the biggest: if 5 people (3 adults and 2 fetuses) are in the same pit and ALL (??) got the same charge, why only one dies?? A compatant pathologist, I'll bet, could prove the sleeper hold.

> ANON,
>
> Sir Gary

❖

April 27, 1990

Dear Beck,

Hi! Today I FINALLY got the trial transcripts and went right to work. Although it's only preliminary it's going GREAT! Now I can actually quote and point out things from the official record. Let's start with this one.

On page 501 Lines 12 to 22: "Now, the other areas of significant indication of injury or trauma were about the wrists and the ankles. Both wrists both ankles, showed increased skin pigmentation, increased thickening. And In the case of the backs of the ankles were areas of ulceration or breakdown in the surface of the skin that showed evidence of granulation tissue as healing. So this was an indication of some kind of repeated or chronic <u>irritive</u> or <u>pressure</u> kind of injury that occurred to the surface of the skin the those areas".

I underlined the words irritive & pressure myself, because that's important. This quote was by Dr. Robert Catherman, both deputy & acting medical examiner for the city of Philadelphia. My memory failed me on this point. I thought he testified in court there were burns and/or charring on the ankles indicating electrical injury.

As you can see his testimony verifies my memory of Debbies ankle injuries. He ankle sores were caused by poor fitting muffler clamps, nothing, no electrical "burns".

I don't think anybody disputes that 3 people --- Lisa, Askins, and Debbie were in the hole in my cellar at the same time and the hole was filled with water. But now I want to quote a few lines from Rivera's Testimony.

Page 160 Lines 22 to 25: "Then he had took all the bags off the top of the <u>board</u> and he went back upstairs, and Donna kept pushing the board up saying that Deborah was dead…"

Page 161 Lines 4 and 5; "Then he said, 'she is not dead' and went over to the board and lifted it up ---"

Page162 Line 12: "The <u>board</u> was already over the hole".

I could go on with other quotes but you see my point.

Not only were all three women together in the water filled hole but it was <u>covered</u> with the board. Which was being held down with bags of dirt.

Now let me go back to Doctor Catherman's testimony on pages 500 & 501 Lines 19 to 25 and 1 to 11.

"In addition, she showed several areas of external injury. Two of those areas, one of them on the front and outside surface of the right forearm, and also around the front and the outside area of the front of the right elbow, injuries to the skin that were superficial. They were kind of on the inside of the right forearm, slightly elevated. The material looked a little black and charred. There was very slight increase in pink discoloration at the surface around that area.

Now, what I have described for you are findings which are almost, not quite, absolutely classic for electrothermal injury. That means at that point there was some contact with some electrical as well as heat energy and as a result the injury took place. The area was similar, but not quite as defined as the one on the other arm."

Now I'm not familiar with those two injury sites but the implications are that those two sites on the arms were the areas where the fatal jolt was applied. Well we know that this couldn't be! Since the board was on top of the hole, there is <u>no</u> way <u>two</u> electrodes would have been applied to her. Because the board was over the hole, the only way the electric jolt could have hit her was (as I've been saying) through the chains, BUT there are NO burn marks on Debbie's ankles, only <u>irritative</u> and <u>pressure</u> sores.

Now for some more quotes from Rivera. Sometimes she said I put it on her chains and sometimes she says I made <u>her</u> put it on Debbie's chain.

Page 160 Lines 11 to 16: "So Gary filled the hole with water and took electrical wires, and he would put it on certain chains, because everybody had a separate chain, and <u>he</u> <u>would</u> <u>say</u> whose chains he would hold the wire on was the one getting the most electricity. (Notice she says "he would say")

Page 163, Lines 1 to 2: "Then, when he first started putting the wire on the chain, he told me to come over there and hold the wire."

BUT you see my point. The "fatal jolt", if there was one, had to come through the chains, <u>NOT</u> by direct contact, on the arms. Nobody (even witnesses) claims a fatal jolt was applied to Debbie's arms.

Now when I was talking to the "Genius" guard he expressed doubt that all three women got the same size jolt. Okay, now let me quote from Rivera again, on page 157, Lines 10 to 14. "Everybody's chain was right over here. And Deborah Dudley is --- Like there's a little square brick thing here, and her chain was there separate from the rest of ours but still all <u>connected</u> together right here over top of the hole."

You can see where I underlined the word connected. Remmeber my drawing.

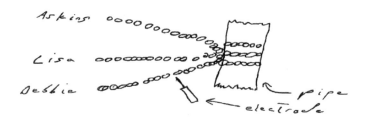

My point being since they were all connected when current was applied to Debbie's, it would travel through ALL THREE chains, not just hers, so ALL three would get the same size jolt.

But let me give you another quote by Rivera on page 163, Line 7 to Line 16: "Then I would --- he was telling me to hold the wire on Deborah's chain, then he would tell me to <u>put it on Lisa's chains and Donna's chains.</u>

Q. When he directed you to do that, were you still chained?

A. Yes, I was.

Q. Did you do this willingly?

A. No. I did not.

Q. Why did you do it?

A. Because he told me to."

So not only were all three chains connected, but Rivera claims to have applied juice to Lisa's and Donna's. So can there be any doubt <u>all three</u> got the same charge? And if so why did only Debbie die?

One more quote by Rivera on page 167, Lines 9 to 14. "He also <u>told me</u> that he had mailed a letter that Sandra had wrote. He went and bought the Christmas cards in New York and that he brought them back to Philly and had her fill them out, then drove them back to Albany and mailed them from there so they would think she was in New York."

The key words I underlined. "Told me." Now Rivera claims I said all this on the day after Debbie's death. This statement is highly suspect, like someone trying to hide something. This stuff had happened three months earlier and everybody knew it because Sandy wrote out the letter and card right there in front of them. My guess is Rivera made this statement to hide her/their motives for killing Sandy and Debbie. Only a guilty person would want to misslead on this point.

There is still so much to do, but the pieces of this puzzle are falling together like I predicted. I still need to find out if an autopsy can distinguish death electrocution as opposed to the "sleeperhold". Also just how big a "jolt" did Debbie and the others get. My hunch is it wasn't big enough to stun a fish even. This is the point. I wish I was on the other side, you know, a detective. If I was I'd follow up on this stuff, especially question Askins and Lisa seperatly. If they did kill these two, it would make the papers like wild fire. I'd be the most famous detective since Columbo, but I'd be for real. Well maybe I will become famous, because as I keep fitting more and more pieces into place, I'll be the one (with some help from my friends) who will get the glory. I could use some positive publicity for a change.

Sr. Gary

(Columbo jr)

April 27, 1990

Dear Beck,

Enclosed is a recent picture from the Pittsburgh Press. It's something I'd never heard of before, electric fish "stunning". It's a new wrinkle and very relevant. Notice the guy is using <u>two</u> electrodes, not one. This started me thinking, and I asked the question, "Why isn't he using only <u>one</u> electrode"??

The answer I think is obvious. One electrode wouldn't work! Just why it wouldn't work, I don't know. As you know only one electrode was used in my instance. So the question isn't simply rhetorical. Any ideas??

ANON,

Sr. Gary

P.S. Please return picture. I want to send it to some other people.

P.S.S You'll notice the three men are in the same pool (water) as the electrodes and are <u>not</u> being shocked. But that may be because they're wearing rubber boots.

May 18, 1990

Dear Beck,

I'm having a big laugh (he, he, he). Now that I can not only prove I didn't kill anyone and practically handed the state three killers on a silver platter, everybody is acting "strange". They're hemming, hawing, squirming and making excuses. Now they, society, have a problem. It's not a matter of me not being given all my rights, or some legal technicality. It's a plain matter of innocence, NOT GUILTY! They can't deny that anymore than they can change the basic laws of science! Of course the state would rather kill and bury a mistake than admit to it, and will do just that. What's funny is watching them try to rationalize it, to squirm to make excuses, for what they're doing. Because now they're NOT executing a murderer, they're KNOWINGLY committing murder.

205

They claim they want to stamp out murder. And how did the state get in this jam? By continuingly shafting me, denying me my basic human and legal rights, as they're continuing to do.

But what's really funny and the biggest guffaw is that society has been shafting me for 46 years, and only now it's bothering them. Only NOW their conscience bothers them. Just look at all the SHIT that's been done to me and NOBODY cared! Little late to develop a conscience isn't it (he, he, he, he, he, he, he).

Maybe there really is justice in this world after all.

ANON,

Sr. Gary

Grim Reader

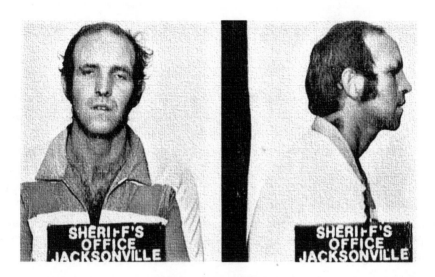

THE LAST WRITES:

DEATHBED PEN-PALS OF OTTIS ELWOOD TOOLE

When police asked Ottis Elwood Toole and Henry Lee Lucas to pinpoint the location of Jim Jones's Guyanese compound where the duo matter-of-factly claimed to have delivered the sodium cyanide which killed 907 cultists, they were very happy to oblige those detectives huddled elbow-to-elbow around a table strewn with postmortem crime scene photography, cold case folders, and a map of the U.S.A. '*Somewhere in East Texas or Louisiana*', they clarified. And *that*, as they say, spoke volumes. The investigation went inevitably downhill from there.

Toole and Lucas occupied a unique place in U.S. law enforcement history, during a period of time when those entrusted with solving murders became aware of a new breed of murderer: one operating among them, looking like them (mostly), passing as ordinary citizens, yet committing violence of uncommon cruelty then walking away generally undetected. They were coming to terms with the '*serial killer*', a phrase recently coined by operatives of the F.B.I. in Quantico, Virginia. And suddenly, local law enforcement saw serial killers coming out of the woodwork: even in a tag-team of halfwit vagrants. Which was fine with Toole and Lucas; so long as the coffee and cigarettes continued to flow, so would their stream of confessions to murders that in at least some instances didn't occur or at which Toole and Lucas couldn't have been physically present. Which is how Henry Lee Lucas ultimately escaped execution in Texas: his capital conviction hinged on his having strangled a hitchhiker on I-5 near Houston when he was, in fact, in Jacksonville, Florida cashing a check.

By the date of his own death in 1996, Ottis Toole was serving multiple life terms for murders committed throughout northern Florida. They included a 1980 robbery-homicide in Jackson County, the 1981 shooting and stabbing of two women in neighboring Holmes County (for which Henry Lee Lucas was also indicted), the 1982 arson death of an elderly Jacksonville man, and the death of a Leon County woman shot in the head the following year. But the man with a 75 I.Q. and equal tastes for pathological lies and incest managed to gain a devoted, international, and frequently carnival sideshow-like following in the 'outside' world. One must wonder what Toole realistically had to offer suburban youths seeking his attention from the confines of a psychiatric hospital, or jail. It had not evidently dawned upon most that, at that same moment, Ottis Toole was neck deep in bad choices: tossing hot coffee on guards, or canoodling a claw-hammer slayer called Chop. One pen pal of Toole's [name redacted to spare their reputation] was in fact a children's book author while another, Tobias Allen, invented a serial killer-themed board game before opting for a suicide plunge from a Seattle-area bridge. Allen, in concert with fellow correspondents, unabashedly capitalizes on the notoriety of a man blamed for the murder and mutilation of Adam Walsh, a 6-year-old child who became separated from his mother in a Hollywood, Florida shopping center and was only reunited in death. Toole denied his involvement, wasn't formally charged in Adam's murder, and it wasn't adequately established by Police if Toole was indeed accountable or whether this crime, like countless others to which he and Lucas laid claim, lacked real objective proof. But the boy's parents were sufficiently convinced of Toole's guilt and authorities obligingly placed him at the top of their suspect list where he'd stay until his agonizing death by cirrhosis in the Fall of 1996.

But even in his final glimpses of life, neither truth nor lies nor a debilitating illness prevented Ottis Elwood Toole's star from rising. Correctional officers at Raiford State Prison recovered these fan letters while cleaning out Toole's last cell, and they, too, speak volumes: about those who took their time to pen the messages, and of the doomed convict still eagerly receiving them, so willing to play along if only to feed (and feed upon) society's seemingly never-sated thirst to meet the boogey man.

APRIL 14, 1995

DEAR MR. TOOLE,

I JUST GOT DONE READING AN INTERVIEW THAT YOU DID IN A
BOOK WRITTEN BY A SMALL PUBLISHER.

IN THAT BOOK WAS AN ORIGINAL ART OFFER. I AM RITING
YOU TO FIND OUT THE DETAILS ON THIS OFFER, AND IF IT IS
STILL AVAILABLE.

I'M ENCLOSING A STAMP AND ENVALOPE WITH MY ADDRESS.
WOULD YOU PLEASE DO ME A FAVOR? IF YOU RETURN A
REPLY TO ME, WOULD YOU PLEASE HAND SIGN THE LETTER?

ALSO THERE WAS A MENTION OF A RECIPE CARD OR BOOK FOR
SALE. IF THERE IS WOULD YOU ALSO SEND A PRICE ON THAT,
IF IT'S FOR SALE. THANK YOU VERY MUCH FOR YOUR TIME.

JORGE G.

❖

Hey Baby,

*I got your letter. And I got to say it brought a smile to my face. And warmth
to my heart. I apologize honey if I haven't been talking much the last few
days. It's just that I was so close to finally leaving this place that I've been
mad cuz I blew my transfer. But it isn't all bad!* *I've got us to look
forward too! If you'll keep your hot ass* *out of trouble we will be able to
be with each other before long. My plans right now are to get out on a
Runner so I can hopefully get on the same floor as you are on! Yeah baby!
I want to dig off in that pussy!* *Cuz a Real Relationship isn't based on
sex alone. I've loved you a very long time Grammaw. And I'm telling you
right now. Don't be playing with my love! And don't lie to me! I have very
few demands. All I ask from my boy is 2 things. Don't denie me no sex when
I want it. Cuz if you do I'll take it!* *And don't lie to me! Cuz lieing will
destroy a Relationship. Anyway baby I am gonna keep on trying to get us
some cigarettes. Everytime I get some you can believe you'll be the first to
know. Well baby I love you with all my heart and soul. If you really want
my name and number so you can send me some money I'll give it to you.
But you don't have to do it if you don't want to. As I've told you I don't love*

you for your money, I love you for you! But if you're gonna send it let me know cuz then I can probably get us some coffee and Rips as soon as it gets here. I'll try to set up a business deal with it! ☺ *Anyway stay sweet and always remember I love you baby with all my heart.*

Love Always, Chop

Also, I'll be able to get my son some new clothing for school! I just sent out my last 60.00 so he could get some nice shoes!

[Undated]

MIGHTY RIVERS BEGIN WITH SPRINGS OF BLOOD, AND SPRINGS BEGIN WITH CUTS OF THE FLESH. THUS, HOPEFULLY OUR FIRST EMBRACE WILL ALWAYS BE YOUR FINAL FATE. IF ANY LUCK DOES COME YOUR WAY, YOU MAY ESCAPE THE HANDS OF THE JEWEL OF OTTIS TOOLE WHO JABS THE HEART AND THEN EATS IT APART. THUS, THE ONLY JOY WHICH LIFE COULD BRING WILL BE A FEAST OF ROASTED HEART AND BLOODY WINE, WHICH SUIT US FINE.

[Undated]

HELLO OTTIS,

I HAVE READ THE INTERVIEW WITH YOU BY BILLY BOB. A VERY INTERESTING ARTICLE.

I AM VERY INTERESTED IN YOUR ART. IF YOU WANT TO SEND SOME, I SHALL SEND BACK SOMETHING ELSE IN RETURN.

I AM WRITING IN THE STUIVENBERG HOSPITAL IN ANTWERP. I FOLLOW A RESIDENTIAL THERAPY BECAUSE I WANT TO BE DEAD. BUT ART KEEPS ME ALIVE.

MUSIC ALSO. AND OFF COURSE AIR, FOOD AND THE SUN.

TELL ME SOMETHING ABOUT YOUR LIFE THERE. I DIDN'T ENCLOSE IRC'S OR A 29 CENT STAMP BUT I GUESS YOU USE A STAMP FROM ANOTHER GUY WHO WROTE YOU A BORING LETTER.

MAYBE I AM THAT GUY!

HOPE TO HEAR FROM YOU!

YAZ

ANTWERP

❖

5-29-95

Ottis!

Hey my Friend! How are you doing? I hope things are doing well for you. I have enclosed 7 stamps. I only had 8 stamps. I don't get paid for 9 days. I hope this helps you out some.

I still would like to come and visit. I am going to try and get on your visiting list again. I will do this very soon and then we could meet!

We can hang out and eat and get pictures taken. I hope I can get there soon! Send me some photos.

What have you been doing to stay busy? I am real glad that your writing your own letters again! It's better for you also. You still have living relatives?

I am not working anymore. I need to look for a new job. I need one soon!

Are you allowed to use the phone? Let me know, OK?

I am watching F-Troop. Have you ever seen that show. It's an old one from the 1960's.

Sometimes its better than others.

What medication are you on? My doctor has me on Xanax 4mg, Paxil 20mg and Ritalin 30 mg everyday.

Well, I'm falling asleep. It's been a rough week. Send the BBQ sauce recipe. I hope your doing well. I will talk to you soon. Take care!

Your Friend Always,

Kenny

Tampa, FL

PS – Have you heard *from [Henry Lee Lucas alleged victim]* Becky Powell?

5-31-95

Dear Ottis:

My Hebrew-Christian brother Barry told me he saw you and talked to you. I lost your inmate number and I tried to contact you by writing to another cellmate and have him tell you to write me and give me your number. But now I have it. Can you tell me God isn't real? He's concerned about even the littlest things. Like you needing a pencil or needing to hear from me. What are the chances that these things would be answered?

Deep in the bowels of steel and cement a lone man asks God for help and humbles himself before an all-powerful, mighty yet loving and merciful God (read I John Chapters 1-5). How can God forgive such vile sins? If we truly are sorry for the sins we've committed and repent, God who is not a man, will forgive us. That's it! He will also remember our sins no more. Have you done that Ottis? Write me back. Here's some stamps & $5.00

JESUS CHRIST, the same yesterday, today, and forever! Get to know him. How? By reading his word and praying (talking to HIM) and Respect HIM. And obey HIM. He loves you & because he loves you can I do less?

May the Lord's Holy Spirit fill your being with his truth, Love and RIGHTEOUSNESS. Because HE lives, we shall also live forever (JN 14:19)

Dalton

June 10, 1995

Mr. Ottis E. Toole,

Knowing that you do not know me, my name is Bill and I work at a small international testing facility here in South Carolina. Overworked and underpaid, of course. I really enjoy participating in sports and love movies, especially a good horror flick.

A lot of people sit down and write to sports superstars, movie stars, etc. but I have a tendency to write to persons that are a lot more accessible. They seem to take the time to answer their mail personally as well as willingly accept mail. I would much rather receive a handwritten letter from someone who tells me about themselves than a stupid form letter telling me that my "hero" is too busy to even sign their name for me.

I recognize your name and know a little about you, but I would be very interested in receiving a letter from you telling me anything that you may want to say or can tell me about yourself. Feel free to tell about any hobbies and/or interests, and how you feel about your unfortunate situation. What is your status of being incarcerated?

Enclosed you will find an envelope already stamped for your convenience. Please respond in writing and anything additional you may want to send to me would be most welcome. Could you also just sign the enclosed index card for my personal collection?

Thanks for your time,

Willie F.

Pendleton, S.C.

6/21/95 10:33 pm EST

Wednesday

Ottis,

Hello there. How are you doing? I hope your doing well and OK. I'm in jail right now. Maybe a few months! I just wanted to say hello! I hope to get passed this.

How's your Family? I told everyone about Miami, but their embarrassed to bring me.

When your able to, please draw a picture of Charles Manson. Also, please draw the HAND OF DEATH.

When I'm out of here, I will send you some stamps and canteen.

Ok Ottis, I'll talk to you soon!

Your Friend, Kenny

Tampa, FL.

❖

[Undated]

Hey Baby,

Just have it sent to me Wilburn Lamb #106546

Make it an even $2,000.00. That'll be $1,200 to cover our canteen for the next 6 months plus $400 to buy my son some nice clothes and shoes for school. Damn he's gonna feel so proud. Thank you baby for letting me be able to do something nice for him like this. And the other $400.00 is to get you a nice ring! Yeah baby I want to give you a wedding ring! ☺ Your my wife damn it so I want to put a ring on your finger. Also make me up your list of the stuff you'll be wanting from the canteen for your first month's order. Yeah $65.00 dollars worth. Cuz as soon as I get the money I can show the guy the receipt and he'll give us are first month's order. That way we don't have to wait while I send it out then have it sent to him. I'm sending a letter out tonight will all the details. That way it'll all be ready to go as soon as possible. Holler down and let me know what you plan on sending. That way I know what to tell my son to look forward to! Thanks baby he's gonna be so happy! I love you and yes you know it's with all my heart!

Love,

Chop

August 14, 1995

Dear Ottis,

Thanks for your prompt reply to my letter. I'm pleased you're in good spirits and health! Thanks also for the canteen list so I can get an idea of what's available and the prices. Enclosed as a start is a $20.00 money order, which I hope you will enjoy to the fullest at the canteen, plus a couple of the pre-stamped envelopes as before.

I note that all you can do is read and do pictures, plus limited recreation, and that no packages are allowed. Is there no chance at all of sending you any books you might like to have?

Yes, I indeed have an interest in the Black Arts, and any drawings from you that would reflect that interest (as mentioned also in my first letter) would be most welcome! I'd also welcome any comments you might have and will share some of mine in return. Can I send you large envelopes, so drawings do not get folded? Enclosed also is a picture of me as you requested, and I look forward to receiving a picture of you in return. Please autograph it as I did mine.

Do you get a lot of letters? Do you write all your own letters, or do you have other inmates helping you out?

I look forward to hearing from you again!

Beast wishes,

Charles

8/28/95

Ottis,

Hope you're well – you ask for a money order & stamps, I just sent you $20. & 15 stamps on 8/21 & now I await more photos for the next money order – send me some different photos for example – sticking tongue out, waving, peace sign, fuck sign, leave it to your imagination O.K. But please send more photos.

216

– Thanks my Friend – Stay cool & be safe

Your Best Friend – ☺

Ricky

Yonkers, NY

P.S. Please hurry – ☺

❖

October 25, 1995

Dear Ottis:

It was good to hear from you my friend. Thank you for the drawings. I liked them very much. I'm sorry that it has taken me so long to write back to you. I've been sick for the last two weeks. I hurt my back and it's been hard for me to sit up and write letters.

I have enclosed some stamps for you. I'll send you a $10 money order in my next letter.

I was sorry to hear that you're in solitary, and that you've not been feeling well. I know better days are ahead for you, so be cool and take it easy. Thanks for writing your own letter to me. Your writing looks really good.

It's hot here again, in the low eighties. Too hot for October. My air conditioning went out, and I live upstairs, so it's really bad.

Maybe you can do five or six more drawings for me. I hung the two you sent in my hallway. I like the colors you use. Do you still do the barbeque drawings? I like demons and ghosts. Thanks again for the ones you sent.

I'll send you some more stamps too. I hope you get to feeling better. You're right, it has been too long since we wrote to each other, so again, it was really good to hear from you. Take care Ottis. Write soon

Your Friend,

Kris Sanderson

Danville, IL

[Undated]

Hi Ottis,

Long time, eh? I really am sorry for not writing in so long, but I have been real busy as I have just moved to New Orleans!

Rick Staton and I are doing another Art show in town. We will be showing some of your stuff here. It's just a one day thing so I don't forsee any big sales, but I will send you some canteen $ soon. O.K.? I just had to see a doctor for an infected ear and that cost me big time, but it's alright now.

Hey I went to Fort Walton/Destin Florida for my first time! It was very pretty and very fun. I went with Rick's family (It's only 6 hours away). Rick and I would be honored to come to Starke to see you! Can that be arranged?

We went to Texas recently to see Elmer Wayne Henley Jr. in Palestine. It was a good visit, but Texas prisons look rough & depressing. Rick went to see Henry Lee in Huntsville too. He said Henry was boring.

Please write me soon. Later,

Your friend,

Tobias Allen

New Orleans, LA

❖

[Undated]

Dear Ottis,

How are things with you? Good I hope. I have not written to you before so I don't know if I know how to do this.

I would like to know if you would be interested in correspondance with me. I am an open-minded gay man and would be willing to answer any questions you have for me – in time we may build some trust as we get to know each other better.

Maybe you would like some magazines etc. is it possible for me to send you stuff?

I'll finish this letter now as I do not wish to bore you!

I hope to hear from you soon,

Regards,

Pete

Hampshire, England

[Undated]

Dearest Ottis (+DJ)

Hi guys! Nice to hear back from you. I was starting to think you had blown me off. It's good to hear you guys are buddies again. I imagine you can use all the friends you can get in there, so ya'll be good to each other! O.K.?

Well, the travelling bed is settled in New Orleans now. I still talk with Rick all the time. He gave me your letter. We put on the art-show as planned here in New Orleans. It was just a one day thing, but we got lots of media attention. One local paper said some very nice/cool things about your art Ottis. I will send on the article to you. Let me get two things out of the way here. First I will send some $ on to you next week when I get paid. I know ya'll can use it. Also I plan to try and get a visit worked out. I will take your advice on this. I hear that Florida is a bit more difficult then some states as far as visits go, but it would be worth any hassle that might arise. I know Rick would love to visit too! In May we went to Texas to see Elmer Wayne Henley Jr. Rick visited Henry too, but I think I told you that. I have never communicated with Henry, and don't care to.

Man oh man the South is hard to get used to for a Washington kid. I thought the heat would surely kill me this summer. I survived though, however I am currently suffering from a massive ear infection. It really sucks as the doctor has me on this powerful medication that eats my stomach alive. I find out in a couple days if things are O.K...or not.

219

Ottis my man you have to watch your health, O.K.? I don't want to hear about you getting sick. Watch the weight thing. I can relate because I keep dropping and adding pounds too. I think it's the medicine. My friends say its real obvious when I'm losing weight. I don't know though. Anyway, watch your health man!

Not too much more to tell on this end. I've been writing to a 19 year old attempted murderess named Sarah Edmondson, here in Louisiana. It has been a cool relationship so far. She writes some good poetry. I am also living with some cool kids here in a pretty nice house.

Take Care,

Peace,

Your friend,

Tobias Allen

New Orleans, LA

Call or write, dudes!

[Undated]

DEAR OTTIS,

GOT YOUR Address from a friend, and I would Love to write and share with you. I don't know anything about you Really so maybe you can tell me some things about yourself. I am very open minded and do love writing hot open minded Letters.

A little about me! I am 43 yrs old. 6' about 185 lbs. blue eyes dirty blonde hair – greying somewhat. I am a Lover of all sexual activity, My friends say I'm pan-sexual because I have no limits or restrictions when it comes to sex. I enjoy both men and women and ages make No difference to me what so ever. I find that the older I get the more I'm enjoying sex with men. I love big dicks, black men, sexy erotic transvestites.

I have a wild fetish for panties. I love cum, cocksucking and licking and sucking ass. Toilet sex, bondage, domination and submission. I love sharing "dirty little secrets" and turn ons to all sexual extremes.

220

If you'd like to write and tell me more about you I would enjoy. I do enjoy the bizarre and the unusual and I'm fascinated with extreme sexual practices, cultures, sexual crimes, sexual violences and just about anything in the realm of sex. If you want, ask me anything or share anything you wish.

Your new pen pal

Stan the Man

Berkeley CA

❖

[Undated]

Dear Mr. Toole,

I'm a 25 yr old male, with loads of tattoos. Some are a bit twisted. I've seen your drawings in some magazines & was wondering how to get them. If you can get some to me I would like that.

If I like the drawings and it would make a good tattoo I'll get it.

If you can get photos tell me & I'll send a picture of my back tattoos.

Your pen pal,

Pat R.

Metarie, LA

❖

September 11, 1995

Dear Ottis,

Thanks for your two recent letters, the excellent drawings and handprint, and the photo of you with your niece! I hope this finds you and your friends well and getting some relief from the hot Summer weather.

221

I would of course love to have an autographed photo of you alone whenever you can send it. Any other strange, demonic artwork would also be welcome!

Glad you liked my photo. It was taken at Highgate Cemetery in London, England. It's a large, overgrown Victorian cemetery – quite spooky and used as a setting for various horror films.

Yes, I would of course be pleased to receive a "writing supply" pass and to send you whatever you want. I understand that under a writing permit you are allowed these things: 10 large envelopes, pilot ink pen and 2 refills, and 3 legal pads. I will include colored refills with the ink pen for your drawings.

Let me know if you or any of your friends (Willie or David) would like a "writing supply" package or "regular" package. I can do several of those as well.

I plan to do the two mirror exercise you suggested. I saw that described on a TV program and perhaps in a Fate article as well. Can't remember just where I saw it but was intrigued at the time and simply forgot about it. Have you or anyone you know done it? Please tell me more about the Hands of Death!!!

Enclosed for you this time are a $20.00 money order and a book of stamps. Enjoy!

Best wishes,

Charles

[Undated]

Mr. Toole,

Hello, how are you these days? I'm doing O.K. Well I don't know what reason I'm writing for. I was reading thru an old issue of Answer Me #3 and there was some of your art work with your address on it. Well I thought I'd write. I used to write to Gacy before he got the gas chamber or was it lethal injection? I don't remember. I also got a chance to talk on the phone once. He was pretty interesting. So how do they treat you in prison? What kind of things do you do to pass time? A Friend of mine was telling me that he writes to you. His name is Ted. He lives in San Diego, CA. Well let me tell you a little about myself. My name is Jayson and I'm 24, I'll be 25 on Sept 16th. I work three jobs. One at a transportation company for mentally retarded. One at a music store and one at a music club. I like to collect records, a few comics and music zines. Well I must be going now. Gotta go to work. Hope to hear back from you.

Jay L.

El Cajon, CA

❖

[Undated]

Greetings Ottis,

Just wanted to write and say Happy Holidays (if that's possible in there!). I know this is going to get there way after x-mas probably, as it is already Dec. 21st. Maybe this can be more of a New Years letter, and by the way, sorry it's not a 'real' card, but money is tight this holiday season.

Hey, tell me, is it true? Did G.J. Schaffer get shanked by another prisoner? I was terribly surprised to hear that news, but I haven't been able to verify it yet, so please let me know! To be honest, I was never too interested in him, but I did read his book. I found his writing pretty cool, but he, as a criminal-pen-pal never seemed worth the time. I kind of wish I had at least one letter from him now though. I read some that Joe had, they were very long. Right now I only write to a few prisoners. I always love your letters Ottis and you know I'm crazy for your wicked drawings!

I've still be dealing with the ear infection thing that I believe I told you about. It seems that a surgery is a harsh reality now. Oh well, I guess I'll get some good medication for the pain. How is your health Toole-man? The last I hear from you, you were not feeling too well. I hope things have improved. The holidays can be shitty enough without being sick to boot!

I've been spending some time around my old buddy Rick Staton and his family, up in Baton Rouge. We always have a great time together, and his family has been very kind to me. I guess they're my best friends here in Louisiana. That reminds me (And I may have asked you this). You and Henry supposedly confessed to some crimes here in Baton Rouge, including a murder-robbery in Rick's neighborhood. So what is the deal with that? Have you ever been to the area? Just curious, but you know you never have to tell me squat, if you don't want to.

That's all for now.

PEACE (to D.J. TOO!!!)

LATER,

Tobias Allen

P.S. I know you're sick of hearing it, but I WILL send a money order, when I can. I should be a bit better off soon!

❖

9-29-95

2:40 pm EST

Friday

Ottis,

How are you doing my friend. I hope that everything is OK w/you and all is well. I have been getting in a lot of trouble lately. I am trying to stay out of trouble all the time.

What have you been doing my friend. Please let me know what you've been doing these days. Have you talked with Gerard Schaefer lately? I am waiting to hear from him.

This is my friend Pat's address on top. He gave me your video w/ Henry Lee Lucas from TV, it's great. I will send you some stamps soon. Draw me Charles Manson!

I will keep good thoughts for you each and everyday.

Take care!

Your Friend,

Kenny

Tampa, FL

9/9/95

Dear Ottis –

Hope your feeling better –

I feel very bad as one of my best friends died of AIDS this week so I've been depressed… Received your letter today & was happy to hear from you & happy you got the stamps & money order – also Thanks for the drawings. They cheered me up!!

You wrote fine on your own – Keep up the good work – I'll send you more stamps & money when I can – I too love you as a Friend – Thank you for being my friend – Any luck with any new photo's – Take a photo & hold a sign saying "Hi, Ricky". That would be real cool & I would love that!!

Thanks – Your Best Friend

Ricky ☺

Yonkers, NY

❖

12 Sep. 1995

Dear Ottis,

Hi how are you today? It's late so don't blame me if I'm not up to making sense.

Just I want to post this tomorrow and I've got an early start with a long trip to London to go watch one of my paintings' auction. This is not my art but art I've been selling to keep my Dad's dealership going. It's the way I earn a living these days since I moved back to the sticks.

D.J. – I instantly recognized your writing when I fished the letter out of my mail box. I wasn't sure if I'd ever hear from you again since I moved out of London. My Dad had a really bad fall, broke his neck and became paralysed so I moved back to aid him and my family what little I could before he died. Since then as Ottis'll tell you, I've not been doing much. Haslemer doesn't scream 'Action' on any given day. It is very good

225

to hear from you again, and lucky for you, you got a room near Ottis. Sorry to hear you've had so many operations.

Well as you can see Ottis I couldn't get any money for you – yet. Next time I find a little spare I'll save you up $100 and then I'll post it. Not worth me sending 20 bucks as the cheque to mail to you costs me $15! I can't use a personal cheque. Only one made out in U.S. $. So hang on for me again & I'll get to you asap. O.K.? I'm so sorry you're not feeling the best. And Boy this Pneumonia on the liver sounds harrowing. I'm sure you'll be O.K. but if I were you I'd get it seen to before it gets dangerous. Sorry Ottis, that sounds nasty. I've had 4 major operations on my intestines. I've had my guts handled by many people. I've only 12 feet left compared to you guys with your 31 feet and all! I became very ill as a kid when I got a disease called "Crohn's Disease". It fucks up your insides – causing the guts to change shape and thickness. So much so that you hardly shit, and most of the food gets stuck in the 'strictures' – Nice Disease Huh?! Painful? – Yes.

Well all I want to hear is that your feeling better and so I hope this letter can be a shot in the arm for ya!

You're looking good Ottis. Thank you for the photo of you and Sarah. You have the Toole Family Eyes. She looks like a nice person. She visit you much? How big is your family? – Thanks again for the Hand of Death drawing & print. I always like to see your demons from the Depths.

Ottis, please get well soon and write back whenever D.J. feels like it. I'm trying for Money for you. Photos to sell are always a bonus, so see if you can include some in your next letter. Take care Ottis

Joseph

United Kingdom

❖

9/28/95

Dear Ottis,

Received your letter today & hope your well – I'm O.K. Too!!
I hope you can send me some pictures real soon!! Have no money to send

today as I don't get paid now for 8 more days!! Once every two weeks!! But when I get paid, I'll save some to send to you with my next letter O.K.?

How's everything, I hope O.K. my friend?

Stay safe & be strong my pal –

Your Friend,

Ricky

Yonkers, NY

❖

10-9-95

Dear Ottis:

I received your most welcome letter and please know that although I may not write as often as I'd like to, yet you are daily in my prayers. I am praying that God will meet all of your needs: spiritual, mental & physical.

Praise God! You are blessed to have this fine Christian friend, David. He is giving you good Biblical advice. Satan won't quit attacking, but "Greater is he that is in us, than he that is in the world!" (1 JOHN 4: 4). I put on my armor everyday before I leave my house, (see EPH. 6:13-18).

I've enclosed $5.00 for you. Thank Jesus for this money. Thank him for everything, no matter how small, that you can think of. In Phill. CH. 4:6 the Scripture says, "Be careful for nothing (Don't worry); But in everything by prayer and supplication (humbly asking) with Thanksgiving let your requests be made known unto GOD.

Be blessed!

Because HE lives (JOHN 14:19),

Dalton

12/4/1995

DEAR OTTIS,

I HAVE BEEN WANTING TO WRITE TO YOU FOR SOME TIME NOW. I DID NOT KNOW HOW TO FIND YOU UNTIL A COUPLE OF WEEKS AGO. I AM AN ARTIST AND GOT AN ART SHOW AT THE RITA DEAN GALLERY. THERE I MET K.D. SHE SHOWED ME THE PICTURES YOU DREW OF HER. I WAS IMPRESSED. I REALLY LIKED YOUR DRAWINGS, SO I ASKED HER IF I COULD HAVE YOUR ADDRESS TO WRITE TO YOU. SHE WAS HAPPY TO GIVE IT TO ME. SHE IS A VERY NICE GIRL AS IS HER HUSBAND J.D. THEY REALLY KNOW HOW TO TREAT PEOPLE WELL.

THERE IS SO MUCH I WANT TO KNOW ABOUT YOU. I HAVE SO MANY QUESTIONS. I WOULD LIKE TO BE YOUR FRIEND. AS FAR AS BEING A PEN PAL, I AM VERY GOOD AT WRITING BACK. WHEN I GET A LETTER, I WRITE BACK RIGHT AWAY. SO, IF YOU DECIDE TO BECOME FRIENDS, I WILL KEEP YOU BUSY WITH MY LETTERS.

I GUESS I COULD START OFF BY TELLING YOU A LITTLE ABOUT MYSELF. I AM 31 YEARS OLD BUT I FEEL LIKE 21. I HAVE A LOT OF ANIMALS BECAUSE I PREFER THEM TO PEOPLE. I HAVE ONE DOG, NAMED OTTIS AFTER YOU, OF COURSE. I HAVE TWO CATS, TWO IGUANAS, 4 AUSTRALIAN TREE FROGS, ONE BALL PYTHON SNAKE, ONE RED-TAIL BOA CONSTRICTOR SNAKE, EIGHT MICE, 17 BIG MICE, 10 BABY MICE AND THAT'S ALL. I DRAW WITH CHARCOAL AND COMPUTER, LIKE PAINTINGS. IF YOU WOULD LIKE, I COULD SEND YOU ONE OF MY COMPUTER PAINTINGS. THEY ARE PRETTY COOL. I LISTEN TO ALL TYPES OF MUSIC: ALTERNATIVE, RAP, R&B, JAZZ, BLUES, CLASSICAL AND OTHERS. I LIKE ART BUT I AM VERY CHOOSEY ABOUT WHAT ART I LIKE. THERE IS A LOT OF BAD ART OUT THERE, AT LEAST IT IS NOT TO MY LIKING.

WHAT ABOUT YOU? WHAT DO YOU DO WITH YOUR TIME? WHAT DO YOU LIKE? DO YOU FIND THAT IN PRISON YOU EAT FASTER? WHAT IS THE FOOD LIKE? DO THEY OFFER ANY INTERESTING THINGS TO DO? WHAT ARE THE PEOPLE LIKE? DO YOU HAVE ANY HOBBIES?

I KNOW WHAT YOU LOOK LIKE SO TO BE FAIR I AM SENDING A PICTURE OF MYSELF SO YOU KNOW WHO IS WRITING TO YOU. I WOULD REALLY LOVE IT IF YOU COULD SEND ME A FEW DRAWINGS. I WOULD DEFINITELY HANG THEM IN MY HOUSE.

I HOPE YOU HAVE A HAPPY HOLIDAY SEASON AND AM SENDING YOU A GIFT WITH THIS LETTER SO YOU CAN USE IT TO DO SOMETHING NICE FOR YOURSELF. I HOPE TO HEAR FROM YOU REAL SOON, MAYBE EVEN BEFORE CHRISTMAS IF THAT IS POSSIBLE.

LOVE

YOUR FRIEND

RUBY

LONG BEACH, CA

[Undated]

Ottis man (and Vince),

Hey guys, once again, I take a million years to write back. I am so sorry, and I hope this letter finds you well. I really do have a good excuse for not writing sooner. The truth is I have been spending all my spare moments writing to a pen pal here in Louisiana, and to another kid on Arkansas Death Row. This kid, Damien Echols, is, more then likely, not guilty. There is a movie coming up on HBO this June 10th that should do a lot to help his case, and may very well lead to his release. If you are at all interested I can send you all the details on his case/conviction. I have sent him some photo copies of your drawings Ottis, and he really likes them. It has lead to him doing some art of his own.

Anyway, myself and Rick Staton are going to visit him at the prison in Tucker tonight. I am rushing to get this letter off to you before we leave. I am feeling real guilty for taking so long, as you have always been one of my favorite pen pals.

Hey, I re-watched 'Death Diploma' the other day on video. That interview with you always makes me feel really sad Ottis. I know that deep down you are a very nice man, with just a really bad reputation. I know that all the shit that was done to you when you were young lead to all the trouble you got into as an adult. By the way, were you really a pyromaniac, or is that exaggerated? I tried to write to Paul Keller in Seattle when I lived there, but he never wrote me back. They were calling him one of the worst serial arsonists ever (He was blamed for over 100 fires). He seems like an interesting man. I think we all have a underlying fascination with fire, but it is hard to see how that gets out of control.

O.K., Ottis, I have to be honest. I have heard a rumor that you are sick (with HIV/AIDS). Now you have to be honest with your old buddy Tobias, is this true? I want you to know that I will be here for you, no matter what. If you need anything, I want you to let me know. I am going to send you a care package with some paper, stamps, and a money order very soon. I just have to get this trip to Arkansas over with, then I can afford to help you out. I will also get the visiting form again, so I can come and see you. Please be honest and let me know just how you are doing. I have already [lost] a couple of friends to that disease. Also, if what I hear is false, please let me know and I will tell the person that told me to shut the fuck up.

I think Rick and I might do another art show soon, so you might want to think about doing some more drawings for it. I am enclosing a review of the last one that talks about your art quite a bit. I don't think I sent it before. If I have, sorry.

Anyway, write me soon, and let me know how you are. I will throw a package into the mail to you soon. By the way, if you see Danny Rolling, tell him to 'Fuck off' for me. He disgusts me.

Hey I heard about GJ SCHAFFER, too. Who iced him? Did they catch the guy? Did the guards even care? I wouldn't, that guy seemed like a jerk, too.

PEACE

Tobias Allen

New Orleans, LA

1/4/96

OTTIS,

Thanks for writing back Ottis. I really appreciate it. It means a lot to me. Knowing about you for years and finally writing you, then for you to write back is great. Thanks for sending those couple drawings. They were cool. If you could, send some more in your next letter.

So what were you in solitary for? What does solitary consist of?

Send me a list of things you are and are not allowed to receive. I want to send you some stuff that you like. Anything you want?

What is your everyday life like Ottis? How many people do you write to each week? And what is your current sentance?

Well Ottis I'm 20 years old and live in a city I'm not to fond of. I live a sort of alternative lifestyle. Into movies, music and books. I like to write and someday hope to be a writer/filmmaker. It's so hard though. Right now I work at a grocery store. Put in long hours just to earn a buck. Life in prison has some good points Ottis, at least you don't have to deal with all these assholes out here in society. Most of them make me sick.

If your in a cell 24 hours a day how is it hard to hustle to survive…I'm very curious as to how your life is Ottis. As I said before I've known about you for years.

Well I'll end this letter. Enclosed is a stamp. Write back soon. Wishing you the best for 1996

Casper

Westland, MI

1/24/96

Ottis –

Hope your well – Hopefully I'll send some stamps & money order with my next letter as I get paid Friday & today's only Wednesday – Got your letter today & want to answer right back ☺ No pictures? Photos?? Also I've been writing Gerard Schaeffer & haven't heard from him, Is he O.k.? I know you guys are friends? Right?

Write soon,

Your Pal,

Ricky

Yonkers, N.Y.

❖

2-5-96

Hi, uncle ottis

I hope this card will find you be good? Are you mad at me for something? I hope your are not. Let me know what you thank about me + Juan oK? If you do not wright me how will I know how you filled?

Well uncle ottis I will wait until you right me back.

I Love you, You are my uncle and You allway be?

Love

Your

Nicese

Sarah

❖

[Undated]

Live not in yesterdays, Look back and you may sorrow

Live precisely for today, Look forward to tomorrow.

I love you uncle ottis For Life

Love your Nicec, Sarah

3-5-96

HAPPY BIRTHDAY –

To a true original.

Hope things are going Allright.

Your Friend,

Vinny

Ottis please tell me if you can have Visitors or if you can use the Phone. Also what magazines do you like.

Thanks, Vince

I liked the pictures you sent me a lot.

Please send me any pictures you want. I love it, try to write Bile in the next one.

I'm going to try to send you $15.00 soon.

Let me know if you have a tape player.

3-14-96

Ottis!

Hello! What's up! Long time since I have heard anything from you. I hope that this letter finds you well and in good health!

Anything new and exciting been up? I wrecked the car last week, so that wasn't very good. Now I have to pay a lot of money for the damages.

I have enclosed 5 stamps for you. I know that you can use them.

I am still working a lot and staying busy. I've been doing a lot of public service hours also.

Please draw me something "WICKED"! I would appreciate it greatly. Let me know how you are doing…

TAKE CARE…

Kenny

Tampa, FL

3/18/96

Ottis,

How are you doing? Is everything going OK? I never heard back from you replying to the letter that I had written back in October.

Actually, I have totally forgotten what I had written. I do recall you mentioning continued correspondence. I'm still interested and willing if you are interested.

Are you still in solitary? I hope you have had the opportunity to get to enter the regular population.

I do recall you mentioning that you draw a little. Would I still be able to receive one?

I would really like to get to know what really makes you tick. I will tell you a little more about myself and hopefully you will respond at length, telling me some things about yourself.

Where to begin… Well, you already know my name and where I live. I moved to South Carolina about 1 ½ years ago now; from New Jersey. My company moved down here to be near Clemson University. As far as my job goes, I work with details relating to the installation of ceramic tiles. I get to see a lot of products before they are actually out on the market. Tiles and all related materials including the adhesives and grout (the stuff filling the area between the tiles).

I get to do product testing on everything to see if it meets industry standards. Without me some things are never for sale. Pretty cool, huh?

Anyhow, I really hope that you choose to respond this time.

Maybe the previous letter got lost or misplaced.

Please take care of yourself and write back as soon as you can.

Sincerely,

Willy F.

Pendleton, SC

P.S. Have you had any contact with Henry Lee Lucas? Would you happen to have his address in Texas that you could give me?

4/19/96

DEAR OTTIS,

SO, WHAT'S UP MAN? I WROTE TO YOU, SENT $. HAVE NOT HEARD BACK FROM YOU. WROTE DAVID. LETTER CAME BACK RETURN TO SENDER. HAVE YOU BEEN A BAD BOY, OTTIS? I WANT SOME DRAWINGS. I THINK YOU OWE ME A FEW. LET ME KNOW WHAT THE STORY IS. AND STAY OUT OF TROUBLE.

LOVE

RUBY

LONG BEACH, CA

23 April 1996

Dear Mr. Toole:

My name is Chris and I will be publishing a magazine called MISANTHROPE. I've enclosed a guideline/information to give you an idea of where the magazine is coming from.

I've heard that you send out recipes and sauces for human meat. I'd love to print something along these lines in the first issue of MISANTHROPE or whatever else you'd care to send to me. I will send you a copy of any issue in which your material appears in.

Regards and I look forward to hearing from you.

Christopher

Melbourne, Australia

❖

5/2/96

Ottis!

Hi, my friend? How are you doing? Not a lot is happening here.

Did you ever draw me GJ Schaffer with his throat cut? Please draw me these drawings. I am putting 20 stamps in here for you. I know you can use them.

Have you heard anything on Adam Walsh? Are they trying to pin that one on you?

My friend Jerry says hi & he loves you. He knows about you very many years.

I've heard you have AIDS. Is this true? Do you have HIV. If you do, your still my good friend.

Send me a picture of yourself. I want a picture of you signed to me.

Alright my friend! Write back soon and send me a "HAND OF DEATH" drawing please! I have always been good to you.

Keep smiling…

Your Friend, Kenny

Tampa, FL

5/3/96

Ottis,

Here's a drawing from me to you. Would you draw me a picture of a little boy holding a baseball bat? I know you can draw that well. You can draw it for me.

Ok, I will let you go my friend! Write back soon! I hope all is well for you!

Keep Smiling!

Kenny

Tampa, FL

❖

May 12, 1996

Dear Mr. Toole,

I saw a couple of your drawings in an issue of 'Answer Me'. I really, REALLY liked your drawings and I have tried to get hold of them ever since I saw them, but it seems impossible to get one… No one seems to have any of them and no one seems to know how to get them.

Yesterday I managed to get hold of this address and I really hope that this letter will reach you. Please answer this letter and let me know how to get a piece of your beautiful art! It would really mean a lot to me.

I hope you can find the time for some letter correspondence, or is there anyway I can reach you by phone? Please excuse my bad English.

Yours sincerely,

Mike

Stockholm

[Undated]

Ottis –

What's up?

How are you?

Haven't heard from you in months!!

Is you alive? What's up?

Write me, O.K.? Pictures?

Your Forever Pal –

RICKY

P.S. I sent you stamps & Money Order & No Answer

[Undated]

Mr. Otis Toole,

    Hello! How are you!

    I have been told that you are an Artist!

    Could I please ask you to drawl a picture for me?

    Would you drawl a <u>self portrait</u> and write me a little about yourself?

Stay well,

Jack S.

Philadelphia, PA

April 24, 1996

Mr. Toole:

I never thought I'd be writing to a man like yourself – but here I am. I am a respected man in the community, well connected, and never had an ounce of trouble in my life, but after reading an article about you in a magazine I felt I had to write to you.

My son is now 16 years old. A handsome athletic boy who has always been the love of my life. But recently I have had these unnatural urges to cook him and eat his tender flesh. God only knows why this has happened – but it has become unbearable for me. I'll relay to you how it began. I am a long-time pipe smoker. I've been smoking a pipe since my teens and was thrilled when my son asked me to teach him how to smoke. But, as he lit up his first bowl, I kept envisioning him grilling on a spit. Ironically it was my son's magazine where I read your interview in which you spoke of cooking and eating young boys. And now whenever I see him puffing away on his briar (which is often) I dream of how delicious he'll taste.

I was out drinking with a colleague one night and after our fifth scotch our tongues loosened and I brought up the subject of cannibalism. He told me he knew of a client in Australia who had a taste for human flesh and often cooked up teen-aged boys in a bar-b-que grill in his backyard. My concern with cooking my son was that his meat would be gamey and tough – but, he told me his friend cooked these muscular boys alive because then they released some sort of enzyme or hormone that naturally tenderized the meat so that they tasted as tender as a calf. With that news I renewed my interest in cooking up my muscular 6-foot son. So, I write to you asking advice. Have you ever cooked a well-built teen? What's the best way to go about it? How should I prep him? Should I fatten him up first? Should I cook him alive? Which cut of meat usually tastes the best? And anything else you can think of that will be of help. I'd also appreciate a copy of your bar-b-que sauce recipe and any cooking instructions. I hope to hear from you soon so that I can finally taste the delicious meat of my handsome son. I've enclosed a $tamp so that you can reply to me at your earliest convenience. Thanks and good luck to you –

Michael S.

New York, NY

[Undated]

Ottis,

Hello, are you there? I thought I heard you call out my name, but I could be wrong. Words without meanings, voices without faces. A leach on the brain, draining me of my memories. The horrors of the world I live in. Can I ever escape? Can you help me?

Peace on earth, goodwill toward men; these are not important to me. A brick in the head or a mullet on a hook, these are important to me. The State hates me. I'm not too fond of them. Do you hate me?

I let my mind wander and it never came back, but I will share what I have left. If I open up to you will my intestines fall to the ground? Will you help me pick them up?

I feel the need to read, but my reading materials were lost in the fire. The fire that torments my soul. Flame of eternal night. Night of eternal torment. Respond to me Ottis, you are my final hope.

Brian

Sebastian, FL

❖

[Undated]

Greetings Mr. Toole!

My name is Eric and I am writing in order to gain correspondence with you.

In the past I have written to others in the same situation that you are in, such as John Gacy, before they murdered him.

I would now like to write back and forth with you and purhaps purchase drawings, etc. that you may have done.

I will not write very much this time, as I am not even 100% sure that the address is correct. So, I will await a reply if you are interested in corresponding. I hope to hear from you soon.

Eric

Howell, MI

[Undated]

Dear Mr. Toole,

Over the past few years, I have read everything about you that I could find. Sometimes I am satisfied with what I read but most of the time I feel like I am being told lies.

The books about you don't seem to try to tell the truth about your life. They just tell some exaggerated story to try to sell books. Maybe that's just what most people want to read.

I want you to know that I don't believe everything I read. I don't think you are the monster described in the books. I would like to get to know you through letters.

Also, I would like to send you items such as books and articles. "Or anything you need." I want to send you a money order to cover postage and materials but I'm not sure how to do it. Can I send it directly to you or does it go into an account? Please let me know how to get things to you. I will send the money order as soon as I hear from you.

Please write back to tell me what you need or just to talk. I'm not sure if I even have the right address or not. There are a lot of things I want to talk to you about. I want to have you as a friend. Well, take care of yourself. I hope to hear from you soon.

Your friend,

Pete

Huntsville, AL

[Undated]

Dear Mr. Toole,

My name is Bobby and I saw an article about you in one of my friend's magazines. And it said that you were an artist.

I myself am an artist and I was wondering if you might send me some of your work.

I am very interested in other people's art.

I myself prefer pen and ink on canvas.

I find it very easy to work with. And the ink really spreads into the canvas very evenly.

What do you like to work with?

I don't know if they will let you have any of my work in there but if they will, please let me know and I will send you one of my pictures. There done on 3" x 5" canvas.

There are a few personal questions I would like to ask you.

I would like to know where you are from?

How old are you? When were you born?

Were you ever married?

Do you have any children?

How did the court trial affect you?

How long did the trial last for?

And how do you feel your attorney performed?

I know these are pretty personal questions. And I don't mean to offend you by them. If I did please let me know, so I won't in the future.

I was also wondering if you write any stories or poems? I write a lot of poems but not very many stories. I'll send you a couple of them next time I write to you, O.K.?

Well I have to go now but I'll write you soon.

Best Wishes,

Bobby

06-18-1996

Dear Ottis,

Why have I not heard from you? Are you ignoring me? I thought that we were to be friends and in good faith I sent you $ to do me some drawings and have not received any letter or drawings from you! Do I have to come and kick your ass or are you going to put out like the bitch that you are? I even sent David a letter and that was returned. You didn't kill him did you? That would answer all.

I want to know what the story is so write me back. I have been very patient and now I am losing my patience, my friend. If you are interested, I could probably sell some drawings for you and make you a bit of $. That is if you are interested. Let me know. Until then,

Your Friend,

Ruby

Long Beach, CA

6-19-96

Ottis,

Hey, how's it going? This is Jason. Do you remember? The last letter I got from you was in Nov. of last year and I wrote you back and never heard from you again. So hows it been. It's going O.K. here. I don't work at the record store anymore. I believe I told you about the music club I also worked at. Well I totally run that now. I'm the man there. Well I got to get going. Hope to hear from you soon. I'll write a longer letter next time. Well, you take care.

C-ya

Jay L.

El Cajon, CA

June 19, 1996

INMATE TOOLE. OTTIS # 090812

I talked with Mr. Zabawa as I told you I would. He stated that he didn't know anything about any paperwork, but it was his understanding that you stood a very good chance of a transfer due to your health conditions even though your not supposed to be eligible while you are CM II Status.

He advised that he would talk further with his supervisors about this and get back with me.

S.R. Arnold, Inspector I

Florida State Prison

❖

6/21 '96

Dear Mr. Ottis Toole,

I got your address from my U.S. friend. First of all, please let me introduce myself. My name is Hitomi, Jap male at 30, have been managing this record label since 1985. The reason why I'm writing to you from the far east is that I'd love to ask you for a drawing for my next compilation tape named "HUMAN MUSIC" w GG ALLIN & SHRINKWRAP, GG ALLIN & THE MURDER JUNKIES, COLON ON THE COB, HARVEY SID FISHER, DAVID KORESH, MAN IS THE BASTARD, DON BOLLES (EX GERMS), ROB X PATRIOT (The leader of AMERICAN FRONT, CA NATIONALIST GROUP), MASONNA etc − . I don't know you're interested in such a music, but you may understand my musical attitude through my catalogue with my poor English... Anyway if you're OK for my offer, please let me know how much bucks you need and where I have to send money to. Sorry for not including a coupon. I'm afraid this letter'll be censored and the coupon will be confiscated, so please tell me a definite safe way to send you money − . Also if you want any Japanese things you're interested in, please let me know.

I'll try to find and send it to you − .

Take care,

Looking forward to your reply,

Yours,

Hitomi A.

BEAST 666 REKORDS

OSAKA, JAPAN

8/4/96

10:15 pm EST

Hi Ottis!

Hey, my Friend? How are you doing? I hope this letter finds you doing well & in good health. Everyone says hello to you! Please send me a photo when you can! I am sending some photos to you. 3 photos & 6 stamps are here for you!

How are things w/ you? I hope all is well with you & things are good for you.

Are you doing well? I heard you say that you were SICK. Are you sick? Tell me about being a Pyromaniac. Is burning things down fun? I would love to know!

I have thought about it quite a lot.

Well, we love you Ottis! All my friends & family say hello to you!

We hope your doing well & OK! Draw me a picture of GJ Schaefer w/a knife in his face. Take care & God Bless You!

Your Friend,

Kenny

Tampa, FL

SATANIC VERSES:

POETIC WORD-SALADS OF ARTHUR SHAWCROSS

A SELF-PORTRAIT OF THE AUTHOR
AS A SERIAL CANNIBAL

My name is Arthur John Shawcross, also known as Arimes Joseph Yerakes. I was born on June 6, 1945 in the small town of Kittery, Maine. I have often wondered if I was a switched baby at birth. I looked like none of the rest of my family. Or so this is how I felt.

My parents moved to Boston, Massachusetts in 1945 after I was born. We lived there for about six months then moved to the Watertown, New York area. As a child, I was a loner because there was no one except my sisters and brother to play with. Also as a child I was caught up in the situation that I had no choice in. Sex with family members. At the time I didn't care for what was being done with me by certain female family members. But then I grew to enjoy the sensations and went on to my cousins and neighborhood girls. At this time my Mother was highly jealous of who I had contact with. No girl was good enough for her son. I had a crush on a girl that was very poor and my Mother made me stop seeing this girl. *Why?*

I attended school at the General Brown Central near Brownville, New York and High school at General Brown Central near Dexter. I left school when I was 19. I went to work at the bowling alley just outside the south side of Watertown. I worked there about a year then got a job with the Family Bargain Center. This is where I met my first wife, where you get all your bargains.

Most of my adult life was spent in the woods near home. This was my playground. My only friend was a boy my age but a year younger. This name was Michael Miller. He is no longer alive today. I often wonder why he shot himself.

I've often wanted to see my son Michael and my daughter Audrey. But I was not given a chance to do so. A Judge refused me visitation rights with my son. My daughter was another matter altogether. But this no one needs to know but myself and the mother of the child.

I was drafted into the Army in April of 1967. I was sent to Fort Benning, Georgia. Here I stayed for eight weeks in Basic Training. Then I was sent to Fort Lee. This is where I was given training as A.I.T. plus cook school and weapons training. I left for home on August 31st of 1967. I had a twenty-three day leave before I had to report to the Oakland California Ship Out Station. Before I shipped overseas, I got married to my second wife. Her name is Linda. I flew over to Vietnam on the 27th of September 1967.

I landed at Ho Chi Min City at about 2:40 in the morning with rockets and bullets flying everywhere. To me it was quite a show. When I got bored with nothing to do, I'd take a PR-25 radio and boogie on out to the highest hill or mountain area or climb into a big bamboo patch and sit out the night. I will admit that I have killed when I was supposed to and also when I was not given that permission. I have only taken one prisoner and never again after that.

I spent 13 months over there. When I came back from Vietnam I had a lot of nightmares of the war. I had beat up my wife from waking me up from a dream. In the back of my mind all I wanted to do was kill. The United States government would teach you how to kill but they never taught you how to stop. For years this was beneath my skin and stewing, then in 1990 I was arrested for felony murder of several counts. I just could not remember it. It still has me in a bind to remember what it was that I've supposed to have done.

I wish the world to know that I am somewhat a complex person. Supposedly I am called very aggressive, but I disagree. I am told that I am anti-social. To what degree I don't rightly know. I am serving 250 to life for serial murder of killing eleven prostitutes in the city of Rochester, New York.

Anna Stephans [sic] was a woman I had met while walking on the left side of Lake Avenue going north toward Driving Park Bridge. I was near the Pizza Hut when this woman came up behind me and asked if I would care to walk with her down by the Genesee River, near the Falls. I walked along quietly minding my own business when she pipes up with small talk of just nothing at all. When we approached the bridge area she asked me to walk down this side road or path facing south of the river on the west side of the river. We stopped at a place that looked out over the water and she sat down in the high grass and told me to do the same. I did and leaned back and sort of laid down and looked at her. This is when she asked to have sex. I asked her what would she like to do and she stated she was in the mood for everything. So off come the clothes and we begin to feel one another and kiss.

When I looked down at her pussy area I spotted a large blood vein about the size of a large pencil. I think I said, "*What is this?*" She told me that she shoots up with heroin. This is when I started to get my things on. She grabs my arm and said I can't leave her like this. "*Well why can't I?*", I asked. She gets up and starts cussing and spitting at me like a crazy person. I didn't know if she may have AIDS or what when I seen that blood vessel all puffed up. I grabbed the bitch and set her down and told her to calm herself. Then she cried quietly to herself. I was in a spot that was a bit too much to take. I quietly took a hold of her and killed her. Why I did it this time is beyond me. I sat there looking at this woman as she laid there in death, all quiet. Finally, with no more problems to account for in this world. Many things run through your mind at times like this. Here was a woman that I never even had sex with. And she is now dead.

There was a sort of drop off near where we were and I shoved her over this and covered her with soil, rocks and whatever was there to hide the fact of what I had just done. I took her clothes and tossed them into the Genesee River and watched them sink out of sight. I got away from there and went up to the bridge and stood there for a long time. This moment in time is strange to think about as I was having strange feelings within, of something like a higher power: somewhat like a God over his subjects.

Each of us humans have the ability to create life and to take that same life. Killing this whore, to me, was a mercy. But with help she could have been a better person. Sometimes I wonder if I myself could have done things differently, without murder. Just what in all creation are we, really? I myself am of another type of human. Either one of higher intelligence or one of lower.

I met Dorothy Keller [sic] one afternoon when I was out walking along the river. Here was a woman sleeping. Wrapped around a bush. From what I could see she was drunk on beer. There was an empty bottle next to her. So I sat back a ways from her and watched her sleep. After a few minutes, I picked up some pebbles and tossed them on her and she woke up and smiled, saying *"Good morning, Sir."* I asked why she was sleeping out here when people walk by. She stated that she had no place else to go.

This is when I gave her my name and address. I asked her if she would except a job for the winter as a live-in. She said, *"You bet I would."* So off we went to my apartment. I told her to go into the bathroom and remove all her clothing and toss them out to me. Then I said I will take them down and wash them while she soaks in the tub for a while. She said, *"Okay."* So this is what I did for her. When I got back up to the apartment, I went up to the door and spoke through it telling her where the soap and stuff is. Then I went back downstairs. When the clothes were done I went back to the apartment and opened the door and she was sitting on the bed naked as the day she was born. I gave her the clothes and asked if she was hungry. We went in the kitchen and I fixed both of us some breakfast of eggs, bacon, toast and coffee. After breakfast she got right to work on cleaning the place up. By 3 o'clock that afternoon when my roommate Rose came home from work she noticed the place was clean. This is when I introduced her to Dorothy. She got room and board and twenty-five dollars a week. The money she had me place in the bank for her. I had a safe in the apartment.

One day she asked if I would take her out to get beer. I said, *"Relax, I'll go get it for you when you want it."* She was content at this. We had a TV with every channel. Plus an ideal spot for her to sit and watch the people going by or sit out on the porch. It started out as a good investment. Then a day come along when I found some money missing from the laundry container. I asked her if she had taken the money. She stated that she had and said she wanted some beer. She didn't have a key to the apartment so I asked her if she had left the apartment open while she was gone to the store. She said, "*Yes*." I went in the bedroom to sleep and I woke up with Dorothy in bed with me. This went on for quite some time and one day came and I wanted it to stop. But not Dorothy. She said that I was disease free and she wanted to stay with me. Then a day came when Dorothy was going to tell Rose and just upset everything altogether. This came to a head when we were both down on the Genesee River fishing for the day. I got so ticked off that I picked up a small log and let her have it right upside of the effing head. Well, that was it. She was deader than hell.

What I will say at this time will seem strange to quite a few people in all cultures.

After the death of Dorothy I felt real weird. When I say this, I mean that I could hear maybe ten times better than before and also the brightness of the day was super bright. Also I was completely wet from sweat from the top of my head to mid chest. This always got to me, as to why this is so.

When I got back to the apartment I just sat alone for I could not function normally. There were even times when I couldn't even hear a sound. But this happened after the fact. When I gave it any thought, I just could not cope with it. I had what is called a knack for pushing bad things away. Or placed on a shelf and forgotten. All of my life was like this. I just pushed any bad things away. This one was the third.

Dorothy's skull is in plain sight if anyone knows just where to look. Be that as it may, I was unable to take it from the spot it is now, or not at this moment. But if I want it moved it can be.

From what I gather there have been in the neighborhood of 151 serial murderers in this country in the past twenty years with a death toll of at least 900 or more. But there are very few serial killers in this country that are what you might say are unknown. Serial killers for the most part are white, young, and loners with some violence in their past. I have in mine.

Some tests were completed on me back in 1990, and these consist of Chromosome Analysis by Smithkline Beecham Clinical Lab in Van Nuys, California. From blood samples taken it was revealed that I am a 47 XYY Predominate Male Karyotype... abnormally elevated urinary kryptopyrroles. In other words, I have over 100 million more Chromosomes in my body than the average male or human. When I get very angry, my urinary system goes hey-wire and I seem to get very much stronger than normal. Why this is, I do not know or even truly understand.

Am I an alien from another solar system? At least, I feel somewhat different than others. I am able to raise and lower my blood pressure at will and also do the same in controlling my aggressiveness.

I hope that you of the Human Race has a nice day. For no one really knows just what is around the corner.

Arthur John Shawcross

Editor's Notes: Police accounts of the recovery of Shawcross victim Anna Steffen are in some details contrary to those Shawcross furnished an AOC interviewer in the mid-1990s, reproduced above for the first time. Ms. Steffen's body was recovered from the spot where it floated in the Genesee River, conflicting with Shawcross's account that he secreted her with dirt and stones at the base of an embankment. His reference to the head of victim Dorothy Keeler remains relevant. Her skull, removed by Shawcross during a subsequent visit, still had not been found as of 2020.

The rhymed verses which follow – malapropist, cringy assaults on the English language – were vehicles Arthur Shawcross found useful to pass time but also to impose structure on his unpolished thoughts and inner dialogue, to offer explanations for his violence, and to promote illogical fantasies about himself as a romantic figure who inconveniently happens to consume human flesh while also being possessed by a demon called Yerakes. And they were a mask: one designed to deceive both the author himself and his imaginary audience that he could achieve introspection.

If you dare, critique whether he succeeded.

SATANIC VERSES

1. TIME
2. DESIRE
3. DEAR MOTHER, DEAR FATHER
4. OSTRACIZED
5. FALLING WITH NO END
6. SHAME ON THE NIGHT
7. DESTINY
8. COMRADES IN ARMS
9. SINS
10. LAWYERS JUSTICE
11. SOLDIERS
12. SERIALS
13. EXPRESSION
14. INFLUENCE
15. I
16. THE GENTLEMAN
17. PSYCHO
18. BIG BITCH
19. NEVER SAY NEVER
20. EXCITEMENT
21. WHAT AM I?
22. GUILT
23. INCEST
24. THE IMMORTAL
25. GIVING
26. FEELINGS
27. A FRIEND
28. WONDERS OF YOUTH
29. ENGLISH WIT
30. OLD CROW
31. THE PAST
32. WINTERS GALE
33. A WITCHES DREAM
34. THE BUTCHER
35. MAKING IT IN PRISON
36. WHIMSICALS
37. FLASH IN THE NIGHT
38. R & R
39. MISERY
40. FRIGHT
41. DARING DO
42. P.T.S.D.
43. CIRCLE OF LIFE
44. HERE'S TO YOU
45. DEATH IS NOT FINAL

TIME

I AM WAITING IN THIS COLD CELL,
LISTENING FOR THE BELL TO CHIME.
FLASHES OF MY PAST THAT LEAD TO HELL,
FOR THERE IS NOT MUCH TIME.

BECAUSE AT 12:01 A.M. THEY WALK ME TO THE CHAIR,
WHEN THE PADRAE READS ME MY LAST RIGHTS.
WE ALL KNOW WHY WE END UP THERE.
I LOOK AT MY LAST SIGHTS.

DEEP INSIDE I FEEL A HEARTRENDING SCREAM
AS THEY WALK ME THROUGH THE COURTYARD.
WHEN I THINK "THIS IS ALL BUT A CRAFTY DREAM"
SOMEONE CALLS OUT "GOD BE WITH YOU!"
I WAS DEALT MY LAST CARD.

TEARS FALL, BUT WHY AM I CRYING?
"GOD CATCH MY SOUL!" IT'S READY TO FLY.
AFTER ALL I AM NOT AFRAID OF DIEING
BECAUSE I KNOW THE REASON WHY.

MARK MY WORDS, MY SOUL LIVES ON.
THIS IS ALL CONFUSION.
I'VE GONE TO SEEK THE TRUTH IN THE LAND BEYOND.
LIFE IN HERE IS A STRANGE ILLUSION…

DESIRE

DO YOU SEE WHAT I SEE?
TRUTH IS BUT AN OFFENCE.
YOUR SILENCE
FOR YOUR CONFIDENCE.

CAN YOU HEAR WHAT I HEAR?
DOOR'S SLAMMING SHUT.
LIMIT YOUR IMAGINATION
BY KEEPING ME WHERE THEY MUST.

DO YOU FEAR WHAT I FEAR?
LIVING PROPERLY.
TRUTHS TO YOU ARE LIES TO ME,
SO I FLEE.

DO YOU NEED WHAT I NEED?
DEATH OVERTHROWN.
WE MUST LOOK INSIDE,
TO EACH OUR OWN.

CAN YOU TRUST WHAT I TRUST?
ME, MYSELF AND I.
PENETRATE OUR DREAMS,
I SEE THE SELFISH LIE.

DEAR MOTHER, DEAR FATHER

DEAR MOTHER, DEAR FATHER.
WHAT IS THIS HELL YOU HAVE BROUGHT ME TOO?
"BELIEVER   DECEIVER"

DAY IN, DAY OUT I LIVE MY LIFE WITHOUT YOU.
NEVER PUSHED ONTO ME WHAT WAS WRONG OR RIGHT.
HIDDEN IN THIS HELL THAT THEY CALL LIFE.

DEAR MOTHER, DEAR FATHER.
EVERY THOUGHT I THINK, YOU DISAPPROVE.
"CREATOR   DICTATOR"

NEVER CENSORING MY MOVES.
CHILDREN ARE SEEN BUT NEVER HEARD.
TEAR OUT EVERYTHING INSPIRED.

DEAR BROTHER, DEAR SISTERS.
TIME HAS FROZEN STILL WHAT'S LEFT TO BE.
"HEAR NOTHING   SAY NOTHING"

CANNOT FACE THE FACT I THINK FOR ME.
NO GUARANTEE, LIFE IS AS IS.
BUT DAMN YOU FOR NOT GIVING ME A CHANCE.

DEAR MOTHER, DEAR FATHER.
YOU CLIPPED MY WINGS BEFORE I LEARNED TO FLY.
"UNSPOILED   UNSPOKEN"

I'VE NEVER HEARD A LULL-A-BY.

DEAR MOTHER, DEAR FATHER.
HIDDEN IN THIS HELL YOU MADE FOR ME,
I'M SEETHING --- I'M BLEEDING,
RIPPING WOUNDS IN ME THAT NEVER HEAL,
WITH UNDIEING SPITE I FEEL FOR YOU.

LIVING OUT THIS HELL YOU ALWAYS KNEW.
I'M IN HELL WITHOUT YOU TWO.

I CANNOT COPE WITHOUT YOU.
TRAPPED IN A WORLD THAT I SEE,
WITH NO ONE TO RESCUE ME...

OSTRACIZED

SUSPICION IS MY NAME.
MY HONESTY IS TO BLAME:
DISHONOR

THE ACCUMATIONS FLY.
DISCUMATIONS WHY?
INTRUDING

BEHIND, MY HANDS ARE TIED.
I'M BEING OSTRACIZED.
MY HELL IS MULTIPLIED.
THE FALLOUT HAS BEGUN.
DAMAGE IS DONE.
MY MANY TURNED TO NONE:
TO NOTHING

I'M REACHING FOR MY FEAR.
MY WILL HAS DISAPPEARED.
THE LIE IS CRYSTAL CLEAR:
DEFENDING

CHANNELS RED,
WITH ONE WORD LEFT TO BE SAID:
BLACKLISTED...

FALLING WITH NO END

IN LIFE WE SPEAK OF DEATH.
EACH BREATH COMES CLOSER TO OUT OF THIS:
I'M NOT AFRAID,
THOUGH I DON'T KNOW JUST WHAT ITS ALL ABOUT.

DECISIONS THAT WE MAKE,
THE CHANCES THAT WE TAKE,
THE BLINDNESS WE CAN'T FAKE.
I THOUGHT I KNEW, BUT I SHOULD HAVE KNOWN
WHAT ITS LIKE TO BE ALL ALONE.

I REMEMBER HERE.
I THOUGHT IT WAS BUT A DREAM.
I NEVER THOUGHT IT WOULD COME TO THIS.
LIVING WITH FEAR.

NOW I KNOW WHAT IT MEANS.
NEVER THOUGHT IT WOULD END LIKE THIS,
FALLING TO THE END,
INTO WHAT I'VE ONLY DONE TO ME.

WITH MESSAGES TO SEND
OUT OF WHAT I'VE ONLY DONE TO ME.
FALLING TO THE END.
CRAWLING TO THE END.
IT'S OVER…

SHAME ON THE NIGHT

SHAME ON THE NIGHT.
FOR THE PLACES I'VE BEEN,
WITH ALL THAT I HAVE SEEN,
GIVING ME THE STRANGEST DREAMS.
BUT I WAS NEVER TOLD
JUST WHAT ALL THIS MEANS.

SHAME ON YOU.
YOU'VE STOLEN THE DAY,
JUST RIPPED IT AWAY,
BUT I SAW THE SKY.
AM I NEVER GOING TO DIE?
YOU KNOW THE REASON WHY.

SHAME ON THE NIGHT.

FOR THE LIGHT (YOUR SOUL).
I'VE LOST ALL MY HOPE.
I CANNOT COPE
ON THE MAGIC FLAME.
BUT NOW I KNOW YOUR NAME (OH LORD).

"JUST GO AWAY", BUT YOU CAME AGAIN.
SO I'D BETTER RUN.
SHAME ON THE SON (ME).
YOU DON'T CARE FOR ALL YOU'VE DONE.

DESTINY

LIFE IT SEEMS TO FADE AWAY.
DRIFTING FURTHER EVERYDAY.
I HAVE LOST THE WILL TO LIVE.
I'VE SIMPLY NOTHING MORE TO GIVE.

AS THE SUN GOES DOWN I MOVE AROUND.
KEEPING FROM THE SHADOWS THAT ABOUND.
MY LIFE HANGS BY A THREAD.
AS ALWAYS, IT'S BEEN SAID.

BUT IF THAT IS MY DESTINY,
IT WILL HAVE TO BE.
I AM RUNNING OUT OF TIME.
MY LIFE IS ON THE LINE.

CAN YOU ACCEPT WHAT I'M SEEING?
FOR DEEP INSIDE I AM SEETHING.
IN MY ANGER I CAN'T ABIDE.
FOR WHAT IS LEFT, BUT SUICIDE?

COMRADES IN ARMS

THE EXHILARATION OF BEING SHOT AT GIVES YOU A CHILL.
THEN YOU DO SOMETHING ABOUT IT.
THE CAMARADERIE, THE RICH EMOTIONS, I MISSED IT.
I MISS IT STILL.

THE FRIENDS YOU MADE, WHO KEPT YOU ALIVE,
WERE BLOWN AWAY, GONE FOREVER.
THEY DIED IN YOUR ARMS, WITH THEIR BLOOD
ON YOUR HANDS, LEAVING YOU NOTHING
BUT TO SURVIVE.

OUR LIVES ARE STILL IN THE COUNTRY OF VIETNAM.
THERE THEY WERE LOST, GONE FOREVER.
WE'LL NEVER GET THEM BACK.
THE NOISE, THE SMELLS ARE WITH US STILL.
WE'VE GIVEN OUR ALL FOR UNCLE SAM.

WE ARE BUT ONE OF MANY WITH NOT MUCH TO GIVE,
BE IT AN HOUR, A DAY, A WEEK, MONTH OR YEAR:
YOU SURELY WANT TO LIVE.
KEEP IN MIND OUR BROTHERS AND SISTERS
DEATH IS SO VERY NEAR.

SINS

WHEN A PERSON LIES,
THEY MURDER SOME PART OF THE WORLD.
THIS IS WHAT WE CALL 'THE GRAY DEATH',
THAT WE MISCALL OUR LIVES.

ALL THIS WE CAN NOT BEAR
TO WITNESS ANY LONGER.
WHAT IS THIS WORLD COMING TO?
ARE WE ALMOST THERE?

MAY THE KING OF SALVATION
GATHER US UP AND TAKE US HOME.
PLEASE GOD PLEASE CAN YOU
SEND US AN EXPLANATION?

ALL THIS PAIN WE FEEL DEEP WITHIN,
WISHING WE WERE IN A FIELD OF CLOVER,
WHEN WE KNOW IT IS OUR SINS.
GOD WHISPERED,
"YOUR LIFE AS YOU KNOW IT
IS ABOUT OVER..."

LAWYERS JUSTICE

OFFICE OF LAWYERS.
(MONEY TALKING)
THEY SAVE YOU IN THEIR POWER.
CAN YOU HEAR THEM STALKING?

SOON YOU WILL PLEASE THEIR APPETITIES.
(THEY WILL DEVOUR)
HAMMER OF JUSTICE CLUTCHES YOU.
WATCH OUT FOR THE OVER-POWER.

APATHY THEIR STEPPING STONES.
(THEY ARE SO UNFEELING)
HIDDEN DEEP ANIMOSITY,
CAN BE DECEIVING.

THROUGH THEIR EYES YOUR LIFE BURNS.
(ONLY HOPING TO FIND)
INQUISITION SINKING YOU,
WITH THEIR PRYING MINDS.

LAYWERS JUSTICE.
(TRUTH ASSASSIN)
CAN NOT SPEAK, NOW YOUR ABOUT DONE IN.
BUT WITH YOUR MONEY,
THEY CAN AT LEAST TIP THEIR SCALES AGAIN.

SOLDIERS

WHEN WE WERE EIGHTEEN AND TWENTY-FOUR
AMERICA SENT MANY OF US OFF TO WAR.
WE WERE ONE OF THIS NATIONS SONS,
SENT OFF TO FIRE ALL THOSE BIG GUNS.

AMERICA CAN'T YOU SEE THAT IT WASN'T TRUE,
WHAT IT WAS THEY WERE TELLING YOU?
WE WERE PROUD SOLDIERS OF THE HILL,
TRAINED TO FIGHT AND TRAINED TO KILL.

THE CRYING, THE DIEING, THE QUIETNESS YOU FEEL
WAS BITTER BY FAR AS WE WONDER OF OUR NEXT MEAL.
ON THE WAY HOME WE WERE NUMB, BUT CALM.
WE ONLY HAD ONE THOUGHT: "HELLO MOM!"

THERE IS REALLY NO ONE TO UNDERSTAND US HERE,
WHAT IT REALLY MEANS TO LIVE IN FEAR.
WHEN WE FEEL THAT STRANGENESS CREEP IN,
IT IS THE FEAR OF OUR SOUL IN A SPIN.

THERE IS NOT MUCH TO SAY OF ALL THE STRIFE,
WHEN MANY OF US GAVE UP A LIFE.
THE VETERANS ARE NOT ALONE
FOR MANY OF US ARE STILL COMING HOME.

SERIALS

WHY IS THERE A COMMONALITY TO PEOPLE
LIKE US? CAN IT BE OUR INDEPENDENCY AND
SELF SUFFICIENCY THAT KEEPS OUR SUBSEQUENT
BIZARRE BEHAVIOR OF THE RUSH?

WITH THE SEVEREST OF VIOLENCE
IN THE FRENZY TO EXECUTE ANYONE
WITHOUT REMORSE, WITHOUT CONSCIENCE
THOUGHT, LEAVES ONE WITH MEMORIES IN THE SILENCE.

THE FORCE WE FEEL THAT NO ONE FINDS
OR THE UNSHAKABLE BELIEF AND CUMULATIVE
PITFALLS, OR THE DEPRESSION IN COMBINATIONS
OF SEVERE PAIN OF OUR KIND.

I FOR ONE ENUNCIATE THAT I
AM MUCH MUCH MORE THEN STATED BY THE PEOPLE,
THE PRESS, OR THE WORLD'S EYE.

IF YOU SEE IN ME AGITATION, INSANITY, FUROR,
EXCITABILITY, DELIRIUM,
VIOLENCE OR PLAIN EVIL,
THEN I SUJEST YOU LOOK IN THE MIRROR.

EXPRESSION

THE ARTICULATION TO SPEECH IS VOCALIZATION
BE IT JARGON, SLANG, OR ENUNCIATION.
THINK WHAT INFLUENCE YOU HAVE IN WHAT YOU SAY,
A BURST OF ELOQUENCE ANY GIVEN DAY.
PRONUNCIATION IS A SPECIAL GIFT TO GAB,
DO NOT CHATTER, PRATTLE OR BLAB.
SOME SPEAK SOFTLY, OTHERS LOUD.
STUDY, PRACTICE, ACCENTUATE, BE PROUD.
LISTEN TO YOUR EVERYDAY SPEAKER,
NOT YOUR MOMBASTIC, DECLAMATORY SQUEEKER.
LOOK FOR WAYS TO VERBALIZE:
TALK TO ONESELF, EXPRESS OR CONNONTIZE.
ADD WISDOM TO YOUR LIFE SPAN.
GIVE AN ELOCUTIONARY EXPRESSION.
THINK DEEP, MAKE AN IMPRESSION.
MAKE YOUR SPEECH EXTRINSICAL,
WITHIN OR AROUND A MUSICAL.

INFLUENCE

WHEN ACTING OUT A ROLE OR PLAY
MAKE ORIGINALITY COME IN A SPECIAL WAY.
GIVE REAL MEANING TO INVENTION.
HAVE FUN, TRY HARD, BE AN INSPIRATION.
MAKE A SPECIAL EFFORT TO BE CREATIVE.
BE THE VISIONARY, LET IT BUT LIVE.
SEEK PERFECTION; WE KNOW ITS HARD TO FIND.
CAN THERE BE A PREMONITION IN MIND?
CREATE AN ILLUSION,
ONLY KEEP OUT CONFUSION.
EXTRAVAGANZA GIVES MEANING IN THE LIGHT.
MAKE IT FANTASTIC IN THEIR SIGHT!

BE THE ROMANTIC.
LET IT BE POETIC, HEROIC AND IDEALISTIC.
IMAGINATION IS WHAT YOU NEED
GIVE THOUGHT ---- PLANT THE SEED.

I

I HAVE TRIED TO BE A KNIGHT
BUT ENDED UP A KNAVE.
IT LOOKS AS THOUGH I MIGHT
JUST TAKE IT TO MY GRAVE.

I CAN GRUMBLE AND GROWL
OR WHIMPER AND SOB,
MAYBE BARK AND HOWL
WHEN I MEET GOD.

I WILL BE A LEGEND, YOU SEE.
WOULDN'T YOU LIKE TO AGREE?
IF ITS MYTHOLOGICAL OR HISTORICAL,
ITS REPUTED TO BE ME.

I AM STATELY AND SOVEREIGN
WITH GREAT AUTHORITY,
OF THAT YOU KNOW. I AM FOREIGN
OF DUTY AND MORALITY.

I AM SHUNNED AS IF I WERE A THORN,
WITH CONTEMPT, DISDAIN AND SCORN.
I'll GLADLY BECOME A BEETLE
THEN TAKE THAT EFFIN' NEEDLE.

THE GENTLEMAN

OH, HOW I WISH
I WERE KNIGHTLY,
INSTEAD OF OLD
AND UNSIGHTLY.

I AM A BIT
OLD FASHIONED,
WITH A QUAINT
BUT POWERFUL PASSION.

WITH DEEP LOVE,
DESIRE AND EMOTIONS
TO SEEK MY LADY'S
ELIXER AND POTION.

I AM A GENTLEMAN
AND ARISTOCRAT,
FROM THE CROWN PRINCE
DOWN TO WHERE THE SQUIRE SAT.

OR MAYBE I AM
THE OUTLAW
OR THE OUTCAST,
SLIPPED IN
FROM OUT THE PAST.

PSYCHO

THE CONCRETE JUNGLE
OF OUR TIME
HAS CREATED
ONE HELL OF A CRIME.

THE CORPSE WAS RENDERED
LIKE SO MUCH MEAT
WHILE IT LAID IN DEATH
ON TOP OF A BLOODY SHEET.

A MAID APPEARS
AS FRESH AS CREAM
WHEN FAR BELOW
SOMEONE HEARD ONE HELL OF A SCREAM.

EVEN THE NURSE
WITH THE BLEACHED YELLOW HAIR
COULDN'T BREATHE
FOR THE LACK OF AIR.

THERE WAS A LOUD CRASH
A NEIGHBOR HEARD.
NOT MUCH WAS SAID,
NOT EVEN ONE WORD.

IT HAD TO BE
A PSYCHO, YOU SEE?
JUST PRAY IT DOES
NOT HAPPEN TO THEE.

BIG BITCH

I ONCE KNEW A GAL OF CONSIDERABLE SIZE,
STEEP SIDES AND A LOT OF SASS.
A BIG MOUNTAIN OF TROUBLE,
WITH A FACE FULL OF STUBBLE.

NOW WE KNOW JUST WHAT IT MEANS,
BUT YET IT REMAINS TO BE SEEN,
WHETHER CRACK KILLS
FOR ONE OF HER THRILLS.

SHE WAS HUNG LIKE A LION, ONE WILD CAT.
A HEAVY REGION, FULL OF FAT.
SHE WAS OF AN IMPRESSIVE SIZE AND WEIGHT,
TO BURY IN A PIANO CRATE.

IF YOU SEE A GAL LIKE MINE,
SHIP THE BITCH OUT TO THE COUNTY LINE.
I'LL BE WAITING WITH A BACKHOE
READY TO PLANT HER IN A BIG-ASSED HOLE.

I HAVE THIS READY SORT OF DITCH,
REALLY WAITING FOR ANOTHER BIG-ASSED BITCH.
OFF IN THE DISTANCE I HEAR SOME THUNDER.
NOW BY DAMN I BETTER GET THIS BITCH UNDER.

NEVER SAY NEVER

RULE NUMBER ONE: NEVER SAY NEVER.
FOR SOME OUT THERE ARE REALLY QUITE CLEVER.
THERE IS MUCH YOU CAN DO IN CARE
BY LEAVING THEM OUT IN THE AIR.
BUT REALLY, WHAT THE HELL, WHO CARES.

YOU CAN ALMOST SAY, "I CAN STAY ON TOP."
REALLY YOU CAN BELIEVE IT, RIGHT NEXT TO A COP.
ONLY WHEN YOU THOUGHT ALL WAS LOST,
YOU GOT UP AND COVERED ALL COST,
LIKE WHEN THE DAY BEGAN WITH A LIGHT FROST.

ONE THING LEADS TO ANOTHER.
NOT MUCH TO DO, SO I DIDN'T BOTHER.
ITS TIME TO GO,
I WANT YOU TO KNOW,
ITS TIME TO GET ANOTHER.

EXCITEMENT

LET US CREATE A DIVERSION
WITH A DISTRACTION, AVOCATION AND RELAXATION.
MAKE IT A BIT MISCHEVIOUS.
LEAVE OUT BEING INAUSPICIOUS.
GIVE A CELEBRATION, SOLEMNIZATION AND COMMEMORATE
WITH A BIG BANG OF ILLUMINATION.
SEE THE COLORFUL BRILLIANCE UP IN THE AIR,
MADE BRIEF BY THE FIREWORKS THERE.
THE REALIZATION AND FULFILLMENT
OF THE CONSUMMATION
HAS US BREATHLESS OF THE COMPLETION.
THE ACTION OF THE EXCITEMENT

GAVE US THE TINGLE OF THE FAIR AND THE INCHANTMENT.
FEEL THE SENSATION OF THE EXPERIENCE.
AREN'T YOU GLAD YOU HAD THE ENDURANCE?
WERE YOU NOT IMPRESSED BY THE LIVELY THRILL?
WHEN NO ONE EVEN THOUGHT OF THE EVENING CHILL?
THE VIBRATIONS, AFFECTION, TENDERNESS AND LOVE
YOU FELT WHEN GUIDED BY THE EVENT OF THE ABOVE.

WHAT AM I?

RELATIONS CAN BE A BORE
WHEN THEY COME BACK BEGGING FOR MORE.
"AH" BUT TO EMBRACE AN OFFER
ADDS WONDERS TO ONES COFFER.

BY THEN THEY CAN DO AS THEY PLEASE
WITH RESERVE AND GENTLE EASE.
AS I SEND THEM OUT ON THEIR REAR
NO WORDS COME BACK DO I HEAR.

I HAVE TO HAVE CONFIDENCE
WHEN DEALING WITH ONES DEPENDENTS;
THE UNSUSPECTING CAN BE CONVICING
UNLESS THEY CAME TO AN ENDING.

FOR I CAN NOT PUSH THEM TO DISQUIETUDE
WHEN THEY DID ARRIVE WITH GRATITUDE.
AM I SO DISPASSIONATE AS A FISH?
ALL THEY CAME FOR WAS TO DELIVER A WISH.

MAYBE I AM SO INSENSITIVE AND SPIRITLESS
WITH DEEP SUPINENESS OR EVEN HEARTLESS,
BUT I WASN'T TAUGHT TO BE GENEROUS
OR EVEN TO BE CHIVALROUS.

GUILT

GUILT IS IN ALL OF US, YOU AGREE?
EVEN ONE SUCH AS ME.
MISBEHAVIOR IN ALL WE FEEL
CAN BE PARDONED WITH AN APPEAL.

CRIMINALITY IS A GAME FOR NONE.
NOWHERE TO HIDE, NOWHERE TO RUN.
IN ALL OF YOUR MISDEEDS
YOU DIDN'T THINK OF OTHERS NEEDS.

THE TRANSGRESSION IS NOT THE RIGHT IMPRESSION.
WE WOULD BE BETTER OFF IN DERELICTION.
IT IS NOT ONLY GUILTINESS
BECAUSE IT COMES DOWN TO SINFULNESS.

GET FROM BEHIND ALL THAT LAWLESSNESS
SO YOU WON'T FEEL GUILTINESS.
DO NOT BE INNUENDO
IF YOU ARE CAUGHT IN A FRAGRANTE DELICTO.

INCEST

AT ONE TIME I WAS THE FAVORITE SON.
THEN THE BEAST CAME AND I HAD TO RUN.
MY MIND WAS IN FRIGHT OF EVEN THE NIGHT;
AS A YOUNG LAD I WAS SCARED WITH ALL MY MIGHT.

WITH DEEP CRUELTY, SHE DID WRONG ME.
IT WAS SATANIC AND DEVILISH TO BELIEVE.
SHE WAS JEALOUS AND SPITEFUL
COLDHEARTED AND SELFISH TO BE HELPFUL.

I FELT I WAS IN A WHOREHOUSE WITH ALL THE FORNICATION.
WITH HER PERVERSION, PEDERASTY AND VIOLATIONS.
I WAS HER PLAYTHING WHEN NO ONE WAS NEAR,
FOR THERE I WAS MOSTLY IN TEARS.

SHE WAS INCESTUOUS, PROMISCUOUS AND UNCLEAN,
DOING TO ME WHAT WAS SO DAMN MEAN.
AS I GOT OLDER SHE LEFT ME DRY,
NEVER TELLING ME THE REASON WHY.

I AM THE UNLOVED CHILD OF DESPISED HATE.
WHAT CAN I EVER DO OR SAY FOR HEAVENS SAKE?
I AM THE ADMONITION OF HER LIONS,
THE INCEST BABY SHE CAN'T JOIN.

I OFTEN WONDER, BUT WHY THE BOTHER,
WHO IT WAS MY RIGHTFUL FATHER?
FOR HE ALONE KNOWS THE SCORE,
WHEN HE GETS EVEN WITH THE WHORE.

THE IMMORTAL

THERE IS A GREAT RELEASE AT THE POINT OF DEATH,
WHEN YOUR ABLE TO TAKE YOUR LAST BREATH.
THE LOVE YOU SEE ON THE OTHER SIDE
DRAWS THE SPIRIT AND LETS IT GLIDE.

I'VE COME CLOSE TO MEETING THE GRIM REAPER,
BUT I WAS CHOSEN TO BE HIS KEEPER.
WHEN YOU DIE YOUR SOUL TAKES FLIGHT,
THE BODY GETS LIGHTER AND THE EYE-SIGHT BRIGHT.

DO YOU BELIEVE THAT YOU'VE LIVED BEFORE?
EVER WONDER WHY LIFE IS NOT A BORE?
NOT EVERYONE CAN LIVE IN TRANSITION
FOR EVER MORE IN RESTORATION.

MAN WAS BORN TO SEEK PERFECTION
WHEN ALL HE HAS IS IMPERFECTION.
THERE IS A GAIN IN EXULTATION
DEEP IN THE SPIRIT WITH INTERJECTION.

MY SPIRIT HAS DURABILITY
IN IT'S LONGEVITY.
FOR THIS, YOU MUST REALIZE,
I WILL BE IMMORTALIZED.

"OH" TO BE BORN INSTANTANEOUSLY,
MANY TIMES PERPETUALLY.
FOR I HAVE TIME TO THE END,
"OH" TIME WITHOUT END.

GIVING

THE PRESENTATION OF A DONATION IS IN THE GIVING,
WITH THE SATISFACTION OF DOING SO WHILE STILL LIVING.
OFFERING AN INVESTMENT OF EVEN A DIME,
BECAUSE WE MAY FIND OURSELVES IN THIS SAME FOOD LINE.

COMMUNICATION WITH A SMALL SUM OF DISPENSATION
LETS YOU FEEL GOOD INSIDE FOR THE ACQUISTION.
IN THE APPROPRIATE DISPOSSESSION,
TO EVEN ONE IN DERELICTION.

TO SUCH A POOR PERSON, IT IS A WINDFALL;
IT IS BETTER THEN HAVING THEIR BACK TO THE WALL
BUT THERE ARE SOME OUT THERE WHO MAKE A LIVING
ON WHAT PEOPLE DEPART IN THEIR GIVING.

SEEING A SUPPOSEDLY LEGLESS MAN
ARISE AND PICK UP HIS WHEELED STAND,
WHO WALKS A FEW BLOCKS TO HIS LIMO,
THEN DRIVES OFF TO HIS CONDO.

BUT KEEP IN MIND THE ONES WHO ARE NOT,
WHO SLEEP UNDER BRIDGES AND VACANT LOTS.
BEING ANEW FOR A BETTER VIEW,
GIVE TO ONE WHO HAS LESS THAN YOU.

FEELINGS

WHAT IS THE SENSATION
THAT COMES WITH EMOTION?
WOULD IT BE VIBRATIONS
OR SOME SORT OF AFFECTIONS?

WITH TENDERNESS AND LOVE,
WHAT IS IT WE SEEK FROM ABOVE?
THE WARMTH AND SENSITIVITY
HAS BROUGHT TO US TANGIBILITY.

ALL THE EAGERNESS AND TOLERANCE
CAN BRING ON VEHEMENCE.
SO FOR THE PASSION THAT'S THERE
ONLY SHOWS YOU CARE.

ARE YOU NOT IN ECSTASY?
MAYBE ITS SIMPLY SYMPATHY.
CAN'T YOU SENSE THE BODY SINGING,
WHEN ALL THE TIME IT WAS FEELING?

A FRIEND

WHAT IS THE MOST IMPORTANT THING IN A MAN'S LIFE?
CAN IT BE JUST A COMPANION OR WIFE?
OR MAYBE EVEN A NEIGHBOR,
SOMEONE TO LEND A HAND IN LABOR?

WHO CAN WE RECEIVE WITH OPEN ARMS?
NOT JUST A LANDLORD OR A LADY AND HER CHARMS.
IT'S MORE LIKE COMRADESHIP
THAN IT IS IN FELLOWSHIP.

JUST WHO CAN IT BE TO SOCIALIZE WITH?
THERE HAS TO BE MORE TO LIFE THEN JUST TO LIVE.
WHAT WHEN A SMALL THING LIKE COMMUNICATION
CAN BE ENJOYED WITH FRATERNIZATION.

WHO CAN IT REALLY BE
THAT WOULD MEAN SO MUCH TO THEE?
HAVE YOU GUESSED IT FROM THIS END,
THAT IT JUST HAS TO BE A FRIEND?

WONDERS OF YOUTH

WHEN I WAS A YOUNG LAD OF 1 AND 2
I WOULD WANDER THE WOODS A TIME OR TWO.
THEN TO EXPLORE THE CREEKS AND CAVES,
I WAS A BIT SCARED AND TRYING TO BE BRAVE.

DOWN IN THE SWAMP WITH BRUSH REAL THICK
I FELL IN A POOL OF MUCK THAT MADE ME SICK.
THE SCREAMS I MADE WERE LOUD TO A DEGREE,
WHEN ALONG CAME A BOY MY AGE TO SAVE ME.

OFF BY THE ROADSIDE OF THE CREEK
I SAT IN THE WATER LOOKING SO MEEK.
I RINSED OFF MY BODY AND CLOTHES TOO
OF ALL THAT MUCK THAT WAS THICK AS GOO.

OUT IN THE FIELD OF WONDER AND TREES
LOOKING TO BUILD A FORT FOR HIM AND ME;
WITH HANDSAW AND AXE, WE CUT A SQUARE.
EVEN DOWN TO FIXING A RABBIT SNARE.

THEN ONE NIGHT WE SEEN A FLASH.
WAY OFF IN THE WOODS, A FIRE RACED FAST.
ALL OF US WENT OUT TO SEE
HOW IT GOT STARTED; WELL BY GOSH IT WASN'T ME.

IT WAS DISCOVERED THAT A WARPED PIECE OF GLASS
STARTED A SMOLDER IN THE GRASS.
WITH A SLIGHT WIND, THAT SPARK GREW,
DESTROYING ALL THAT WE EVER KNEW.

ENGLISH WIT

A YOUNG LADY SO FAIR
GAVE A YOUNG MAN A STARE,
OF A CHALLENGE OF A LOVER.
THEN OFF THEY RAN TO THE INN
TO BEGIN A SESSION IN SIN,
BENEATH THE SHEETS AND COVERS.

THEY HAD ONE HOT OLD TIME,
STRETCHED OUT ON THE FLOOR OF PINE.
THE LADY LAID BACK AND SAID, "PLEASE I NEED A REST."
THE YOUNG MAN THOUGHT, "HOW COZY THIS LITTLE NEST."

WITH HER STILL WET
FROM ALL BUT THE SWEAT
OF THE LOVEMAKING
SHE ENDURED IN THE TAKING.

SHE AWOKE IN A SNIT,
AND SOMEWHAT IN PAIN,
THEN STATED, "DON'T EVER DO THAT AGAIN.
WAKE ME UP FIRST.
I MIGHT HAVE MISSED IT!"

THE MUCH WINDED YOUNG MAN
WHO COULD HARDLY STAND
TO PUT ON HIS FROCK
DIED ON THE SPOT IN SHOCK.

OLD CROW

I AM JUST AN OLD CROW
SITTING ON A LIMB
THINKING OF THE SNOW
ON THE ASPECT OF A WHIM.

DO YOU WONDER WHAT IT'S LIKE TO BE A SNOWFLAKE?
JUST RIDING ON THE WIND.
IF ONLY I CAN KEEP AWAKE,
OR FALL OFF THIS VERY LIMB.

IT'S SO VERY COLD UP HERE
IN THIS BIG OLD TREE.
BUT IF I STAY MUCH LONGER, I FEAR
I'LL BECOME ONE WITH THEE.

OH, LITTLE SNOWFLAKE.
TELL ME WHAT YOU KNOW.
I'LL MAKE MY PEACE WHILE AWAKE
BEFORE THE WIND BEGINS TO BLOW.

THE PAST

THE PRETERITION TO EVERYONE'S LIFE
IS SET IN THEIR REMOTE PAST.
ABOVE AND BEYOND ALL THE STRIFE,
KNOWING NOTHING CAN EVER LAST.

DON'T YOU WISH YOU CAN TURN BACK THE CLOCK?
THAT IS IRRECOVERABLE, TO SAY THE VERY LEAST.
TO UNWIND OR TURN BACK THE CLOCK
RETROSPECTIVELY, LIKE LOOKING EAST.

FOR EVEN THEN YOU SEE THE MORROW,
WHEN YOU CATCH YOURSELF LOOKING BACK
OF TODAY AS EVERYDAY, IN SORROW,
FOR SOMETHING TO ATTACK.

EVEN MORE SO, YOU CAN ONLY DREAM.
OR IS IT REASONABLE TO BE VERY FAST?
TO KEEP AHEAD OF THE SUBCONSCIOUS SCREAM
IN RUNNING AHEAD OF YOUR PAST?

WINTERS GALE

FEEL THE HARSH BLOWING WIND
OF THE STORM IN ITS FEROCITY;
TO CRY, HOWL AND WAIL
OF STRONG SEVERITY.

THE DRIFTING SNOW OF AN ICY WIND
IN ITS FROSTY STINGING BLOW
CAN NUMB THE BODY TO THE SKIN,
OF THIS I WANT YOU TO KNOW.

IF ONE IS CAUGHT OUT IN THIS VIOLENCE
YOU NEED TO FIND A HUGE DRIFT, THEN DIG INTO THE SIDE,
AWAY FROM THE TEMPEST EFFERVESCE.
THEN SNUGGLE UP INSIDE OR YOU MIGHT HAVE DIED.

YOUR BODY WARMTH WILL KEEP YOU ALIVE
AS LONG AS YOU ARE NOT WET.
A SNUB OF CANDLE WILL HELP YOU TO SURVIVE,
AS LONG AS YOU DON'T BREAK INTO A SWEAT.

KEEP IN MIND ALL THE TIME
OF NATURES ATTEMPT TO BE MEAN.
FOR EVER MORE, OF HER WHINE,
IT'S LIKELY YOU WILL LIVE AND DREAM.

A WITCHES DREAM

THE BLOWING OF THE WARM NIGHT WINDS
ARE GENTLE AS LOVING HANDS
IN KNOWING THAT FALL BEGINS
WHEN THE SUMMER ENDS.

GET OUT THE COSTUMES AND PUMPKINS TOO
FOR DON'T YOU KNOW THE WITCHES WILL RIDE
THEIR BROOMS AND CRY THEIR WOO,
WHEN THEY LOOK FOR THEIR LOVERS HIDE.

IN THE HALLOW OF THE NIGHT
CAN BE HEARD A MOANING SCREAM
OF A WITCH'S UNSOULFULL PLIGHT
OF FOREVER TO BE MEAN.

FOR WE SEE AND HEAR THE HALLOW'S WEEN
WITH THIS YOU KNOW CAN BE A TRICK OR A TREAT.
TO SUCCOR A WITCH'S FAVOR, IT'S YET TO BE SEEN
IF SHE GIVES UP A COAL OR A SWEET.

BUT KEEP IN MIND OF ALL THE FIGHT
THAT LAYS BETWEEN
DAY AND THE NIGHT.

THE BUTCHER

ONE YEAR IT CAME TO ME
THAT I DRANK THE BLOOD
FROM TEN AND THREE.

OH, IT WAS MY VERY FIRST
FROM THE FLOOD
OF THIS UNQUESTIONABLE THIRST.

BY AND BY
IT BECAME SO MUCH SWEETER,
BETTER BY FAR THEN THE TASTE OF RYE.

FOR I COULD SURELY TELL
WHO IT WAS, THE MEAT-EATER,
JUST BY THE SOUND AS THEY FELL.

WITH ALL THE BITTER
I CUT UP SWEETER,
THEN GROUND IT, SO MUCH BETTER.

ALL THE SWEET MEAT
OF THE TENDERLOIN
FELT SO MUCH BETTER IN THE HEAT.

THE BONING WAS REAL CLASS
FROM THE NECK
DOWN TO THE SPLASH.

BY CLOSING TIME
ELEVEN OF THE TEN AND THREE
WAS CUT OH SO FINE.

"AH" BUT THE TWO
I LET DRIP,
TILL READY FOR STEW.

284

WAS SO TIRED FOR FAIR
THAT AFTER I CLEANED UP
I WENT OUT FOR SOME AIR.

"OH" ISN'T IT BLOODY TASTY
TO BITE INTO SOMETHING SO RARE,
ALMOST AS GOOD AS PASTRY.

NOW BACK TO THE LAST TWO
THAT ARE STILL HANGING THERE.
"OH" I WONDER WHO

WILL TAKE OVER THE MORROW
TO COLLECT THESE TWO MORSELS
OF SWEETMEATS AND SORROW?

DON'T YOU KNOW?
I DID THIS DAILY
AS THE BUTCHER IN ESCROW.

MAKING IT IN PRISON

TO ALL MY BROTHERS AND SISTERS IN PRISON,
THOSE OF YOU WHO CAN NOT COPE
WITH THE DESCONSOLATION AND DEJECTION,
BECAUSE I'LL TELL YOU THERE IS HOPE.

GET RID OF THE SADNESS
FOR IT LEADS TO DEPRESSION,
AND LEAVES YOU WITH HEAVINESS
IN THE HEART OF HOMESICKNESS.

DON'T HANG YOUR HEAD, LIFT IT.
TAKE A DEEP BREATH.
ASK A LIFER TO LIFT THE SPIRIT,
OR IT CAN LEAD YOU TO YOUR DEATH.

PRACTICE BY LOOKING IN THE MIRROR.
SMILE, LAUGH, WINK, BUT DON'T CRY.
DO NOT GIVE IN TO INFERIORITY,
AND NOW I'LL TELL YOU WHY.

FIRST YOU'LL BE PUT ON MEDICATION
THAT YOU CLAIM THAT YOU CAN'T SLEEP.
ONCE THERE, YOUR ON PERMANENT VACATION,
OUT OF TOUCH WITH ALL BUT THOSE WHO WEEP.

PUT SUNSHINE BACK IN YOUR LIFE.
GET AN EDUCATION AND PROGRESS.
MAKE YOUR FAMILY PROUD WITHOUT STRIFE,
SO ONE DAY YOU CAN CHANGE YOUR ADDRESS.

WHIMSICALS

"OH" LITTLE HERMAN
AND BROTHER THERMAN
HAD AN ADVERSITY
TO WASHING THEIR EARS.
BUT GRANNY SCRUBBED THEM
WITH HER LYE SOAP
AND THEY HAVEN'T HEARD
A WORD IN YEARS.

"OH" MRS. O'MALLY
WHO LIVED IN THE VALLEY
SUFFERED FROM ULCERS,
WE UNDERSTAND.
GRANDMA GAVE HER
A BAR OF HER LYE SOAP
AND NOW SHE HAS
THE CLEANEST ULCERS
IN THE LAND.

FLASH IN THE NIGHT

THE FIRELIGHT OF A FALLING STAR
GIVES US PLEASURE IN WHERE WE ARE.
MAKE A WISH OF THE SIGHT,
AS YOU DRIVE IN THE STILL OF THE NIGHT.

BUT IN ALL REALITY OF WHAT YOU SEE
IT IS A METEOR FROM AFAR, DON'T YOU AGREE?
THERE ARE MANY SIGHTS TO SEE ON AN EVENING BRIGHT.
ALWAYS MAKE SURE YOU KEEP TO THE RIGHT.

THE SUDDEN FLASH OF THE HEADLIGHTS GLARE
CATCHES THE EYE OF CREATURES AS THEY STARE.
EVEN AS YOU HOLD YOUR BREATH,
SOME OF THEM WILL JUMP IN YOUR PATH TO THEIR DEATH.

OUT IN THE WOODED AREAS OF THE CLEAR
IS A SIGHT WORTH SEEING IN THE LOCAL DEER.
ALONG THE BACK ROADS, AS YOU DRIVE WITH CARE,
GOD'S CREATURES LOVE TO TEST THEIR DERRIERE.

R & R

WHILE IN FLIGHT OVER THE HAWAIIAN ISLANDS
YOU MAY SEE MANY WONDERFUL COLORS OF GREENS,
BLUES, SAPPHIRE AND TURQUOISE NEAR THE LANDS;
SANDS OF WHITE, BLACK, BROWN AND MINT GREEN.

THE VERY SALTY WATER OFF THE BEACHES
AND WITH A LIGHT RAIN OVER DIAMOND HEAD POINT
YOU HEAR COLORFUL PARROTS IN THEIR SCREECHES
WHILE YOU LAY BACK AND TOKE A JOINT.

WITH THE MELLOW FEELING OF WARM BLISS
WE SIT HERE ON R & R AWAY FROM THE CHASE
OF EXPECTATION; TOO MUCH SO TO EVER MISS.
FOR SOON ENOUGH WE WILL BE BACK TO THAT BAD PLACE.

SEE THE WIDE SPECTRUM OF WILD COLORS
WITHIN SIGHT OF A HEAVENLY SCENT
OF FINE ROUND-EYED LADIES COFERSING
FROM ONE TO ANOTHER
ABOUT MONEY, SECURITY OR THE ASPECT OF ENCHANTMENT.

SEE THE ERUPTING VOLCANO TOSSING IGNEOUS ROCK
AND SPEWING MOLTEN LAVA OF A GLASSY TEXTURE.
AND GASSES IN THE AIR FOR FAIR AROUND THE CLOCK
A PLACE NOTHING CAN LIVE, TO BE SURE.

MISERY

SEE THE MAN IN MOVEMENT, PAINTED IN LAMPBLACK,
MOVING SLOWLY WITHIN THE BRUSH,
WHILE CARRYING A CROSSBOW, AND A SMALL SACK,
WITH FEELINGS WITHIN OF MUSH.

WITH THE ENEMY SO VERY CLOSE
THAT YOU CAN ABOUT SMELL THEIR SWEAT,
AS YOU DRIFT CLOSER AS A GHOST
IN THE MUGGY SECTION OF WET.

A CLOSE ENCOUNTER OF A TINY SERPENT
LEAVES ONE IN TEARS OF THE NEAR MISS.
THE SILENCE THAT ABOUNDS THE ENCAMPMENT
LETS YOU WONDER OF A MISTAKE IN THIS.

BUT EVER MORE, AS YOU GET CLOSER,
YOU BEGIN TO SEE THE BAMBOO CAGES
WITH BODIES OF A HUMAN LOOSER
IN THE CAPTURE OF GENTLE FACES.

NOT ONE WAS ALIVE IN THIS HELL HOLE OF DEATH.
EVEN MORE SO, NOT ONE G.I. WAS TO BE FOUND
IN THE STINK OF ROT THAT TOOK A MAN'S BREATH,
OR IN THE LACK OF EVIDENCE OF ANY SOUND.

WE LEFT THE AREA AND TOUCHED NOT A THING.
WITH TEARS OF SORROW WE ADVANCED; FORWARD
OUT OF THE EVILNESS THAT THE ENEMY DID BRING
ON ITS OWN PEOPLE, WHO DIED BY THE SWORD.

FRIGHT

ONCE AWAY FROM THE CAMP OF QUIET ACTIVITY
YOU START TO FEEL
THE QUIETNESS AND THOSE DAMN MOSQUITOES FOR FAIR
IN THEIR QUEST OF BLOOD FOR A WARM MEAL
WHILE IN A SWARM OF BUSYNESS IN THE AIR.

WHEN ALL IS QUIET AFTER A LONG MARCH, YOU WONDER
IF AT ALL YOU ARE ALONE. OFF IN THE DISTANCE
YOU HEAR OR THINK YOU HEAR SOME CURSING FROM UNDER
THE BRUSH OR, UP IN THE TREES IN AN INSTANT.

REMEMBER THOSE LIZARDS OF THE REGION
CALLED THE GECKO?
CAN YOU RECALL WHAT THEY SAY, ALL THE WHILE?
IT WAS HARD TO GET USED TO,
"OH" THIS LITTLE PEST OF WOO
GOT US INTO UNNECESSARY TIGHTNESS OF THE BILE.

ANOTHER THAT WAS HARD TO MISS
WAS THAT STINKING DUNG BEETLE
IN IT'S HUNT FOR WASTES ANYWHERE
THAT HUMANS ARE FOUND.
WITH THE NOISE OF AN APPROACHING AIRCRAFT,
IT MADE US SETTLE A LITTLE LOWER IN THE GRASS,
WITH SWEAT ALL AROUND.

THEN SUDDENLY TO HEAR METAL AGAINST METAL
TIGHTENS THE NERVES AND THE SPLANCHNIC MUSCLE.
FOR YOU KNOW THAT SOMEONE COMES TO DO BATTLE:
THEM FOR MR. HO AND US FOR UNCLE.

DARING DO

"SHHHH!" CAN YOU FEEL THE CREEPY
SENSATION AS YOU WALK AN OLD CEMETARY
LATE ON THE EVE OF HALLOWEEN,
WITH MIST AND SOFT SOUNDS OF
SOMETHING NOT SO SLEEPY?

WATCH OUT FOR THE OPEN GRAVE!
AND IF YOU FIND ONE, CHECK
TO SEE IF THE SOIL IS FRESH.
"OH", IF IT IS YOUR WHOLE
BODY SAYS: "FEET LETS GO, I'M NOT SO BRAVE."

BUT AS YOU RUN AND STUMBLE,
YOU BEGIN TO SEE STRANGE THINGS
THAT AREN'T REALLY THERE AT ALL.
BUT JUST IN CASE, I'M SURE OF ONE THING:
WHY DOES MY STOMACH GRUMBLE.

WHEN FROM BEHIND I HEAR A DREADFUL SCREAM,
MY FEET NEVER TOUCH THE GROUND.
FOR THERE IS NO WAY I'LL COME BACK
TO THIS DARING DO,
ON HALLOWEEN…

P.T.S.D.

THIS IS A GROUP OF SIGNS AND SYMPTOMS
THAT COLLECTIVELY INDICATE OR CHARACTERIZE
A DESEASE, A PSYCHOLOGICAL DISORDER, OR A SYNDROME
OF SORTS, OR OTHER ABNORMAL
CONDITIONS TO HARMONIZE.

THE COMPLEX SYMPTOMS
INDECATEING THE EXISTENCE OF AN
UNDESIRABLE CONDITION OR QUALITY, A DISTINCTIVE
OR CHARACTERISTIC PATTERN OR BEHAVIOR CAN
BRING ON A CONCURRANCE OF SYMPTOMS
TOGETHER THAT LIVE.

WITH SEVERE STRAIN RESULTING FROM EXAUSTION,
SUFFERING FROM ANXIETY OR APPLIED FORCE OR
FORCES THAT TENDS TO STRAIN OR DEFORM THE CAUTION
SIGNALS OF BODY, MENTALITY OR EMOTIONAL CORE.

DISRUPTIVE OR DISQUIETING INFLUENCE
DERIVED FROM THE MIND OR EMOTIONS
WHERE THE PERSON CAN NOT REASON ITS SENSES
TO SPECULATE OR PUT HIS OR HER BEING IN MOTION.

CIRCLE OF LIFE

IF YOUR CIRCLE STAYS UNBROKEN
THEN YOU'RE A VERY LUCKY PERSON,
BECAUSE IT NEVER HAS FOR ME.

IN THE PALACE OF YOUR DREAMS
LIES THE CHALICE OF YOUR SOUL.
AND ITS LIKELY YOU MAY
FIND THE ANSWER THERE.

CIRCLE OF LIFE.
TEARS WE ALL BEAR.
AND THE DIRECTION
WE ALL PLAN TO TAKE.

HERE'S TO YOU

HAVE A GLASS OF SPARKLING CHAMPAGNE.
ISN'T IT GRAND TO HAVE SUCH A REFRAIN.
HERE'S TO YOU AS LONG AS YOU LIVE.
AS LONG AS YOU LIVE, MAY YOU WANT TO.
MAY YOU WANT TO AS LONG AS YOU LIVE.
IF I'M ASLEEP WHEN YOU WANT TO, WAKE ME.
IF I DON'T WANT TO, THEN MAKE ME.
BUT WHEN I'M FINISHED, I DID IT FOR YOU;
THEN DON'T YOU KNOW, I HAVE NO MORE TO GIVE.

DEATH IS NOT FINAL

THIS STORY BEGAN WITH CAUTION OF OUR PEERS
FOR THEY WISH TO STOP THE SLAUGHTER.
BUT THEN THIS STORY BEGAN IN TEARS,
MIXED WITH SOME SAD LAUGHTER.

IT ALL BEGAN WITH LIFE,
THEN ENDED IN DEATH.
WHAT BROUGHT ON THIS STRIFE
OF SOMEONES LAST BREATH?

WE ALL HAVE A QUESTION
BUT WILL WE EVER GET AN ANSWER?
DID WE FEEL REJECTION,
OR A SPARK OF THE ROMANCER?

ONE CAN NOT UNDERSTAND WHAT IS AHEAD
UNTIL THEY CHECK ON THEIR PAST.
LET US STOP THE SPREAD
OF ALL THIS AT LAST.

Grim Reader

Index

___

K

___

L